Queer about Comics

Contents

Darieck Scott and Ramzi Fawaz
Introduction: Queer about Comics   197

andré carrington
Desiring Blackness: A Queer Orientation to Marvel's *Black Panther*, 1998–2016   221

Anthony Michael D'Agostino
"Flesh-to-Flesh Contact": Marvel Comics' Rogue and the Queer Feminist Imagination   251

Yetta Howard
Unsuitable for Children? Adult-erated Age in Underground Graphic Narratives   283

Jessica Q. Stark
Nancy and the Queer Adorable in Serial Comics Form   315

Rebecca Wanzo
The Normative Broken: Melinda Gebbie, Feminist Comix, and Child Sexuality Temporalities   347

Kate McCullough
"The Complexity of Loss Itself": The Comics Form and *Fun Home*'s Queer Reparative Temporality   377

Margaret Galvan
"The Lesbian Norman Rockwell": Alison Bechdel and Queer Grassroots Networks   407

ii Contents

Review Essays

Joshua Abraham Kopin

Identity and Representation in US Comics   439

Shelley Streeby

Heroism and Comics Form: Feminist and Queer Speculations   449

**Darieck
Scott
and
Ramzi
Fawaz**

Introduction:
Queer about Comics

There's something queer about comics. Whether one looks to the alternative mutant kinships of superhero stories (the epitome of queer world making), the ironic and socially negative narratives of independent comics (the epitome of queer antinormativity), or the social stigma that makes the medium marginal, juvenile, and outcast from "proper" art (the epitome of queer identity), comics are rife with the social and aesthetic cues commonly attached to queer life. Moreover, the medium has had a long history as a top reading choice among those "queer" subjects variously called sexual deviants, juvenile delinquents, dropouts, the working class, and minorities of all stripes. Despite this, comics studies and queer theory have remained surprisingly alienated from each other. On the one hand, classical comics studies' tendency to analyze the formal codes of sequential art separately from social questions of sexual identity and embodied difference has often led to a disregard for a nuanced queer and intersectional critique of the comics medium. On the other, the prevailing assumption that mainstream comics (namely, the superhero genre) embody nationalistic, sexist, and homophobic ideologies has led many queer theorists to dismiss comics altogether or else to celebrate a limited sample of politically palatable alternative comics as exemplars of queer visual culture. In this logic, "Queer zines, yes! Superhero comics, no!"

This alienation—at times even antagonism—evinces a failure of recognition in the current development of scholarship rather than a true gulf between the foundational questions and concepts of the two fields. The conceptual and historical intersections of queer theory (and sexuality more broadly) and comics culture, in both its visual and narrative production and its fan communities, are rife and rich. At every moment in their cultural history, comic books have been linked to queerness or to broader questions of sexuality and sexual identity in US society. In the 1930s and 1940s *Wonder Woman* visually celebrated S-M practices and same-sex bonding between women, metaphorized through the image of the chained, shackled, or bound submissive; in the late 1940s and early 1950s crime and horror comics presented what was arguably the most antisocial critique of postwar domestic life outside of noir cinema, spectacularizing forms of violence, gore, and criminality that radically upended the ideals of nuclear-family harmony and the sublimation of desire in material goods; in the late 1950s *Mad* magazine elicited affective pleasure in the satiric critique of the nuclear family and its blatant refusal of the Cold War security state; in the 1960s and 1970s Marvel Comics revitalized the superhero comic book by infusing its art with the visual politics of gay and women's liberation while the artists who contributed to the *Wimmen's Comix* anthology (1972–92) brought a radical sexual politics to the visual culture of comic books; and from the 1960s to contemporary times, gay, lesbian, and queer culture has taken up comics as sites of sexual pleasure, such as in the graphic sex narratives of Tom of Finland and the cartoonists inspired by him, many of whom testify to beginning their cartooning by tracing and imaginatively redrawing the male figures they encountered in superhero comics. These latter crosscurrents now flow strongly in both directions, as evidenced by the recent proliferation of explicitly LGBTQ characters and scenarios in contemporary comics from the X-Men's "legacy virus" (a potent metaphor for HIV/AIDS) to the lesbian Batwoman and the gay Green Lantern. Moreover, the ubiquity of the medium—comic books being among the most mass-produced and circulated print media of the twentieth century—alongside its simultaneous stigmatization as the presumed reading material of a small slice of immature youth and social outcasts, models Eve Kosofsky Sedgwick's (1990) now-classic formulation of queerness as both a universalizing and a minoritizing discourse: anyone and everyone can be queer, but actual queers are a minority group in the larger culture; similarly, comics end up in the hands of nearly everybody, but comic book readers are a niche (read: queer, nerd, outcast, weirdo) group.

As this broad sketch of comics' queer attachments suggests, rather than needing to be queered, comics themselves "queer" the archive of US culture. Encounters between queer theories and comics studies potentially offer broader historical assessments of how the literary medium of comics, and its larger aesthetic and production history, might be understood as a distinctly queer mode of cultural production that has functioned *as* queer history, rather than its serialized supplement. When we understand the history of sexuality and the history of comics as *mutually constitutive*, rather than merely reflective or coincidental, we can gain insight into the ways that the comic book medium's visual structures not only lend themselves to questions of sexuality and sexual identity but have also taken shape historically in response to transformations in the history of sexuality.

The coeditors' aim for this special issue has been to elicit sustained theorizations of the pairing of queerness and comics, and explorations of the implications of that pairing for reading American literature as well as for queer theory, queer politics, and comics studies. Among the questions we consider to be fecund for exploring what's queer about comics—and what aspects of comics represent and give meaning to queerness—are the following: How might a medium made up of the literal intersection of lines, images, and bodies capture the values of intersectional analysis? How do comics' attention to the visual orientation of images in space model a conception of *sexual orientation*—especially in relation to race and gender, since all these are coordinates of embodied being not truly "present" on the two-dimensional page but signified and referred to by combinations of text and image? How might the medium's discontinuous organization of images map onto disability's discontinuous relationship to heterosexual able-bodied existence? How might the medium's courting of marginal and outsider audiences allow for the formation of queer counterpublics? How do the comics medium's formal properties provide material analogies for or creatively materialize and literalize seemingly formless experiences of nonnormative erotic desire, pleasure, and intimacy? These questions only begin to scratch the surface of productive encounters between comics studies and queer studies, but they suggest a synthetic approach to comics that considers the medium's queerness as opening out into a variety of formal and narrative experiments that have attempted to deal with the problem of being literally and figuratively marginal or "queered" by social and political orders.

In the interest of developing some of these links, we would like here to map a few of the primary sites where we see queerness as a social/ affective force intersecting productively with comics as a medium. This list functions merely as a starting point for identifying those locations where queerness—understood variously as a social force, a complex network of erotic and affective ties, or an entire shared culture— appears intimately bound up with the formal and narrative capacities of the comics medium.

1. The status of comics as marginal literature and art, as well as the assumed immaturity of its audiences (associated with childhood or arrested adolescent fantasy), situates comics as an outsider medium that elicits attachments from perceived social delinquents, outcasts, and minorities. Comics readers and fans construct their relationships to these texts on the basis of the medium's marginality and often their own sense of disconnection from the expectations of normative social life. Comics is a medium that thus hails counterpublics. Per Michael Warner (2006, 56):

   > A counterpublic maintains at some level, conscious or not, an awareness of its subordinate status. The cultural horizon against which it marks itself off is not just a general or wider public but a dominant one. And the conflict extends not just to ideas or policy questions but to speech genres and modes of address that constitute the public or to the hierarchy among media. The discourse that constitutes it is not merely a different or alternative idiom but one that in other contexts would be regarded with hostility or with a sense of indecorousness.

   Comics counterpublics are shaped in large part by the development of a variety of alternative and often egalitarian and grassroots forms of sociality among readers, creators, and textual content including fan clubs, letter-writing campaigns, zines, and comic art conventions. What Fredric Wertham (1954, 189–90) presciently captured in his derision of the homosexual undertones in Batman and Robin in the mid-1950s was the same queer spirit that he would later celebrate in his embrace of comic book fan communities and their egalitarian practices in the 1960s and 1970s; in both comic book content *and* fan culture ran an ongoing critique of normative social relations that exhibits itself in both comic books' visual content and their solicitation of nonnormative counterpublics.

2. The expansive representational capacity of the medium queers it. As a low-tech medium primarily composed of hand-drawn images, the representational possibilities of comics vastly outrun those of other media, requiring little to no special effects or technical equipment in the most classical sense. (It might be said, too, that this low-tech quality makes comics either fundamentally democratic or especially available to democratic practices.) Both the protocols of writing/drawing and reading comics dictate that anything that can be drawn can be believed—often if not most times with little or no attention to verisimilitude between what is represented on the page and what we perceive in the three-dimensional world beyond the page. This has made the medium especially effective as a space for the depiction of an array of fantastical characters, worlds, and social interactions (among humans, mutants, aliens, cyborgs, and other "inhuman" figurations). The fantasy aspects of the medium have historically lent themselves to the depiction of a vast array of nonnormative expressions of gender and sexuality—from the most metaphoric (in hyperbolic camp visuality or the metamorphosing of human bodies into forms that call into question traditional gender norms, etc.) to the most literal (the actual depiction of queer bodies and erotic attachments).

Such figures are possible to read as refractions of social and political possibilities. As coeditor Ramzi Fawaz (2016) shows in *The New Mutants: Superheroes and the Radical Imagination of American Comics*, a perhaps unexpected example of comics' refractory fantastic can be found in *The Fantastic Four* (1961), the first commercial hit of mainstream superhero comics giant Marvel during Marvel's revival in the early 1960s. In that series, the three male characters' physical mutations run up against and undermine their ability to embody normative masculinity even as their commercial dominance and fan response presented them as exemplars in a tradition of representation whose intention (after Wertham's Comics Code Authority) was to produce heroic masculine role models. Instead, the heroes were freaks: Mr. Fantastic's pliability was a sign of "softness," the Thing's rocky body rendered him fundamentally androgynous, and the Human Torch's flaming body functioned both as a figure of hypermasculinity and as a visual signifier of the "flaming" homosexual of Cold War America. The extraordinary transformations that made them "super" and "heroes" also unraveled their traditional performance of gender and sexuality—or, as Fawaz suggests, such unraveling might even productively be seen as a necessary part of how it was possible to *think* heroism (for the cultural producers who were putatively straight, educated white males) on the cusp of the vast social changes coalescing under the signs of the civil rights movement and, later, black power, second-wave feminism, the sexual revolution, the rise of the American Left antiwar movement, and gay liberation.

3. The unpredictability of serial narrative and narration and the visual structure of comics as a set of sequential panels that repeat, but always with a difference, suggest that comics are *formally* queer. Just as the underlying premise in comics that anything that can be drawn can be believed taps into the productivity of human capacities for fantasy, the formal character of comics—the idea that you can have indefinite iterations of a given story that never reproduce a single trajectory—helps clarify the ways that fabulation underwrites our realities, in decidedly queer ways.

Here for definitions we can turn to Saidiya Hartman's (2008, 11) description of the practice of critical fabulation:

> "Fabula" denotes the basic elements of story, the building blocks of the narrative. A fabula, according to Mieke Bal, is "a series of logically and chronologically related events that are caused and experienced by actors. An event is a transition from one state to another. Actors are agents that perform actions. (They are not necessarily human.) To act is to cause or experience an event."
>
> By playing with and rearranging the basic elements of the story, by re-presenting the sequence of events in divergent stories and from contested points of view, . . . [critical fabulation] attempt[s] to jeopardize the status of the event, to displace the received or authorized account, and to imagine what might have happened or might have been said or might have been done.

What is potentially queer about comics' fabulation and thus the formal relation comics bear to queer politics? Take two fundamental conceits of queer theory: In what is perhaps the most oft-quoted line from the inaugural moment of queer theory, Judith Butler (1991, 313) claimed that "gender is a kind of imitation for which there is no original." Only second to this then-revolutionary statement might be Sedgwick's (1993, 8) bracing contention that "one of the things that 'queer' can refer to [is] the open mesh of possibilities, gaps, overlaps, dissonances and resonances, lapses and excesses of meaning when the constituent elements of anyone's gender, of anyone's sexuality aren't made (or can't be made) to signify monolithically." Though both theorists first formulated these claims to describe the instability of gendered and sexual identity, their statements characterize the operation of the comic strip form exactly. As a serialized medium, comics proliferate images that imitate both material or embodied experience and previous images or copies in a sequence; this proliferation, which visually appears as an "open mesh" of pictorial icons organized in countless sequences, underscores the limitless differences produced between an ever-expanding range of images and the figures and worlds they depict. Simultaneously, the sheer number of images, texts, and characters the medium produces renders claims to originality superfluous, as does the presentation of mutant, monstrous, or altogether fantastical characters that have no "original" form in everyday life. Perhaps more than any other literary or cultural mode, then, comics self-consciously multiply and underscore differences at every site of their production so that no single comics panel can ever be made "to signify monolithically." Each iteration of an image, an issue, a storyline, or a world has the potential to disrupt, comment on, or altogether alter the flow and direction of what has come before: in this sense, comics function, to borrow from Sara Ahmed (2006), as queer orientation devices, productively directing readers toward deviant bodies that refuse to be fixed in one image or frame, toward new desires for fantasy worlds that rebel against the constraints of everyday life, and toward new kinds of counterpublic affiliations among readers who identify with the queer, deviant, maladjusted form called comics.

Each of these areas of nexus is rich unto itself and allows scholars working at the intersection of queer theory and comics studies to talk about a range of things—from the cultivation of rarefied fan communities, to the production of queer intimacies between readers and fantasy characters, to formal and representational feats that lend themselves to being articulated to the depiction of nonnormative or queer orientations to the world.

Following is an example of how a reading attentive to these vectors of confluence reveals that the most quotidian—or what we could heuristically propose as paradigmatic—encounter with even mainstream superhero comics is replete with queer meanings. Figure 1 shows the cover of the first comic book that coeditor Darieck Scott remembers buying as a child. This cover features Nubia, the iconic superhero Wonder Woman's black twin sister, who debuted in 1973 (Bates and Heck 1973; the cover artist is Nick Cardy). Nubia was in many ways a failed superhero character. She appeared on this cover and in a part of DC Comics' bid during the bronze age (c. 1970–84) to broaden its

Figure 1 Wonder Woman and Nubia face off in 1973. From Bates and Heck (1973), *Wonder Woman* #206

consumer audience, to capitalize on the apparent success of Blaxploitation films, and to signal that the fantasy world of DC Comics, like that of its rival Marvel Comics, was engaged with "real" contemporary developments like racial integration and the emergence of the site of the black ghetto in US cultural discourse. The character Nubia, however, unlike other DC Comics 1970s assays in racial diversity such as now-mainstay character John Stewart, "the black Green Lantern," gained little traction, disappearing from *Wonder Woman* after three issues and never becoming a frequently recurring secondary or even tertiary character in DC's fantasy world. Yet Nubia's apparent inability to capture the attention of her creators (Don Heck, penciller; Cary Bates, the principal writer; and Robert Kanigher, the editor) did little to prevent the character from becoming a template figure for a range of fantasies of black power and beauty proliferating in a fan counterpublic—a fandom aware of its "subordinate" or "alternative" status within the larger counterpublic of never-quite-mainstream Wonder Woman fans. Typing "Nubia Wonder Woman" into an internet image search nets you pages of fan-created images of the character, as well as references to the web page for "Nubia, the Illustrated Index" (Strickland n.d.). (A recent book on comics by Deborah Elizabeth Whaley [2015], *Black Women in Sequence: Re-Inking Comics, Graphic Novels, and Anime*—reviewed in this special issue—devotes seven-plus pages to considering Nubia.)

Scott, unaware of this context or this future for Nubia when he was first powerfully attracted to the cover image, became an initiate of Nubia's counterpublic in a way that can scarcely be understood without the assistance of queer theory. Having had no previous exposure to Wonder Woman as a six-year-old in 1973, Scott was entranced by, desirous of, and identified with this image of a dark-skinned, glamorous, powerful black woman warrior. Nubia was the kind of black and queer object of desire that contributor andré carrington describes in his essay, "Desiring Blackness: A Queer Orientation to Marvel's *Black Panther*, 1998–2016." It was also, significantly, and in the paradigmatic manner in which comics provide sources of fantasy for their readers of whatever age, an *education* instantiating such desire, before Scott could have named black and queer as objects of desire, in a world that, of course, makes the satisfaction of such desires exceedingly difficult. Scott's attraction to this cover image and to Nubia's story inaugurated a fantasy of black power and black beauty, conjunctions that could not appear as other than at least partly if not wholly fantastic within what was apparent even to a child as an antiblack "real" world. Here, then, we see a comic operating precisely as a queer orientation device, productively directing young Scott and other readers both then and later toward new desires for fantasy counterworlds that rebel against the constraints of everyday life.

But of course the cover image is also shot through with the discourses of antiblackness, signaled by its use of well-worn tropes that enable a much more demoralizing reading. Above we note that queer orientation devices direct readers toward "deviant bodies" as much as new desires, and here we can discern, not without dismay, the price that deviance pays even in fantasy, when measured on a scale of value that pushes against but cannot escape the racist contexts of its creation. Apart from the interesting choice of "Nubia" as the character's name, the otherwise glorious leopard-skin skirt here functions, through signifying wildness, animality, and their overdetermined exemplars the "jungle" and "Africa," as though it were a kind of transnational or supranational costume of blackness—a blackness and an Africa made powerful by the fact that Nubia is powerful, a wildness and animality rendered glamorous by her superheroic aura. These associations open the image to fully justified accusations of caricature and stereotyping. (Importantly, this costume appears only on this cover, where Nubia's identity has to be established with a minimum of text or story contextualization; in fact, Nubia never appears in this costume in the comic books and instead wears feminized Roman armor.) At the same time, this concatenation of effects and affects is flanked by the presence of the sword and the Roman-helmeted villain in ghost form looming behind, linking them to the familiar imagery of the classic ancient world and to classical evocations of mythic heroism: in such a way that the combined Barthesian *studium* and *punctum*, as it were, of the image achieves what Kobena Mercer (1994, 200–201) says (provisionally) of some of Robert Mapplethorpe's photographs of black men, where men "who in all probability" come from the disenfranchised, disempowered late-capitalist underclass are "in the blink of an eye" "elevated onto the pedestal of the transcendental Western aesthetic ideal."

On *Wonder Woman*'s cover Nubia appears historyless, except insofar as her history is that of repeated iterations of racialized types—with all their dangers, harms, and eked-out pleasures—and of largely (but not only) malignant metonyms. The frisson of excitement and pleasure beholding Nubia in 1973—and even now—is the effect of the projections her mute two-dimensional figure invites. As an entirely new superhero then and a rarely featured one now, her image is an example of how the comic book form or the sequential graphic narrative form appeals for and requires the participatory imagination of the reader-viewer. We are invited to imagine the world that makes a powerful black Wonder Woman possible, and from there, we are asked to imagine her presence in the "real" world and the wrongs that her power and beauty might right. Moreover, we are, perhaps, even encouraged to identify with both this black Wonder Woman and her potential power (which may lie ultimately in her very ability to incite endless fabulation on the part of the viewer).

Introduction 207

Figure 2 The reconstituted X-Men appear as a tower of heroic figures on the holographic cover. From Kelly and Peterson (1998), *X-Men* #80

In a different time and context, yet with parallel resonance, Fawaz remembers his own first comic book reading experience in 1998, when he encountered the X-Men, a cadre of mutant outcasts gifted with extraordinary abilities due to an evolution in their genetic makeup. Fawaz was thirteen years old when he picked up *X-Men* #80, the series' thirty-fifth anniversary issue (Kelly and Peterson 1998), at a local comic book shop in Tustin, California, and beheld its radiant holographic pink cover depicting a tower of dazzling, disco-attired superheroes (see fig. 2). At its center appears the steel-plated Colossus carrying the puckish warrior Wolverine aloft his impossibly muscular arm, with the teleporting blue elf Nightcrawler leaping upward near their feet; surrounding this trio are an explosive group of superhuman woman warriors, the intangible Shadowcat, the weather goddess Storm, the nigh-invulnerable powerhouse Rogue, and the bone-wielding rebel Marrow. Growing up in a queer family, sibling to a gay brother, and bullied to tears on a daily basis for his own exuberant gayness, Fawaz immediately connected with the words "A team reunited . . . a dream reborn" emblazoned on that cover, which spoke to him of the promise and possibility of queer kinship and solidarity in the face of overwhelming odds. Above all, what struck Fawaz about that cover was the sheer variety of characters depicted—how could a man made of steel, an intangible woman, a white-haired weather goddess, a butch teen girl with bones sticking out of her skin, and a teleporting blue elf be any kind of a team? Who were these people, and what dream did they share? Almost demanding an act of critical fabulation from its reader, the image elicits a desire to understand how disparate, monstrous mutant heroes might act in concert. In less lofty yearnings, the fantasy of standing atop the arm of a muscle-bound Adonis surrounded by powerful mutant women, in pink holographic form, was at least one gay boy's dream come true.

Like so many readers of the *X-Men* series over the decades, no character drew Fawaz in more than the weather goddess Storm, a Kenyan-born immigrant to the United States, the first black woman superhero in a mainstream comic book, and the X-Men's team leader by the 1990s. In that same anniversary issue, at a low point in the team's battle with an imposter group of X-Men, Storm rallies her bruised and beaten comrades by reminding them that what defines their bond is a set of shared values, a chosen kinship maintained through mutual love and respect, not by force or expectation. With his budding left-wing consciousness, on one side, and his attachment to queer family, on the other, Fawaz fell in love with this fictional mutant goddess and her team: this was the kind of community he longed for. What was it about the visual and narrative fantasy offered by a mainstream superhero comic book circa 1998 that could allow a thirteen-year-old Lebanese American suburban gay boy to so deeply and sincerely identify with an orphaned, Kenyan, mutant immigrant X-Man? If one were to try and explain this question by turning to recent public debates about superhero comics, we might put forward the answer, *diversity*. Yet this term and its shifting meanings—variety, difference, or representational equality—would have rung false to Fawaz's teenage ears. It was not simply the fact of Storm's "diverse" background as Kenyan, immigrant, woman, or mutant that drew Fawaz to her but rather her ethical orientation toward those around her, her response to human and mutant differences, and her familial bond with her fellow X-Men. These were distinctly queer attachments in that they were grounded in the terms of alternative intimacy, kinship, and belonging. Both the cover image and the narrative that unfolded behind allowed for multiple queer attachments to intermingle at once, from affective aspirations for alternative community, to burgeoning erotic desires for a range of superhuman male bodies, to cross-gender and racial identifications.

These two examples of readerly identification and fabulation underscore a well-worn yet endlessly generative fact about the comics medium: the participation of the reader in completing the story usually is invited to occur between separate panels of images, in the "gutters." Scott McCloud (1993, 60–74), a pioneer in theorizing the comic book form, calls this structural element in sequential-art comic book storytelling "closure." McCloud identifies six different kinds of panel-to-panel transitions that insist on the reader's imaginative contribution of completion to story elements: moment-to-moment transitions; action to action; subject to subject; scene to scene; aspect to aspect; and non sequitur (i.e., no apparent sequential relation). To return to Scott's example, Nubia's cover image is not strictly speaking an instance of this kind of structure of graphic storytelling, since Nubia here is iconic, presented in the recognizable postures of the adored superhero, rather than placed in a sequence. Yet the function of the gutter is taken up within the "panel" itself by Nubia's clear mirroring of Wonder Woman in all but skin color and costume, a repetition with a difference that asks to us to consider the sibling relationship announced in the caption between the two characters and to ponder at once the possibilities and the limits of their equality. It is possible to see that in fact there *are* transitions from McCloud's taxonomy in operation: an implied action-to-action transition, because Wonder Woman and Nubia have their swords raised and appear to be charging each other; a subject-to-subject transition, because the characters are divided by the sword and because they are presented as radically differentiated mirror images of each other; and perhaps even a non sequitur transition, precisely because of the image's invitation to see the characters as so radically different, a difference underlined and intensified by the unnecessary presence of the leopard-skin skirt, which acts like a multiplier of racialized difference and an elaborate stage-hook begging us to pull stereotypes into the frame.

Once you open the cover and read the story within, Nubia's history is the same modern reimagining of the mythological as Wonder Woman's—she, too, was fashioned from clay and breathed into life by the gods, just darker clay than that of the pink-skinned Diana. The dividing sword and its gutter-within-the-panel function may illustrate how Nubia's character and image are engaged in an act of "crossover," just as pre-hip-hop black recording artists like Diana Ross, Michael Jackson, and Prince were often measured—and criticized—by the fact that the buyers of their records were not just black but included a significant white fandom. As such a crossover (though in reverse with respect to the positions and numbers of creators and consumers), Nubia registers in ways that always retain an element of being seen as different from white. She provides a template for a fantasy wherein blackness and black woman-ness are powerful, beautiful, and glamorous but largely within the limits of a perspective founded in Negrophilia (at best) and Negrophobia (at worst). This is not without powerful affective charge, especially in a genre like superhero comics in 1973 (and now), where the image of a black woman as heroic or powerful is uncommon and arguably actively repressed; but the image's *work* at the level of empowering anti-antiblack fantasy is perhaps either foreclosed or too much deferred by its appeal to either a notion of equality that smuggles in alongside it whiteness as the standard or to a fairly simple inversion of black-versus-white values. The cover image's formal comic book queerness, though, throws open and makes at least ephemerally manifest what racialized modes of beholding foreclose and defer. The repetition within the cover image, its mirroring and reversal of mirroring, is also an education about the proximities of the supposed gulf between races (the image makes Nubia's difference from Diana one of coloring process and costume only) and as a microcosm of the seriality of comics representation, where the stories and images, as they extend and repeat with alterations from issue to issue, in the hands of different pencillers, writers, inkers, and colorists—both professional and fan—allow for no fixity of image, form, or meaning.

Hence, we can find in reading this image and the palimpsest of many readings that layer it from 1973 on, or in a holographic *X-Men* cover and the affective aspirations of its teenage viewer, paradigms of comic book fandom—a young boy buys a comic book and falls in love with superheroes—and an illustration of how that paradigm, by usual accounts masculinist, covertly raced along the lines of white supremacy (i.e., baseline human is white), and imbued with a nostalgia conducive to any number of wicked conservative politics, is far queerer than it may appear. The stories we have recounted are actually that of a black and a Lebanese American boy's introduction to superhero comics happening via identification and disidentification (in the sense of José Esteban Muñoz [1999, 31]) with an image of a female character presented as "black" and in a context where this image is a novelty within the pantheon of superheroic images, since few black-appearing characters grace comic book covers (significant exceptions being Marvel's Luke Cage in 1972 and John Stewart on a *Green Lantern* cover in 1971). In this light, the marginal appearance in a marginal, dismissed-as-childish genre of representation rendered that marginal world of comics a world *for Scott's and Fawaz's own differences*—of blackness in an antiblack world and of cross-gender identification in a misogynist world that punishes boys for "girly" behavior as it constantly punishes cisgendered girls as "inferior." Thus, this particular paradigm of comics fandom is a story of queer intimacy among character, reader, genre, and form.

What is most striking and generative about the collection of essays brought together in this special issue is the vast range of conceptual maneuvers they accomplish. Some of the essays provide fully formed queer theories of comics form. Others develop meticulous close readings attuned to the eruption of queerness on the comics page, thereby teaching us how to read comics for their capacity to represent or make visible nonnormative desires, intimacies, and affiliations in ways that might elude other mediums. Yet others track how comics provide an archival visual history of the shifting nature of sexuality in the United States. All make explicit how the formal terms and conceits by which serial comics operate—including sequentially unfolding panels, multidirectional modes of reading, long-form serial narratives, and admixtures of text and image, among others—are repeatedly articulated to the central questions of queer theory, including the relationship of embodiment to desire, the legibility of queer intimacies, and the struggle to make queer modes of living and affiliating both representable and desirable. Rather than offering a single unified queer theory of comics or merely tracking individual representations of queers in comics, these essays *model the variety of ways that comics produce their own visual theories of queer desire.*

"Desiring Blackness: A Queer Orientation to Marvel's *Black Panther*, 1998–2016," by andré carrington, deftly handles the sometimes dissonant registers confronting comics scholarship. The essay takes seriously the notion that something as apparently ephemeral as fantasy and as supposedly childish as superheroes is immersed in, emerges from, partakes of, and comments on lived realities such as race and the discourses that construct those realities. Focusing on the divergent treatments of *Black Panther* comics by authors Christopher Priest (1998–2003) and Ta-Nehisi Coates (2016) of the title character's black female comrades-in-arms, carrington interrogates how race consciousness and colonial legacies inform the discourses of desire operating within the comic. carrington's Black Panther is a fantasy of an African past not subject to European colonialism and of an African utopian present and future that imagine their own forms of queer relationships. carrington brings the often contradictory influences and intertexts shaping *Black Panther* comics together in a meditation on the limits and possibilities of desiring what—from an Afro-pessimist point of view—is structured as the undesirable: blackness. carrington notes how utopian fictions often posit or assume the transcendence of racial distinctions, though the resulting representation frequently, and nigh universally, depicts a kind of assimilation that evacuates racial distinctions of all meaning, such that utopias, if they consider racial conflict at all, usually posit that the horrors of racism are defeated by eliminating the cognizance of race altogether. This common utopia-constituting move at once evidences an emancipatory imagination (and emancipatory politics) and a fundamental antiblackness that can name blackness only as something undesirable. carrington is interested in how the utopian imagination can maintain racial distinction while still fulfilling, or aiming toward the fulfillment of, utopia's promises of a better, more just society; how in the utopian imagination of *Black Panther* comics, though blackness cannot free itself from the anti-blackness that informs and forever subtends it, blackness nevertheless becomes desirable.

In "'Flesh-to-Flesh Contact': Marvel Comics' Rogue and the Queer Feminist Imagination," Anthony Michael D'Agostino argues that the comic book superhero can function as a highly generative conceptual resource for queer theory's investigation of unruly or "rogue" identifications across embodied and cultural differences. D'Agostino conducts a breathtakingly crystalline reading of a single superheroic fantasy figure, the infamous and beloved character Rogue from Marvel Comics' long-running *X-Men* series, which follows the adventures of a cadre of genetically evolved (or "mutant") superheroes who are socially outcast from humanity. Within the long history of superhero comics narratives, D'Agostino argues, Rogue's superhuman ability to absorb the psyches and mutant powers of others has functioned as an extended meditation on the possibilities, risks, and pleasures (both erotic and affective) of coming into contact with those who are unlike us, and consequently it allows us to forge identifications that may alter the very fabric of our being with unexpected results. He compellingly argues, "Rogue coheres as a metafictional figure not just for the specific heroes she touches but for the superhero genre's general conception of superhuman power as consubstantial with a nonnormative body, which is produced through transformative contact that renders differences mobile across a blurred boundary between subject and object." In so doing, D'Agostino suggests that increasingly fraught and defensive postures toward appropriation, assimilation, and other modes of presumably unethical identification with others in contemporary queer politics and theory are productively unsettled by superheroes, fantasy figures with whom we develop deep affective attachment because of their bodily vulnerability to outside forces. D'Agostino sees Rogue not merely as a representational figure for queerness or a fantasy of appropriating "the other" but as a figure who, in her long-running struggles to touch (and hence psychically absorb) others ethically, models a practice of queer intimacy between strangers variously construed. In her various flesh-to-flesh encounters, both coercive and reciprocal, with other mutant and superhuman beings, Rogue's evolving practice of ethical contact surprisingly braids together a wide range of queer, feminist, and queer of color commitments to negotiating and developing lasting ties across differences from the 1970s onward. Ultimately, D'Agostino not only reveals superhero comic books as rich sites of queer theorizing about the electrifying possibilities of identification but trains us to think and be like Rogue, touching our most cherished theoretical and social commitments to identity politics without ever holding on so tight that we become them.

Yetta Howard's "Unsuitable for Children? Adult-erated Age in Underground Graphic Narratives" uses the extraordinarily durable association of comics with childhood reading and entertainment as a starting point for theorizing the graphic narrative's capacity to "radicalize the definitional borders of adulthood and childhood" in distinctly queer ways. Howard explores how experimental queer writers and artists such as Kathy Acker, Diane DiMassa, Freddie Baer, David Wojnarowicz, James Romberger, and Margeruite Van Cook have used the particular formal qualities of graphic narratives to articulate or visualize complex experiences of childhood trauma and abuse from the perspective of queer adults. Howard puts theoretical pressure on the tendency to view comics as a medium that adulterates or taints developmentally "healthy" or desirable reading practices by willfully combining admixtures of text and images in ways that are analogous to the perception of queerness as a mode of being in the world that makes childhood sexuality impure or contaminated. Refusing this normative developmental logic, Howard instead makes a claim for the conceptually sophisticated and aesthetically generative qualities of such visual-verbal fusions. She argues, "Thinking about comics and queerness as adulterated textual and identificatory forms, I wish to mobilize the use of *adulterate*—to make impure by adding inferior elements—in excess of the worsening that it denotes and use *adult-erate* to name the ways that childhoods in the texts are adult oriented but also to characterize how their visual-narrative qualities, in their own contexts, revise and reflect notions of impurity and being worsened as singularly queer ways of being and representing." In the experimental comics texts she analyzes, Howard unpacks how various creators often use adult narrative voices alongside disturbing images of childhood sexuality, including sexual abuse and sex work, to show how "growing older" does not necessitate getting better, evolving into a normative sexuality, or covering over childhood traumas. Rather, childhood itself is revealed as an endless series of images to be incorporated into unfolding serial narratives, collectively forming a picture of how we grow askance from normative expectations. Essentially, Howard asks us to attend to the conceptual possibilities that emerge when an adulterated medium collides with distinctly queer narratives of growing up oblique to all expected routes of normal sexual and social development.

In "*Nancy* and the Queer Adorable in the Serial Comics Form," Jessica Q. Stark uses the iconic comic strip character Nancy as an occasion to theorize how comic strip seriality invites the open-ended play of multiplicitous sequential possibilities that might unfold from a single icon, punchline, or gag. Stark places the original *Nancy* comic strips developed by artist Ernie Bushmiller in the 1920s and 1930s (which depicted Nancy as a sly trickster figure continually upsetting rules or pulling practical jokes on friends and neighbors) alongside the playful, erotic, and sometimes perverse appropriations of the Nancy character by gay artist and poet Joe Brainard. In a series of surrealist comics produced throughout the 1970s, Brainard depicted the pincushion-haired, boyish Nancy in a series of shocking and titillating poses, including having sex, doing drugs, exposing her genitals, inhabiting different genres of art, and taking on numerous shapes and forms. Stark disrupts a traditional mode of queer reading or interpretation that would simply see Brainard's work as a queer appropriation of a staid, normative, or one-dimensional mass cultural figure; rather, she reads Brainard *through* Bushmiller in backward sequential order, to argue that Brainard drew on already existing and proliferating queer possibilities in Bushmiller's serial strips from the midcentury. Both artists, she contends, capitalized on Nancy's cuteness by hyperbolizing the seemingly universally adorable qualities of girlhood to the point of absurdity, thereby making what is cute, adorable, sweet, or lovable about feminine heterosexuality seem hyperbolically ridiculous and consequently open to reinvention and play. Stark's most ambitious intellectual move is to treat the open-ended qualities of serial narratives—their invitation to present multiple, contradicting, and proliferating versions of identity, bodies, and intimacies—as a model for a queerly inflected analysis of cultural texts themselves: she reads the presumed sequence of Bushmiller to Brainard in every possible direction, rather than as a historical teleology from an earlier iteration of Nancy to a later queer one. As she forcefully argues, "Considering these works side by side reveals the paradoxical status of the long-publishing US comics figure writ large as a site for queer knowledge-making that invites revisionary accumulations, serial mobility, playful recombination, and an iconic malleability that underscores the multivoiced site of comics as a characteristically queer medium." In so doing, Stark suggests nothing less than comics seriality as a formal method of queer analysis.

Rebecca Wanzo's "The Normative Broken: Melinda Gebbie, Feminist Comix, and Child Sexuality Temporalities" positions the fantasy erotica comic *Lost Girls*, by Alan Moore—a figure from the comics pantheon in both independent comics and superhero comics for mainstream publishers—and Melinda Gebbie within a genealogy of feminist women's comix from the 1970s and 1980s. Focusing on Moore's *Lost Girls* collaborator Gebbie and her debt to and background in women's comix, Wanzo considers how the inherently fantastic and nonrealist or pararealist representations of sexuality in comics allow us to experience pornography and consider sex in productive new ways. Threading its way through feminist debates about the harms or nonharms of pornography, "The Normative Broken" engages fraught discussions of childhood incest and sexual abuse of children, both of which are thematics that figure centrally in *Lost Girls*, as well as in the major intertexts *Lost Girls* references—feminist comix and three classics of children's and fantasy literature, *Alice's Adventures in Wonderland*, *Peter Pan*, and *The Wizard of Oz*. Wanzo argues that *Lost Girls* and its antecedents in women's comix stage a strong intervention in feminist approaches to female sexuality in their surprising deployment of obscenity. In *Lost Girls* and women's comix, taboo representations of children's sexuality and sexual abuse are central to a theorization in image-text narrative form of how traumatic pasts and the irreconcilable desires wrought by sexual injuries create the conditions that help lost girls find homosocial and queer belonging with one another. The comics are models of feminist temporalities of survival in the wake of trauma, but they also depict utopian futures that are often ecstatic and resistant to normative scripts of what we think of as women's healthy sexual subjectivity. In contextualizing and examining a pornographic comic—albeit one with the prestige that Moore's pedigree brings—the essay implicitly argues for widening the range of comics that comics studies takes seriously, pushing beyond the recognizably literary memoirs and autobiographies praised in studies of Alison Bechdel, Phoebe Gloeckner, Art Spiegelman, and others and beyond even superheroes. Wanzo draws connections among comics studies, pornography and porn studies, feminist approaches to female sexuality, the study of children's literature, and theorizations of childhood and girlhood.

Our two final essays both examine the work of Alison Bechdel, with very different disciplinary and methodological approaches that nonetheless pay close attention to the comics form and its availability to illumination by queer theory. Kate McCullough's "'The Complexity of Loss Itself': The Comics Form and *Fun Home*'s Queer Reparative Temporality" focuses on Bechdel's celebrated 2006 graphic memoir

Fun Home to make broader claims about comics' potentiality for queer world making. McCullough closely reads *Fun Home* using queer theories of temporality—considering notions such as Elizabeth Freeman's "temporal drag," Kathryn Bond Stockton's "growing sideways," scrambled time, and the asynchronies between sacred time and human time. *Fun Home*, McCullough argues, exemplifies queer understandings of the past and of futurity, and invites a reparative reading of family that emphasizes queer kinship's departure from heteronormativity. "Opening up registers of queer time not available in purely prose or purely visual form, comics offer a unique opportunity for the enactment of a queer temporality," McCullough maintains. Bechdel's *Fun Home* mines the formal possibilities inherent in the medium itself to destabilize linear-progress narratives of sexual and psychological development. McCullough's essay integrates a vast body of knowledge in both queer studies and comics studies to inform virtuoso close readings of Bechdel's graphic memoir. The essay's robust analytical attention to both form and content in a graphic work provides a compelling model of how to use existing queer theories to conduct productive new readings of the formal qualities of comics and of how the comics form itself helps enrich our theorizations of queerness.

Alternatively, in "'The Lesbian Norman Rockwell': Alison Bechdel and Queer Grassroots Networks," Margaret Galvan meticulously reconstructs the queer grassroots publishing networks that enabled Bechdel to develop a national following, first with her long-running comic strip *Dykes to Watch Out For* (1983) and subsequently with her award-winning graphic novel *Fun Home*. Galvan uses Bechdel as an iconic case study for thinking about comics as a distinctly queer archive, a medium that weaves its way through larger histories of LGBTQ print and visual media production and political activism. Galvan tracks the origins of Bechdel's developing creative world making, including her beloved serial narrative of a cadre of radical queer and feminist friends, in a vast range of small gay and lesbian periodicals from the early 1980s onward, analyzing them within the larger visual contexts in which they were published such as LGBTQ-oriented advertising and local news stories. Galvan reads Bechdel's archive of comic strips as providing material evidence of LGBTQ cultural and political practices that are often obscured when such comics are reproduced and circulated outside their original print contexts, thereby losing their ties to larger queer collective cultural production. She claims: "I develop new practices of close-reading comics that emphasize relationality and thereby unfurl how queer activisms shape such works.... This approach decenters the individual, honoring the rich history of collaboration in comics by opening a conversation about the multiple ways that communities shape even single-authored works." Galvan's project is groundbreaking first in its extensive use of archival materials from a range of locations, including the Lesbian Herstory Archives, the Sophia Smith Collection at Smith College, and Firebrand Book Records at Cornell University; and second, in its theorization of what Galvan calls "the queer comics archive," which she identifies as both the material sources of LGBTQ comics production and an archival research methodology that reads the unexpected appearance of comics in queer cultural and print materials as formal evidence of larger networks of queer community building.

Galvan's essay provides a fitting conclusion to a collection that functions, in and of itself, as a queer comics archive; taken together, the essays relentlessly place queerness in its comics contexts—where it appears in and circulates around the circuits of comics production and consumption—while also recuperating the social relations and imaginative practices that comics have allowed queer subjects to forge. More than anything, perhaps, they model methodologically what it might mean to be *queer about comics*, to approach this medium through its sexiest, most disturbing, and most viscerally charged expressions without turning away from those boldly deviant serial possibilities. In so doing, these essays offer up a range of queer sequences to follow, perhaps even to places we have never dared to draw in our imagination.

Darieck Scott is associate professor of African American studies at the University of California, Berkeley. Scott is the author of *Extravagant Abjection: Blackness, Power, and Sexuality in the African American Literary Imagination* (NYU Press, 2010), winner of the 2011 Alan Bray Memorial Prize for Queer Studies of the Modern Language Association. Scott is also the author of the novels *Hex* (Carroll and Graf, 2007) and *Traitor to the Race* (Plume, 1995), and the editor of *Best Black Gay Erotica* (Cleis, 2004). His fiction has appeared in the anthologies *Freedom in This Village* (Carroll and Graf, 2005), *Black like Us* (Cleis, 2002), *Giant Steps* (2000), *Shade* (1996), and *Ancestral House* (Westview, 1995), as well as in the erotica collections *Flesh and the Word 4* (Plume, 1997) and *Inside Him* (2006). He has published essays in *Callaloo*, *GLQ*, the *Americas Review*, and *American Literary History*.

Ramzi Fawaz is associate professor of English at the University of Wisconsin, Madison. He is the author of *The New Mutants: Superheroes and the Radical Imagination of American Comics* (NYU Press, 2016), winner of the Center for Lesbian and Gay Studies Fellowship Award and the ASAP Book Award of the Association for the Study of the Arts of the Present. His work has been published in numerous journals, including *American Literature, GLQ, ASAP/Journal, Feminist Studies*, and *Callaloo*. Along with Deborah Whaley and Shelley Streeby, he is a coeditor of the forthcoming *Keywords in Comics Studies* volume from NYU Press. He is completing a new book titled *Queer Forms* (forthcoming, NYU Press), which explores the aesthetic innovations of movements for women's and gay liberation in the 1970s and after.

References

Ahmed, Sara. 2006. "Orientations: Toward a Queer Phenomenology." *GLQ* 12, no. 4: 543–74.

Bates, Cary (writer), and Don Heck (penciller). 1973. *Wonder Woman* 1, no. 206. New York: DC Comics.

Butler, Judith. 1991. "Imitation and Gender Insubordination." In *The Lesbian and Gay Studies Reader*, edited by Henry Abelove, Michele Aina Barale, and David Halperin, 307–20. New York: Routledge.

Fawaz, Ramzi. 2016. *The New Mutants: Superheroes and the Radical Imagination of American Comics*. New York: NYU Press.

Hartman, Saidiya. 2008. "Venus in Two Acts." *Small Axe* 12, no. 2: 1–14.

Kelly, Joe (writer), and Brandon Peterson (penciller). 1998. *X-Men* 2, no. 80. New York: Marvel Comics.

McCloud, Scott. 1993. *Understanding Comics: The Invisible Art*. New York: HarperCollins.

Mercer, Kobena. 1994. *Welcome to the Jungle: New Positions in Black Cultural Studies*. New York: Routledge.

Muñoz, José Esteban. 1999. *Disidentifications: Queers of Color and the Performance of Politics*. Minneapolis: Univ. of Minnesota Press.

Sedgwick, Eve Kosofsky. 1990. *Epistemology of the Closet*. Berkeley: Univ. of California Press.

———. 1993. *Tendencies*. Durham, NC: Duke Univ. Press.

Strickland, Carol A. n.d. "Nubia: The Illustrated Index." *Carol A. Strickland*. www.carolastrickland.com/comics/wwcentral/misc_indexes/nubia/nubia.html (accessed December 12, 2017).

Warner, Michael. 2005. *Publics and Counterpublics*. New York: Zone Books.

Wertham, Fredric. 1954. *Seduction of the Innocent*. New York: Rinehart.

Whaley, Deborah Elizabeth. 2015. *Black Women in Sequence: Re-Inking Comics, Graphic Novels, and Anime*. Seattle: Univ. of Washington Press.

andré carrington

Desiring Blackness:
A Queer Orientation to Marvel's
Black Panther, 1998–2016

Abstract The socially symbolic figure of the superhero comes into close contact with vernacular intellectual critiques of race and modernity through the much-anticipated film adaptation of Marvel's *Black Panther* comics. This article analyzes the implications for queer approaches to black popular cultural production of the knowledge practices that inspire *Black Panther*'s depiction of an African utopia. The intertexts involved include histories, travel writings, and other comics. Focusing on the divergent treatments by authors Christopher Priest (1998–2003) and Ta-Nehisi Coates (2016) of the title character's black female comrades-in-arms, this reading interrogates how race consciousness and colonial legacies inform the discourses of desire operating within the text. The term *desiring blackness* describes an orientation to reading that defers to African Americanist and black diasporic considerations to ground the task of interpretation in conditions that elicit compromise among disparate lines of theoretical inquiry: queer phenomenology, decolonial epistemology, Afrofuturism, and queer of color critique.
Keywords comics, utopia, diaspora, African American studies, queer theory, nationalism

The passionate attachment that often characterizes black and queer orientations to cultural texts can teach us many things. With respect to the role of desire in interpretation, the stories told in comic books prove instructive through their continual reappearance in new forms to appeal to the attitudes of different segments of the reading public. The film adaptation of Marvel's *Black Panther* comics (newly released as of this writing) certainly promises to expand the range of persons implicated in interpreting the set of texts that provide its content. Importantly, this media event also marshals the labors of a considerable number of visibly black persons—actors and filmmakers—whom the viewing audience already regards with some combination of affective dispositions, intellectual interests, and indifference. Familiarity with the prior textual constructions of the film's protagonists heightens my curiosity about how the critical priorities we bring to comics are informed by the anteriority of our relationship to blackness. As a discussion of what is queer about comics emerges in the watershed of a particularly black moment in the production of narratives derived from the medium, it seems fitting to ask what we expect and what we desire in relation to comics in explicitly race-conscious terms.

Some of the persons responsible for the proliferating images of the Black Panther in print and other media include writers Christopher Priest, Ta-Nehisi Coates, Roxane Gay, and Yona Harvey; artists Brian Stelfreeze, M. D. Bright, Alitha Martinez, and Afua Richardson; the late comics and animation innovator Dwayne McDuffie; filmmakers Reginald Hudlin and Ryan Coogler; actors Chadwick Boseman and Djimon Hounsou; and the character's creators, Stan Lee and Jack Kirby. In this discussion, I focus on the comic book series written by Priest from 1998 to 2003 and the first several issues of the most recent series authored by Coates in 2016, because their contributions to the past half-century of *Black Panther*'s textual history play an outsize role in its current reception.

The spectacle of black performance and interpretation accruing to this set of texts will undoubtedly garner renewed attention to the politics of black popular media from all quarters. Before this resurgence, I want to inflect the critical lexicon with a greater awareness of the degree to which the *Black Panther* phenomenon is already situated in a dense network of desiring practices. Heightening this awareness is necessary in order to forestall habits of critical description that circumscribe black textual practices within (racially) unmarked knowledge formations. In the past, such categorical gestures have underestimated the difference between black Marxism and historical materialisms that treat racial identity as epiphenomenal to class (Robinson 2000); they have misrecognized black feminist mobilizations as inimical to black liberation and women's emancipation (Harris 2011); and they have marginalized black artistic responses to the changing conditions of modernity in accounts of modernism and postmodernism (Harper 1994; Dickson-Carr 2013).

In venues like this special issue, queer studies prides itself on overcoming disciplinary preoccupations that eclipse the centrality of race to the construction of sexuality, gender, and its other objects of inquiry (Harper et al. 1997; Duggan 2015). Accordingly, in this article, I argue that reckoning with what is black about this particular comics text is a corequisite for posing the question of what is queer about comics. Facing what is black about the way in which certain comics are queer is a practice of *orientation*. In Sara Ahmed's (2006, 545) words, accounting for our orientation toward objects entails acknowledging how "the world that is around us has already taken certain shapes, as the very form of what is more and less familiar." Habituating ourselves with the distinctly racial attachments of the text is one way to counter what Ernesto Javier Martínez (2013, 116) refers to as the "muted sociality of queerness," which predisposes us to ascribe queerness to that which transgresses familiar arrangements of identity and desire more often than we perceive it in intragroup (e.g., intraracial) terms. Emphasizing the social, intersubjective quality of "queer" over its individuating dimensions enables critical observers to recognize "that queer experiences are actually *coproduced and shared* by larger collectives (even though these collectives often deny their own implicatedness in queer sociality). It also provides an unusually in-depth reminder that some nonqueer people actually work to resist the logic of social fragmentation mandated by homophobic societies and that they do so, at times, by bearing 'faithful witness' to acts of queer social resistance—even when it is dangerous to do so" (16). Recognizing how collective practices constitute queer subjects reminds us that "queer does not have a relation of exteriority to that with which it comes into contact" (Ahmed 2006, 544). Owing to the work that "nonqueer" authors and audiences have done to bring *Black Panther* to prominence, we ought to acknowledge that the implications of developments in black popular culture for queer criticism are entangled with the internal dynamics of black cultural politics.

My effort to preempt queer readings of *Black Panther* arises out of a learned vigilance toward the silencing that can take place when disparate intellectual traditions meet on the plane of popular controversy. For *Black Panther*, the stage for assessments of what is queer about comics has been set by recent interventions in critical theory concerned with epistemic violence around questions of race. The concept of epistemic violence harks back to Gayatri Chakravorty Spivak's radical question, "Can the subaltern speak?" and its corollary, "Can the hegemonic ear hear anything?" (Barrett 2004, 359). According to another feminist philosopher of language, Kristie Dotson, epistemic violence is the silencing we experience when our interlocutors fail, intentionally or otherwise, "to communicatively reciprocate a linguistic exchange owing to pernicious ignorance.... *Pernicious ignorance* should be understood to refer to any reliable ignorance ... that is *consistent* or follows from a predictable epistemic gap" (Dotson 2011, 238).

Critics concerned with the epistemic gaps that result in pernicious ignorance highlight how they are reproduced through institutional and quotidian practices (Outlaw 2007). At best, such practices disregard the nuance that closer attention to marginalized knowledge traditions might yield. But the cumulative impact of silencing marginal texts and repertoires is the subjugation of vital ways of knowing and being in the world (Taylor 2003). These subjugating effects occur when the inauguration of a school of thought, such as new materialism or the posthuman turn, claims to discover phenomena "familiar to, among others, First Nations and Indigenous peoples; to those humans who have never been quite human enough" (Tompkins 2016). They occur when overweening suspicion about the totalizing tendencies of colonial modernity effaces the multiplicity of logics, universalisms, and modernities envisioned among colonized peoples (Mbembe 2003; Quijano 2007). Queer studies is not immune to this predicament. For example, out of a sensitivity to transnational capitalism, some critics trace the articulation of new sexual economies and gender expressions in the global South to US and European influences propagated by globalization; this occludes the more complex genealogies of local sex cultures undergoing transformation (Jackson 2009).

As black scholars have enhanced our focus on sexuality over time, our concerns have converged with queer studies, but we draw from different foundations. Significant cultural production by black lesbian, feminist, gay, and gender-nonconforming activists and artists in the 1980s and 1990s addressed sexuality as a factor in the construction of racial difference and social inequality (Johnson 2014). Yet the provenance of these works—their publication, often by nonacademic presses, alongside poetry and pornography—consigned them to the periphery of the emergent queer studies canon (Macharia 2014). As Roderick A. Ferguson (2012, 224) writes, "Understanding the procedures by which queerness is brought into the administrative ethos means that we have to both comprehend the administrative management of race and gender and theorize the relation of those forms of difference to queerness as an administrative object." As we institutionalize the priorities of black and queer constituencies through academic inquiry, we ought to interrogate continually what textuality and visibility have meant for the way our desires are represented in the popular imagination.

In order to maintain a relation of reciprocity with the intellectual prerogatives that make texts like *Black Panther* legible, queer theorizations of black popular culture must undo the effects of "insistent and profound ignorance of people of color, even in the twenty-first century" (Holland 2014, 804). In the interpretation of *Black Panther* comics that follows, I forward the notion that blackness comprises a "cathectic and world-making" apparatus that is indispensable to understanding the cultural politics of African American popular texts.[1] By offering an orientation to the discourses of desire that inform *Black Panther*'s fabulations, I will illustrate how black and queer critical idioms might speak to one another's respective and mutual interests in the construction of identity, space, and modernity, as well as gender and sexuality.

I posit the present discussion as an instructional gesture toward the incipient queer readings that will attend the explosion of *Black Panther* texts in the years to come. I employ the term *desiring blackness* with an appreciation for its resonance with a similar formulation coined by Aliyyah Abdur-Rahman (2012, 158), who asserts that "there is always already something queer about blackness." My analysis takes exception to this axiom. Rather than presuming that queerness is emerging in a new, black form on the cultural landscape, I aim to orient readers to habits of desiring inscribed in black textuality that should be of interest even if they may never "touch" queerness (Muñoz 2009, 1).

The rhetoric of desiring, rather than defining, what blackness is or what it means emphasizes what blackness *does* and what we, as readers, do in relation to it. Focusing on two formative moments in the textual corpus, I outline the tasks of desiring blackness in *Black Panther* comics in three stages. First, I discuss how a succession of writers approach a signature trope in *Black Panther* to construct a sexual politics that resists overdetermination by race. Subsequently, I take stock of the geopolitical references grounding *Black Panther*'s countermythology, and I argue that its imaginative reinvention of Pan-African and black nationalist agendas holds felicitous potential for queer readers. Ultimately, these dynamics suggest that a dialogue between queer studies and comics will be made more resourceful by desiring blackness: attending to the demands blackness places on interpretation.

Adored Ones

The most recognizable departure from convention in the new *Black Panther* comics by Coates is a lesbian relationship between prominent

Figure 1 From Coates and Stelfreeze (2016), *Black Panther* #1

characters (see fig. 1). The silhouette of two women's heads backlit by a roaring fire in the first issue of Coates and Stelfreeze's series symbolizes both the characters' sexual passion and the stark contrasts communicated by their dialogue. As the shadows of their faces become one against the fire, they speak of themselves as "dead women," in light of their decision to reverse their prior commitments and start a rebellion against the Black Panther. Coates introduces this development in order to revisit a feature of the text inherited from Priest's era. To characterize the dilemma posed by his predecessors' treatment of sexuality, Coates gestures toward the desire to find grounding in history encoded in each iteration of the narrative. Whereas his explanation refers to plot developments that take place between Priest's tenure as writer of the series and Coates's own, I will go on to suggest that both authors are contending with fundamental quandaries posed by the endeavor to portray the setting of the text as both utopian and African.

The female characters engaged in a kiss in the pages of *Black Panther* #1 (Coates and Stelfreeze 2016) are Aneka and Ayo, members of the all-female elite military force that the hero relies on to secure his person and maintain the peace in the fictionalized African nation of Wakanda, where T'Challa, the Black Panther, reigns. This feature of the comics originated with Priest in 1998. Priest's introduction of the all-female elite bodyguards, whom he named the Dora Milaje, a moniker to which he assigned the pseudotranslation "Adored Ones," left a troubling legacy for future writers. The Dora Milaje were central to Priest's first storyline as author of the *Black Panther* series (Priest and Bright 2000). He depicted the women warriors as wives-in-waiting for the Black Panther; they spoke only to him and addressed him as "Beloved." Because tradition prevents the hero from ever consummating his relationship with a member of the Dora Milaje, a pitched conflict ensues when one of their number seeks to win his love. The lovesick erstwhile devotee, Nakia, becomes a deadly rival. On the cover of *Black Panther* #24, artist ChrisCross depicts the sinister turn in their relationship. The hero holds his arms wide open, exposing his chest to the touch of a woman in a tight, wine-colored bodysuit. Unbeknownst to the Black Panther, she holds a serrated knife behind his back; with her eyes half-closed and her head in profile, her face is concealed from view. The block lettering on the cover exclaims, "HER NAME IS *Malice*!" (see fig. 2). Seductive imagery like this, which links physical intimacy with vulnerability to violence, conveys the impression that the Black Panther and his young female charges posed as much of a threat to one another as they offered mutual support.

Coates describes his discomfort with this background in an interview, characterizing the Dora Milaje concept as "a scantily clad troop of female bodyguards devoted to the Black Panther. It felt like a male fantasy, they seemed to me almost to be jewelry for the Black Panther" (quoted in Gray 2016). As the Black Panther's subordinate companions who hope to become his wife, the female attendants make a show of his command over their bodies, surrounding him as objects of an acquisitive desire. But as "jewelry," in Coates's phrasing, they reveal the character's heterosexuality to be excessively demonstrative and his investment in women as objects too literal. Throughout Priest's tenure as author of the text, however, the chaste courtship between the king and his women warriors reinforced the stability of the fictitious nation's traditions even as they faced new challenges. In the period preceding the launch of the series authored by Coates, the fictitious nation of Wakanda has suffered its first-ever invasion, and several crises of

Figure 2 From Priest and Bright (2000), *Black Panther #24*

leadership have led its people to question their monarch for the first time. Coates takes advantage of this instability to articulate his ambivalence about the role of the Dora Milaje in the text:

> Given what I know of men in the real world and what I know of men throughout history, that's a situation that's ripe for abuse. So it occurred to me that some of the Dora Milaje might have issues with that.
>
> Sometimes people are willing to let go of parts of themselves or their desire to have certain rights if you can give them security.... You might have two people who love each other but can never be public about their relationship, who say, "Well, OK, I'm willing to take that loss for my country." But what happens when they don't even have a country anymore? (quoted in Micheline 2016)

Framing their burgeoning relationship as the exercise of a newfound freedom from overly constraining civic responsibilities situates Ayo and Aneka as participants in a new political order. Those who once practiced restraint in deference to their sovereign now turn against him and toward each other.

In Coates's *Black Panther* #1, Ayo and Aneka's manner of speaking to each other foreshadows the transformation of their relationship: they call one another "Beloved" before they kiss, reclaiming the sobriquet from their patriarch. They subsequently rename themselves Midnight Angels. Later, they proclaim their independence by insisting they are "cherished by no man, but 'adored' by the Goddess herself," fastening their "adored" status to the nation's religion rather than its ruler (Coates and Sprouse 2016). While no writers of the series suggest that repression is a pervasive characteristic of the fictitious nation's culture, Coates rationalizes the Dora Milaje's propriety as a function of military discipline. Portraying the characters as mutineers reclaiming their agency from the devices of the state amplifies their role as rivals to the Black Panther. Whereas they had once prioritized their desire for the nation's security over their desire to enjoy certain liberties, the disintegration of the former enables them to invest their energies in themselves, the people, rather than the king.

Though Coates appears to fashion the Dora Milaje's rebellion into a spectacular deviation from heteronormative conventions, closer examination of these figures' history in the text demonstrates their inherent propensity for the education of desire. They display their allegiance to the state and its king through the symbolic reproduction of heterosexuality—an arranged marriage defers consummation indefinitely. Priest introduced the Dora Milaje along with other new elements of the Black Panther mythos in 1998. At first glance, his contributions form an elaborate but superficial edifice of racialized exoticism around a figure who represents the universal ideals of the superhero: altruism, physical perfection, intellectual sophistication, and a strong moral compass. In a subplot that runs throughout his *Black Panther* series, however, Priest portrays the Dora Milaje as participants in coordinated spatial practices that substantiate the Black Panther's legitimacy as a national leader.

When T'Challa betrays his duties by pursuing Nakia, who was then one of his bodyguards, readers learn that the Dora Milaje are akin to

Figure 3 From Priest and Jusco (1999), *Black Panther* #6

deputies from Wakanda's many ethnic groups (Priest and Jusko 1999; see fig. 3). A brief glimpse into Nakia's past, in flashback form, shows her as a young girl fishing in shallow waters while counselors to the king stand above her in judgment, examining her from the banks of the stream to determine whether she can represent her people. After an extreme close-up in which an elder inspects Nakia's teeth to ensure she is "strong and of good stock," an elder proclaims, "In three summers I present her to the king." Nakia reappears as a bride adorned

Figure 4 From Priest and Jusco (1999), *Black Panther* #6

with makeup, jewelry, and golden neck rings evocative of those worn by married Ndebele women in South Africa (Forbes 1998). T'Challa reassures her, "The role of the Dora Milaje is merely ceremonial. Your king shall not make demands of you"—a promise he will eventually break. The flashback insinuates that the Dora Milaje's relationships to the king represent alliances between disparate descent lines, fulfilling a purpose not entirely unlike marriages among the European aristocracy. The betrothal arrangement among villages, regions, and the seat of government sutures heterogeneous social formations within the fictitious country to its principal power center: a religion devoted to the Panther deity, for which Black Panther is the figurehead. Would-be rivals for local dominance are kept at bay through their communities' shared relationship to the throne. At one point, the king even inducts an African American woman with Wakandan lineage into the Dora Milaje in order to secure her local relatives' allegiance to the throne (Priest and Calafiore 2001).

Rather than romanticizing rural girls' affiliation with a metropolitan nobleman like a Cinderella story, Priest emplots the erotic implications of the Dora Milaje's relationship to the Black Panther in a cautionary tale. Under the hallucinatory influence of a character representing the devil himself, the hero fantasizes about his estranged fiancée, an African American woman named Monica Lynne (Priest and Jusko 1999; see fig. 4). Through a sequence of vertically juxtaposed images illustrating a passionate kiss, readers witness the Black Panther unwittingly mistake Nakia for Lynne. The top panel shows only the lower halves of the two lovers' faces, removing the romantic encounter from time, space, and age. The pink lipstick on one of their faces is the only notable detail. The next image, below, shows them to be a man with a clean-shaven face and natural haircut kissing a woman wearing lingerie on a sofa. The two of them are replaced in the following image with figures taking up the exact same pose in a different setting: the man is recognizable to contemporaneous readers as T'Challa, wearing his trademark sunglasses, shaven head, and goatee, but the young woman wearing red lipstick is Nakia—they are in the back of his limousine. Although she is initially taken aback by T'Challa's astonished, embarrassed reaction to his own compromised judgment, Nakia relishes the prospect of attaining the forbidden love of her king. T'Challa dismisses Nakia from her office among the Dora Milaje, and her infatuation turns into an all-consuming jealousy, subsequently becoming malice.

The prerequisite for betrothal between T'Challa and his armed servants is their vow to love, honor, and obey him. In return, he offers the esteem of a nationally revered occupation and a promise not to make sexual advances toward them. Although the Black Panther is free to take other lovers and to marry, the duties of the Dora Milaje apparently preclude those liberties. The line forbidding sexual liaisons is drawn explicitly in structural terms rather than in terms of consent, and the power differential between the king and his companions bars sexual access, rather than permitting it. By introducing the Dora Milaje with a story that immediately flouts the taboos associated with their role, Priest aims to disabuse readers of the discomfiting connotations of their physical appearance. He provides an alternative explanation for these connotations and relegates the presumptions they invite to an exceptional situation that is met with strong opprobrium. Coates's revisions suggest that his predecessor's work to contain the questionable aspects of the Dora Milaje were only partially successful; still, both writers position black women's empowerment as the staging ground for a conflict between value systems. Both authors enlist the female warriors in an affront against a metanarrative that identifies the African present with the European past.

Amazons, Not Vestals

The phenomenon of *droit de seigneur, droit de cuissage,* or *prima noctis,* the feudal lord's privilege of sexual access to a vassal's bride, is the principal foil to Priest's representation of the Black Panther's Adored Ones. In his study of prima noctis abuse in European history, Alain Boureau (1998) finds little evidence in the historical record that attests to its actual occurrence. On the contrary, he notes that nineteenth-century critics of oppressive religious institutions marshaled accounts of this disgraceful exercise of power from the past in order to delegitimize their political opponents, who were, in their view, out of step with modernity. Peggy McCracken (2000, 354) summarizes Boureau's findings thus: "The historical use of the myth of cuissage is always about power and hierarchy: the lord's status in relation to his dependents; the church's legitimacy with respect to traditional and legal custom; the justice of the present in relation to the abuses of the (medieval) past." The disavowal of despicable habits of power as anachronisms, holdovers from a less-civilized era, is instrumental to the construction in history of a less-modern past that gives way to a modern present. Critics such as Samuel Ramos and Octavio Paz describe this demarcation in spatial as well as temporal terms by identifying how it positions the colonial periphery as backward, behind, or catching up in relation to the centers of metropolitan power (Alcoff 2007). This scheme subjects denizens of the global South to "an alienated relationship to their own temporal reality": "The temporal displacement of space, which causes the colonized person to be unable to experience their own time as the new and instead to see that 'now' as occurring in another space, is the result of a Eurocentric organization of time in which time is measured by the developments in technological knowledge, the gadget porn of iPads and BlackBerrys, and the languages in which that technological knowledge is developed" (85). The "Eurocentric organization of time" universalizes milestones in the history of European societies, such as print literacy and market-based economic exchange, as the common itinerary with which all peoples should travel. By the same token, this organization of time constructs deviations from its normative itinerary that are actually taking place simultaneously, but located elsewhere in the world, as relics of a bygone era or even barbaric, uncivilized stages of development. The normativity of a Eurocentric trajectory for civilization organizes phenomena that are conventionally deemed social, political, and economic into indices of development and narratives of crisis. This same logic also annexes "private" considerations, from notions of hygiene, table manners, sexual practices, and gender expression to the notion of privacy itself and evaluates alternative configurations of these habits in terms of their proximity, resemblance, homology, or hierarchical subordination to dominant private/public regimes (Duggan 2015).

In view of this problematic, which Walter Mignolo theorizes as "colonial difference," we might reconsider whether it is mere relativism or if it might in fact be critical to consider a plurality of distinct place- and time-specific explanations for the devotion of the king's bodyguards (Alcoff 2007, 87). For Priest's portrayal of the Dora Milaje's betrothal to the king to appear modern without installing the European feudal past as its point of departure, it must disavow a version of modernity coterminous with coloniality. Of course, this gesture requires constructing an alternative frame of reference that is visible only through the prism of colonial difference.

If the form of the relationship between the Black Panther and daughters from disparate villages favors its feudal European twin, but Priest aims to convey an insistently different vision of subjects' obeisance to their king that would be free from sexual and class-based hierarchy, how might he achieve such a portrayal? The text would have to align itself with histories of desiring that are opaque when viewed through a Eurocentric lens, so that no matter how congruent its artifacts appear to be with oppressive practices, they still somehow signify alternatives.

The critique of the present on which the story of *Black Panther* is predicated is a refusal to internalize contradictions between colonizer and colonized, men and women, medieval and modern, and lords and vassals. These dichotomies function as homologies for the sexual exercise of power in European accounts of *cuissage*. I would therefore argue that Priest is undertaking a complicated revisionist gesture in his portrayal of the women warriors betrothed to the king. The Dora Milaje pose an alternative to the colonial, medieval, and classical ideals their appearance approximates by disidentifying with their European analogues *and* their African precedents.

Many of the historical antecedents that make the Dora Milaje's significance legible use the word *Amazon* to describe troops of women who adhere to obscure martial traditions. Following Viviane Namaste's (1999) demystification of the term *queer* as metaphor and catachresis and J. Hillis Miller's (2007) disambiguation of the multiple significances of performativity, I propose that exploring the associations of the term *Amazon* in contexts like and unlike those of *Black Panther* may help us understand how it functions as an orienting device for the role of the Dora Milaje in the text. Like the term *Amazon*, the terms *black* and *queer* also prove imprecise but evocative as descriptors for the text's utopian orientation to modernity and its multiple geographies.

The nineteenth-century example cited for the etymology of *Amazon* in the *Oxford English Dictionary* illustrates the term's meaning through contrast. When used "in reference to the sexual habits of the Amazons," it connotes qualities that are opposite those of the word *vestal*, that is, "These hinds are amazons, not vestals."[2] Whereas both words have classical origins, they are markedly local. Like the word *homosexual*, abhorred by sexologists for its illegitimate origins as "a bastard term compounded of Greek and Latin elements," the *Amazon/vestal* pairing is an amalgamation (Somerville 2000, 32). One term hails from Greece and the other from Rome. The prototypical Amazons were equestrian archers from the Eurasian steppe; the women who inspired their stories were female members of a nomadic group rather than separatists (Worrall 2014). The vestal virgins' station in Rome, on the other hand, was sedentary, urban, noble, and sacrificial (Lutwyche 2012). The modern juxtaposition of these terms in the defining example comes from the travel writings of English physician George Henry Kingsley, included in a volume by the notorious eugenicist Sir Francis Galton. In his notes on his travels in the Scottish Highlands, Kingsley makes this comparison to describe a herd of deer consisting entirely of female members (hinds) spotted on a hunting trip: "Never by any chance is there a stag in their company, except possibly some effeminate hobbledehoy of a pricket, too weak-minded to take the risks of the hillside. It must, however, be understood that these hinds are Amazons, not vestals, as is evident from the number of calves trotting about amongst them; unless, indeed, they are ladysuperintendents of an educational institution for young stags" (Kingsley 1861, 137). We accrue species-defining characteristics in our own minds when we compare ourselves to nonhuman animals. Kingsley's menagerie emblematizes the use of anthropocentric metaphors to posit the intrinsic humanity of certain expressions of subjectivity: erotic object choice, sexual subcultures, and gender expressions autonomous from sexual physiognomy. His extended metaphor reinforces species difference by using the subjunctive rather than indicative mood: of course, only a male human's awkwardness can make him a "hobbledehoy," and of course, only female humans join Amazon or vestal societies. This fantasy contains a kernel of insight: by fantasizing about, and thereby objectifying, sexuality among nonhumans, we make sense of the subjective and heterogeneous quality of all animals' desiring practices (McHugh 2011, 115–18).

Invoking Greek Amazons and Roman vestals in nineteenth-century Scotland constructs a continuity between classical civilizations and extends it to modern paradigms of female homosocial desire. To use Sylvia Wynter's (2003, 318) phrasing, this fictive continuity is overrepresented among "genres of being human." Like the schemata in which figures like the Mulata Globeleza, Mammy, Jezebel, and Sapphire are embedded, modern Amazons often function as "pornotropes" that objectify female sexuality and gender expression in racially specific terms (Spillers 1987; Soares 2012; Weheliye 2014). These pornotroping traditions literally and figuratively incarcerate women within systems of exploitation. Their echoes resound in Western hegemonic feminism, as well, when colonial and feminist discourses intersect to obfuscate the specificity of third world women's oppression and alienate them from resources for survival and resistance (Hobson 2012, 140–41). An imaginative praxis that militates against the misnaming of black and decolonial desires would cultivate such resources in sacralized and popular traditions.

In *The Sexual Demon of Colonial Power*, Greg Thomas (2007, 22) writes, "While George Padmore once wrote in *Pan-Africanism or Communism?* (1956) that there was a choice to be made, Pan-Africanism can also be construed as an alternative to sexual imperialism." Underlying this assertion is the recognition that Pan-Africanism can be, and has been, articulated in ways that recapitulate heteronormative ideals. In the postcolonial era, the most pathetic of these discourses has decried homosexuality as an affront to "African values" or a symptom of decadence introduced by colonial elites or Islamic aristocrats (Epprecht 2008, 131–32). Meanwhile, the neocolonial desire to rescue "queer Africans in dire need" from AIDS, fundamentalism, and poverty reproduces meanings of sexual conformity and deviance across a broad swath of nations, cultures, and historical epochs (Nyong'o 2012, 46–47). Thomas scrutinizes the antihomophobic rhetoric of the African American and black British bourgeoisie for trafficking in similarly reductive accounts of African and black diasporic ideological tendencies. Pointedly, he writes, "This class of experts take [sic] scant pleasure in Black popular culture and its resistance to the white bourgeois culture of empire" (Thomas 2007, 142). I am less sympathetic to his arguments about where critics find pleasure than I am interested in extending his disidentification with black popular culture as a repository of anticolonial knowledge. While the insurgency of interventions performed in a mass medium like comics is questionable, the Dora Milaje's uncanny correspondence with meanings of blackness that both affirm and defy colonial difference makes them a compelling figure for the alternatives to sexual imperialism we all desire.

The palette with which *Black Panther* paints desirable and desiring blackness as the foundation for a hypothetical national culture reflects a broad spectrum of anticolonial literature encompassing Edward Said's *Orientalism* (1978), Walter Rodney's *How Europe Underdeveloped Africa* (1972), Audre Lorde's "biomythography" (1982), and the Afrocentric school of thought inspired by Cheikh Anta Diop. While the latter body of scholarship is especially marginal in contemporary academic institutions, people of African descent across social classes have reflected on its epistemological significance in ways that do more than imbibing it in undiluted form. Vernacular texts that synthesize disparate currents in American, Africana, and postcolonial thought—like *Black Panther*, Milestone Media, black exploitation cinema, and so-called street lit—ensure that African pasts remain available to the many and varied desires of the black diasporic reading public (Brown 2000, 19–24). As critics, we can harness the insights of popular readership by reconciling its vulnerability to critique and co-optation with its potential to mobilize "radically revisionary epistemological formations that would attribute equivalent efficaciousness to myth, dream, and history" (Russell 2009, 60–61).

Precedents for the Dora Milaje can be found throughout the annals of precolonial African history, and they provide fodder for inspirational fiction and propaganda alike. Notably, author Jewelle Gomez catalogued a number of these figures to contest the whiteness of the feminist movement in science fiction in the 1980s (carrington 2016, 239). The appearance of female aides-de-camp to a warrior-king occur in historical proximity to Priest's *Black Panther* comics, as well. In an affinity with *Black Panther* that may be undesirable, the late Libyan leader Muammar Qaddafi's all-female personal security detail was alternately called the Amazonian Guard and Revolutionary Nuns, evoking members' dedication to the nation and citing their putative chastity as proof (Fulcher 1990; Kokan 1995). Qaddafi's advocacy for Pan-African and Arab unity, as well as his culpability for political violence, amplified the idiosyncrasy of his persona, including the spectacle of his female bodyguards (Falola, Morgan, and Oyenini 2012, 42–45).

In addition to this contemporary likeness, other touchstones for the Dora Milaje are embedded more deeply in the imaginations of readers acquainted with African American letters. Historicizing the trope as neither a dubious homage to a Pan-Africanist patriarch nor an invention cut from whole cloth requires a concerted effort to bridge the gap between black diasporic heritage and its roots. Desiring blackness has always required such fabulation. As Kevin Young (2012, 147–48) writes: "The remapping performed by the enslaved African and the freed artist—turning an Africa of memory, and even of recent experience, into utopia—was pitched against the notion of Africa as 'no place' in the European imagination. . . . Given that the imagination is where the Negro was first questioned and dismissed, why wouldn't black folks also choose the imagination as the site of this struggle and reclamation?" The same willful imagination enables us to construct queerness as an impetus for the recovery of improbable meanings. When Martínez (2013, 114) recommends restoring a sense of sociality to queerness, he highlights the integral role of such willful, context-bound self-definition in communities of color: "Queer people define themselves in relation to some of the same webs of cultural meaning that heterosexuals around them draw from. . . . In this sense, queers are engaged participants in the dialogic production of cultural meanings and therefore fundamentally part of the collective experience and imaginary." We can understand why *Black Panther*'s deployment of African imagery makes sense to readers if we reimagine blackness as a space of plenitude in which longings that go unvoiced elsewhere in popular and academic mediations find some fulfillment. Sifting through the materials out of which readers construct race-conscious historical sensibilities is a necessary gesture toward achieving reciprocity between the "radically revisionary epistemological formations" (Russell 2009, 60–61) invoked by black and queer inquiries.

Wives of the Leopard

The so-called Dahomey Amazons are among the most iconic representatives of military power in precolonial West Africa. The Kingdom of Dahomey (territorially situated in present-day Benin) intimidated its neighbors and rivals by subverting shared conventions of hierarchy, marriage, and violence, especially during the brutal 1890 colonial war with France that deposed its last king, Béhanzin (Hargreaves 1980). Whereas most African women participated in farming, culturally significant rituals, and the management of households, the female soldiers who guarded Dahomey's king and his symbolic wives were notably autonomous.[3] They engaged in their own commerce during peacetime, and they wielded muskets as well as brand-new imported guns in battle, distinguishing them from many of their contemporaries (Bay 1998, 67–69). Like much earlier treatments of the mounted fighters of Scythia, contemporaneous accounts of Dahomey's armed women identified them as exceptions to regional and global norms.

Insofar as its exceptional status reinscribes the norms of colonial thinking, invoking Dahomey as a precedent for Wakanda's fictitious modernity is problematic. As Iris Berger (2003) notes, independence movements that set the agenda for politics and intellectual life in mid-twentieth-century African countries "tied their legitimacy in part to a reimagined past, both colonial and precolonial." Women's perspectives remained marginal to discourses on the formation of national identity. Although African pasts contain resources out of which contemporary readers might fashion a foothold in non-Western epistemologies of gender, race, and power, it can be dangerous to install the marker of colonial difference between an undesirable present and a usable past. It would be tempting to credit twentieth-century authors like Priest with retrieving the glory and egalitarianism of an African society from colonial repression by viewing the Dora Milaje as a postcolonial interpretation of the Amazons of Dahomey. However, that gesture could circumscribe the project of imagining modernity within the boundaries of a conflict between African and European nations. Alternatively, we might appraise the factors that bring Dahomey's palace bodyguards to our attention as modern phenomena in their own right, according to a different understanding of modernity.

The Fon people of Dahomey are situated at an intersection of epistemological considerations important to queer theories and methodologies: for critics concerned with the reliability of various forms of evidence, for theories of how societies reproduce themselves through performance, and for notions of desire as a force that confers meaning—in excess of what can be explained by ideology—on the forms we turn to for interpretation. The kingdom of Dahomey's investment in communication with other polities through writing provides an archive of state interests and social practices that is comparable to its European counterparts in both form and scope. Several accounts from European travelers brought recollections of its history into metropolitan discourse before the late nineteenth-century "scramble for Africa." By the time the people who would be identified with Dahomey in the colonial era put their self-knowledge into forms (stories, linguistic conventions, rituals, and material culture) that were intelligible to their European contemporaries and to readers today, they had already accumulated data that suggest a form of modernity that was augmented, not initiated, by the colonial encounter.

The Dahomeyan state's precursors left traces of their history that referenced roots already firmly established by the seventeenth century for aspects of their shared identity, such as place-names, origin myths, and mnemonics that were communicated to outsiders. One visitor recalls a story of the state's founders: "Danh was killed, and the foundation stone of a palace was built over his corpse. The palace was called Danhomen, *i.e.*, on Danh's belly. . . . This took place in 1625, when the Ffons [*sic*] changed their names to Dahomans" (Skertchly 1874, 85–87). During a period in which they understood their own history to be one of uninterrupted continuity, their neighbors passed into and out of the territoriality of different nations (Monroe 2007, 349–53). To the west was the homeland of Dahomey's founders, which later became the German colony of Togo, and to the east was Yorubaland, including the Oyo Empire that once dominated them politically and financially (Law 1991, 154–66). The kingdom maintained trade with the Islamic world as well, implicating Dahomey in a mercantile and political system that antedated the transatlantic slave trade (Law 1990).

Perhaps the most distinguishing characteristic of Dahomey's social formation was its bureaucracy, made legible in discursive and material terms. Research that synthesizes oral and written sources, along with architectural evidence, attests to complex structures linking the person of the king and his office, his several classes of wives, the women who provided their armed security, the elder female intermediaries through whom men were compelled to address the king at court, and the vast palaces in several cities where thousands of women resided (Morton-Williams 1993, 110–11). While references to various linguistic and cultural traditions inform the representation of the Dora Milaje in *Black Panther*, the Amazons of Dahomey are a compelling example because they present the clearest opportunity to appeal to a precolonial past as the pretext for the narrative's rendition of an African setting. Their trace in the historical record grounds contemporary claims to a concrete utopian orientation to time and space.

The features I cite to characterize Dahomey's modernity are important neither because they illustrate the presence of conventions resembling those of European nations nor because they establish that the state was at an appropriately mature stage in its development when it began to interface with colonial power. Rather, Dahomey's overtures toward its colonial counterparts included its representations of itself *to itself*, which Ferguson (2003, 60) frames in Foucauldian terms as "'the internal discourse of the institution'—the one it employed to address itself, and which circulated among those who made it function." These self-representations, including the reputations attained by the armed women in their ranks, attest to the eighteenth- and nineteenth-century Fon peoples' centuries-long desire to exercise agency over their own and their counterparts' perceptions of their respective places in the world. Reanimating their vision of modernity as part of a utopian intervention in popular culture is a "grounding" gesture, in the sense that Walter Rodney (1969, 60–64) coined the term to describe the work of black diasporic intellectuals. Grounding, viewed as the orientation to world-making that makes the utopian aspirations of Priest and Coates concrete, is "the idea that for people of African descent, connecting with the historical and present conditions of African peoples throughout the Diaspora, rather than aligning with the imperialists, could provide the trust and necessary insight for elites of African descent to lead their own people" (Young 2015).

Black Panther's historically resonant renditions of African Amazons are not unique in contemporary culture. Indeed, another mythmaking endeavor built on imagery from precolonial Benin also utilizes the medium of comics. The United Nations Educational, Scientific, and Cultural Organization (UNESCO) has produced a series of educational modules on women in African history that includes a comic book on the women soldiers of Dahomey. In this narrative, the "elite troops of women soldiers" exit history with the French colonial conquest of the 1890s (Serbin, Joubeaud, and Masioni 2014).

The final page of the comic, illustrated by Pat Masioni, is a single frame juxtaposing three sets of black women who could easily be surrogates for the Dora Milaje (see fig. 5). The centerpiece of the panel features two women in colorful but undecorated wrappers, one with a headscarf, dancing before the Republic of Benin's waving flag. They are flanked on each side by female soldiers. On the left, a group marches in formation wearing camouflage fatigues and carrying bayonetted assault weapons, and on the right, a woman in the foreground strides barefoot on a hillside along with her comrades-in-arms, all of whom bear rifles and wear uniforms resembling an 1851 illustration of a female soldier under King Gezo of Dahomey (see fig. 6). The caption reads: "In addition to the imprint that they have left on the collective memory, the women soldiers bequeathed to the Republic of Benin dances that are performed to this day in Abomey, songs and legends. There are many women soldiers in Benin's armed forces today" (Serbin, Joubeaud, and Masioni 2014, 21). By presenting a dreamlike juxtaposition of women from three hypothetical moments in the "collective memory" of anyone who becomes familiar with Benin's history, the UNESCO comic promulgates an abstract utopia. It enlists readers in furtherance of an educational mission articulated with other UN interventions, like the *General History of Africa* and the International Decade for People of African Descent. These discursive interventions are linked with *Black Panther* comics by the way they mobilize historical references around the aim of desiring blackness. Fictitious and historical texts alike deploy black bodies to new frontiers of the imagination without ever fully extricating us from the prior arrangements that make our images available.

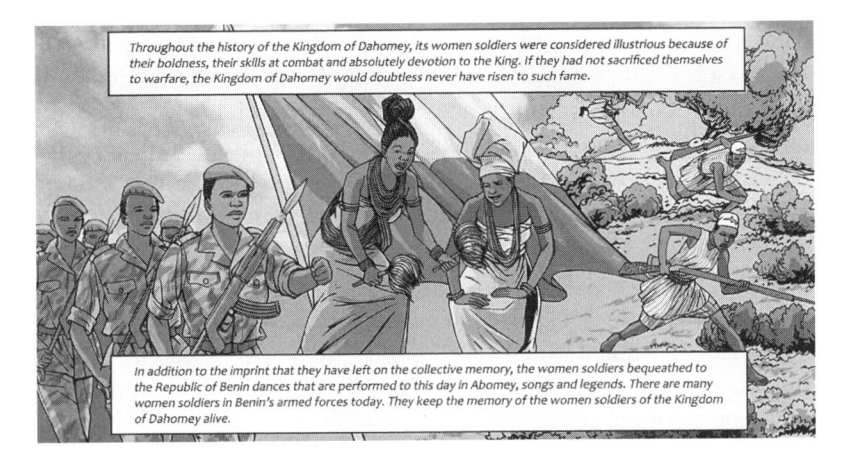

Figure 5 An educational comic. From Sylvia Serbin, Edouard Joubeaud, and Pat Masioni (2014), *The Women Soldiers of Dahomey*

Figure 6 Frontispiece illustration in Frederick E. Forbes (1851), *Dahomey and the Dahomans: Being the Journals of Two Missions to the King of Dahomey, and Residence at His Capital, in the Year 1849 and 1850*

Out of Utopia

Wakanda simulates certain hypotheses about the impact of colonialism by posing a counterfactual example of an African nation that was never colonized. After a fashion, it approximates the namesake of

Thomas More's *Utopia*, the word *outopia*, designating "no place." But the reason Wakanda corresponds to no place is a consequence of its relation to actually existing places: it represents a fantasy collectively authored by a social formation as a means of addressing the unmet needs of our particular historical circumstances. Ernst Bloch marked this specificity as the distinction between a concrete utopia and an abstract utopia (Muñoz 2009, 3–4). In its steadfast rejection of the here and now, *Black Panther* indulges the desires of people of African descent to envision ourselves in an alternative relation to modernity. The outwardly anachronistic appearance of the Dora Milaje gestures toward a history of sexuality that is more desirable than those that have been written.

A critical orientation to the text that accepts racially specific desires as the basis for its speculation demands that we locate African sites on the itinerary of queer futurity and other utopian agendas that might pass them by. African American speculation has always journeyed through diaspora on its way to divining new forms of black life and politics, and new forms of desiring blackness emerge through the same process. The new black queer studies reclaims "histories of many black lesbians and gay men traveling the world as they figured out their hungers, their desires, their ways of being possible" (Macharia 2014). So, too, does Afrofuturism. When authors like George Schuyler (*Black Empire*; 1936), Amiri Baraka (*A Black Mass*; 1966), Ishmael Reed (*Mumbo Jumbo*; 1972), and Octavia Butler (*Parable of the Sower*; 1993) mine the annals of Nilotic, Congo Basin, and Swahili Coast societies to craft satirical and affecting fictions, the overture to the reading public is double-voiced. First, modeling the settings of short stories and novels on selective readings of an eclectic archive allows these authors to establish a dialogue with knowledge of the transnational that cuts across colonial difference and undermines distinctions between institutionalized cultural conventions and everyday life. Concomitantly, to the extent that a counterfactual setting like Wakanda delinks speculations about history from the task of making truth claims, it channels this will to speculate into the task of inspiration.

Clothing the Black Panther in a heroic discourse on the precolonial African past and disidentifying with its present in order to conjure a vision of its future is not necessarily a rational way to mobilize affinities between actually existing Africans and black Americans. In its irrational gestures that transcend antinomies like the overrepresentation of coloniality within the narratives that define modernity, desiring blackness revalorizes a longing for ways of being black that belong to "the no-longer conscious, that thing or place that may be extinguished but not yet discharged in its utopian potentiality" (Muñoz 2009, 30).

By situating *Black Panther*'s invocations of and divergences from potential models for the role of the Dora Milaje as part of a concerted effort to imagine modernity otherwise, I am arguing that the desires we might read as queer within the text are already spoken for—or already arranged—by the term *black*. In light of this consideration, a queer orientation to black knowledge production will always amount to an augmentation of motion already in process. Blackness is not a discrete quantity; it is a desired coherence, a hypothetical trajectory between past and future. Querying a text that represents historically determined forms of this desire, including black nationalisms and other race-conscious world-making endeavors, provides a point of departure for understanding the concrete utopian ambitions of comics. By linking *Black Panther* to the unfinished projects of queering comics and queer futurity, I am commending it as an example of the strivings and failures that Muñoz identified in "the interface between an engagement with the no-longer-conscious and the not-yet-here" (87). Variously described as an unconscious, a repertoire, or "the wake," this symbolic interface is replete with unnamed possibilities for readers and critics concerned about what it means to identify with and desire blackness (Sharpe 2016, 2).

The hesitancy that separates my conceptualization of desiring blackness from the queer approaches to *Black Panther* that we can anticipate in the months and years to come is by no means a contention that the text, its authors, and their implicatedness are *not* queer. It's a suggestion that they are not *yet*. We may never touch queerness. As Muñoz writes, "I suggest that holding queerness in a sort of ontologically humble state, under a conceptual grid in which we do not claim to always already know queerness in the world, potentially staves off the ossifying effects of neoliberal ideology and the degradation of politics brought about by representations of queerness in contemporary popular culture" (2009, 22). Approaching popular texts with foreknowledge of their amenability to queer readings may draw us closer to the utopian potential they have to offer. At the same time, we should know that "because this world is already in place . . . queer moments, where things come out of line, are fleeting" (Ahmed 2006,

565). The "structuring and educated mode of desiring" (Muñoz 2009, 1) that informs my orientation to comics seeks to reconcile utopian ambitions with humble critical designs.

andré carrington is a scholar of race, gender, and genre in black and American cultural production. He is the author of *Speculative Blackness: The Future of Race in Science Fiction* (Univ. of Minnesota Press, 2016) and cofounder, with Jennifer Camper, of the Queers and Comics conference. He is currently assistant professor of African American literature at Drexel University. Follow him online at andrecarringtonphd.com.

Notes

1   Holland, Ochoa, and Tompkins (2014, 396) coin the phrase "cathectic and world-making behaviors" to comment on the way forms of deviance associated with the visceral are "already politicized as points of biopolitical, territorial, economic, and cultural intervention." I cite these descriptors to underscore how politicized habits of desiring characterize blackness as a mode of being and impetus for action. Blackness coincides with queerness as a "structuring and educated mode of desiring" in the sense articulated by Muñoz (2009, 1) in *Cruising Utopia: The Then and There of Queer Futurity*.
2   *Oxford English Dictionary*, s.v. "Amazon." OED Online, June 2017, Oxford University Press, oed.com/view/Entry/6077 (accessed October 8, 2017).
3   "Wives of the leopard" is a translation of *Ahosi*, an honorific utilized in the ethnographic research of Edna Bay (1998) and Peter Morton-Williams (1993) on women in Dahomey.

References

Abdur-Rahman, Aliyyah. 2012. *Against the Closet: Black Political Longing and the Erotics of Race*. Durham, NC: Duke Univ. Press.
Ahmed, Sara. 2006. "Orientations: Toward a Queer Phenomenology." *GLQ: A Journal of Lesbian and Gay Studies* 12, no. 4: 543–74.
Alcoff, Linda Martín. 2007. "Mignolo's Epistemology of Coloniality." *CR: The New Centennial Review* 7, no. 3: 79–101.
Barrett, Michèle. 2004. "Can the Subaltern Speak? New York, February 2004." *History Workshop Journal*, no. 58: 359.
Bay, Edna. 1998. *Wives of the Leopard: Gender, Politics, and Culture in the Kingdom of Dahomey*. Charlottesville: Univ. of Virginia Press.
Berger, Iris. 2003. "African Women's History: Themes and Perspectives." *Journal of Colonialism and Colonial History* 4, no. 1: n.p.

Boureau, Alain. 1998. *The Lord's First Night: The Myth of the Droit de Cuissage*. Translated by Lydia G. Cochrane. Chicago: Univ. of Chicago Press.

Brown, Jeffrey A. 2000. *Black Superheroes, Milestone Comics, and Their Fans*. Jackson: Univ. Press of Mississippi.

Carrington, André M. 2016. *Speculative Blackness: The Future of Race in Science Fiction*. Minneapolis: Univ. of Minnesota Press.

Coates, Ta-Nehisi (writer), and Chris Sprouse (penciller). 2016. *Black Panther*, no. 6. New York: Marvel Comics.

Coates, Ta-Nehisi (writer), and Brian Stelfreeze (penciller). 2016. *Black Panther*, no. 1. New York: Marvel Comics.

Dickson-Carr, Darryl. 2013. "African Americans and the Making of Modernity." *American Literary History* 25, no. 3: 672–82.

Dotson, Kristie. 2011. "Tracking Epistemic Violence, Tracking Practices of Silencing." *Hypatia* 26, no. 2: 236–57.

Duggan, Lisa. 2015. "Queer Complacency without Empire." *Bully Bloggers*, September 22. bullybloggers.wordpress.com/2015/09/22/queer-compla cency-without-empire.

Epprecht, Marc. 2008. *Heterosexual Africa? The History of an Idea from the Age of Exploration to the Age of AIDS*. Athens: Ohio Univ. Press.

Falola, Toyin, Jason Morgan, and Bukola Adeyemi Oyenini. 2012. *Culture and Customs of Libya*. Santa Barbara, CA: Greenwood.

Ferguson, Roderick A. 2003. *Aberrations in Black: Toward a Queer of Color Critique*. Minneapolis: Univ. of Minnesota Press.

———. 2012. "Administering Sexuality; or, The Will to Institutionality." In *The Reorder of Things: The University and Its Pedagogies of Minority Difference*, 209–26. Minneapolis: Univ. of Minnesota Press.

Forbes, David, dir. 1998. *The Long Tears: An Ndebele Story*. Mabhoko, South Africa: Shadow Films.

Forbes, Frederick. 1851. *Dahomey and the Dahomans: Being the Journals of Two Missions to the King of Dahomey, and Residence at His Capital, in the Year 1849 and 1850*. London: Longman, Brown, Green, and Longmans. Library of Congress. http://hdl.loc.gov/loc.wdl/wdl.2527.

Fulcher, Lindsay. 1990. "Unholy Orders: Libya's Self-Styled First Revolutionary Nun." *Guardian*, August 22.

Gray, Jonathan W. 2016. "A Conflicted Man: An Interview with Ta-Nehisi Coates about *Black Panther*." *New Republic*, April 4. newrepublic.com /article/132355/conflicted-man-interview-ta-nehisi-coates-black-panther.

Hargreaves, John D. 1980. "The French Conquest of Dahomey." *History Today* 30, no. 3: 5–9.

Harper, Philip Brian. 1994. *Framing the Margins: The Social Logic of Postmodern Culture*. New York: Oxford Univ. Press.

Harper, Philip Brian, et al. 1997. "Queer Transexions of Race, Nation, and Gender: An Introduction." *Social Text* 15, nos. 3/4: 1–4.

Harris, Duchess. 2011. *Black Feminist Politics from Kennedy to Obama*. New York: Palgrave MacMillan.

Hobson, Janell. 2012. *Body as Evidence: Mediating Race, Globalizing Gender*. Albany: State Univ. of New York Press.

Holland, Sharon P. 2014. "The Practice of Discipline, Disciplinary Practices." *American Literary History* 26, no. 4: 804–12.

Holland, Sharon P., Marcia Ochoa, and Kyla Wazana Tompkins. 2014. "Introduction: On the Visceral." *GLQ: A Journal of Lesbian and Gay Studies* 20, no. 4: 391–406.

Jackson, Peter A. 2009. "Capitalism and Global Queering: National Markets, Parallels among Sexual Cultures, and Multiple Queer Modernities." *GLQ: A Journal of Lesbian and Gay Studies* 15, no. 3: 357–95.

Johnson, E. Patrick. 2014. "To Be Young, Gifted, and Queer: Race and Sex in the New Black Studies." *Black Scholar* 44, no. 2: 50–58.

Kingsley, George. 1861. "A Gossip on a Sutherland Hill-Side." In *Vacation Tourists and Notes of Travel in 1860*, edited by Francis Galton, 116–75. London: Cambridge, MacMillan and Co. catalog.hathitrust.org/Record/006090090.

Kokan, Jane. 1995. "Gadafy's Women Extol His Virtues." *Guardian*, April 18.

Law, Robin. 1990. "Further Light on Bulfinch Lambe and the 'Emperor of Pawpaw': King Agaja of Dahomey's Letter to George I of England, 1726." *History in Africa*, no. 17: 211–26.

———. 1991. *The Oyo Empire, c. 1660–c. 1836: A West African Imperialism in the Era of the Atlantic Slave Trade*. Brookfield, VT: Ashgate.

Lutwyche, Jayne. 2012. "Ancient Rome's Maidens—Who Were the Vestal Virgins?" BBC Religion and Ethics, September 7. www.bbc.co.uk/religion/0/18490233.

Macharia, Keguro. 2014. "Black Queer Studies Now." *Gukira*, August 19. gukira.wordpress.com/2014/08/19/black-queer-studies-now.

Martínez, Ernesto Javier. 2013. *On Making Sense: Queer Race Narratives of Intelligibility*. Palo Alto, CA: Stanford Univ. Press.

Mbembe, Achille. 2003. "Life, Sovereignty, and Terror in the Fiction of Amos Tutuola." *Research in African Literatures* 34, no. 4: 1–26.

McCracken, Peggy. 2000. Review of *The Lord's First Night: The Myth of the Droit de Cuissage*, by Alain Boureau. *Journal of the History of Sexuality* 9, no. 3: 351–54.

McHugh, Susan. 2011. *Animal Stories: Narrating across Species Lines*. Minneapolis: Univ. of Minnesota Press.

Micheline, J. A. 2016. "Ta-Nehisi Coates on 'Black Panther' and Creating a Comic That Reflects the Black Experience." *Vice*, April 5. www.vice.com/read/ta-nehisi-coates-talks-about-black-panther-and-writing-from-a-black-experience.

Miller, J. Hillis. 2007. "Performativity as Performance/Performativity as Speech Act: Derrida's Special Theory of Performativity." *South Atlantic Quarterly* 106, no. 2: 219–35.

Monroe, J. Cameron. 2007. "Continuity, Revolution, or Evolution on the Slave Coast of West Africa? Royal Architecture and Political Order in Precolonial Dahomey." *Journal of African History* 48, no. 3: 349–73.

Morton-Williams, Peter. 1993. "A Yoruba Woman Remembers Servitude in a Palace of Dahomey, in the Reign of Kings Glele and Behanzin." *Africa: Journal of the African Institute* 63, no. 1: 102–17.

Muñoz, José Esteban. 2009. *Cruising Utopia: The Then and There of Queer Futurity*. New York: NYU Press.

Namaste, Viviane K. 1999. "The Use and Abuse of Queer Tropes: Metaphor and Catachresis in Queer Theory and Politics." *Social Semiotics* 9, no. 2: 213–34.

Nyong'o, Tavia. 2012. "Queer Africa and the Fantasy of Virtual Participation." *WSQ: Women's Studies Quarterly* 40, nos. 1/2: 40–63.

Outlaw, Lucius T. 2007. "Social Ordering and the Systematic Production of Difference." In *Race and Epistemologies of Ignorance*, edited by Shannon Sullivan and Nancy Tuana, 197–211. Albany: SUNY Press.

Priest, Christopher (writer), and Mark Bright (penciller). 2000. "Beloved." *Black Panther* 3, no. 24. New York: Marvel Comics.

Priest, Christopher (writer), and Jim Calafiore (penciller). 2001. *Black Panther* 3, no. 34. New York: Marvel Comics.

Priest, Christopher (writer), and Joe Jusko (penciller). 1999. "Hunted." *Black Panther* 3, no. 6. New York: Marvel Comics.

Quijano, Aníbal. 2007. "Coloniality and Modernity/Rationality." *Cultural Studies* 21, no. 2: 168–78.

Robinson, Cedric J. 2000. *Black Marxism: The Making of the Black Radical Tradition*. Chapel Hill: Univ. of North Carolina Press.

Rodney, Walter. 1969. *The Groundings with my Brothers*. London: Bogle-L'Ouverture Publications.

Russell, Heather. 2009. *Legba's Crossing: Narratology in the African Atlantic*. Athens: Univ. of Georgia Press.

Serbin, Sylvia, Edouard Joubeaud, and Pat Masioni. 2014. *The Women Soldiers of Dahomey*. Paris: UNESCO. en.unesco.org/womeninafrica/women-soldiers-dahomey/comic.

Sharpe, Christina. 2016. *In the Wake: On Blackness and Being*. Durham, NC: Duke Univ. Press.

Skertchly, J. Alfred. 1874. *Dahomey as It Is: Being a Narrative of Eight Months' Residence in That Country*. babel.hathitrust.org/cgi/pt?id=uc2.ark:/13960/t8df71v8b.

Soares, Maria Andrea Dos Santos. 2012. "Look, Blackness in Brazil! Disrupting the Grotesquerie of Racial Representation in Brazilian Visual Culture." *Cultural Dynamics* 24, no. 1: 75–101.

Somerville, Siobhan B. 2000. *Queering the Color Line: Race and the Invention of Homosexuality in American Culture*. Durham, NC: Duke Univ. Press.

Spillers, Hortense J. 1987. "Mama's Baby, Papa's Maybe: An American Grammar Book." *Diacritics* 17, no. 2: 64–81.

Taylor, Diana. 2003. *The Archive and the Repertoire: Performing Cultural Memory in the Americas*. Durham, NC: Duke Univ. Press.

Thomas, Greg. 2007. *The Sexual Demon of Colonial Power: Pan-African Embodiment and Erotic Schemes of Empire*. Bloomington: Indiana Univ. Press.

Tompkins, Kyla Wazana. 2016. "On the Limits and Promise of New Materialist Philosophy." *Lateral* 5, no. 1: n.p.

Weheliye, Alexander G. 2014. *Habeas Viscus: Racializing Assemblages, Biopolitics, and Black Feminist Theories of the Human*. Durham, NC: Duke Univ. Press.

Worrall, Simon. 2014. "Amazon Warriors Did Indeed Fight and Die Like Men." *National Geographic*, October 28. news.nationalgeographic.com/news/2014/10/141029-amazons-scythians-hunger-games-herodotus-ice-princess-tattoo-cannabis.

Wynter, Sylvia. 2003. "Unsettling the Coloniality of Being/Power/Truth/Freedom: Towards the Human, after Man, Its Overrepresentation—An Argument." *CR: The New Centennial Review* 3, no. 3: 257–337.

Young, Alden. 2015. "Some Reflections on the Journey from African Studies to Africana Studies: African Studies beyond the Area Studies Paradigm." *Red Sea Notes*, September 7. redseanotes.wordpress.com/2015/09/07/some-reflections-on-the-journey-from-african-studies-to-africana-studies.

Young, Kevin. 2012. *The Grey Album: On the Blackness of Blackness*. Minneapolis: Graywolf Press.

Anthony Michael D'Agostino

"Flesh-to-Flesh Contact": Marvel Comics' Rogue and the Queer Feminist Imagination

Abstract The X-Men's Rogue's ability to absorb the powers and personality of others through "flesh-to-flesh contact" presents an affective figure for the queer potential of the X-Men's metaphor of mutancy as difference. Close readings of Rogue's first appearance, *Avengers Annual* #10, and the end of her first major character arc, *Uncanny X-Men* #185, reveal that this affective figure for queerness is variable and derived from X-Men writer Chris Claremont's ongoing engagement with feminist politics and theory.
Keywords queer theory, X-Men, comics, superheroes, affect

> When ah touch you . . . ah'll absorb your power an' memories as well. Any flesh-to-flesh contact—no matter how slight—will suffice for the transfer.
> —Rogue, *Avengers Annual* #10 (1981)

An original creation of legendary comic book scribe Chris Claremont and penciller Michael Golden, Marvel Comics' heroine Rogue is arguably one of the most recognizable characters in comic book history.[1] Although best known as a member of the X-Men, a superhero team of mutants, Rogue was originally introduced as a villain in *Avengers Annual* #10 (Claremont and Golden 1981). In this now-classic issue, Rogue's close-cropped white-streaked hair and Southern drawl distinguished her visually and verbally as much as she was conceptually distinguished by her mutant power to absorb the powers, memories, and personalities—"the very identity" (Claremont and Romita 1985a)—of those she touches (Claremont and

Smith 1983b). Since she was unable to control her absorptive capabilities, if Rogue stayed in "flesh-to-flesh contact" with another person too long, she ran the risk of permanently absorbing their powers and personality. When her character was introduced, Rogue struggled with the lasting effects of the accidental permanent absorption of the abilities and persona of the heroine Ms. Marvel. Although Rogue possessed the superheroine's alien-derived superhuman strength, durability, and flight, she suffered from debilitating psychological dysphoria, as she was subject to Ms. Marvel's thoughts and emotions, which she often mistook for her own. To mitigate the possibility of inadvertently absorbing the consciousnesses of others, Rogue wore a green jumpsuit that covered her body from head to toe. As of the time of this writing, Rogue's gloves and hood are still part of the character's iconic design.

Isolated from physical affection lest she be brought into ego-destroying intimacy with others, in the 1980s and 1990s *Uncanny X-Men* comics, Rogue cuts something of a tragic sentimental figure. As a brash, beautiful Southern belle who yearns on multiple occasions to feel the touch of a lover, friend, or mother, she dramatizes the psychological isolation and emotional intensity of marginalized difference in superhero form.[2] This essay, however, questions the common understanding of Rogue's absorptive touch as monolithically tragic and performs something of a reparative reading of Rogue and her power of absorption, interpreting them as central to an understanding of the superhero figure's unique effectiveness in analyzing difference. Rogue's powers of alien strength, durability, and flight absorbed from Ms. Marvel resonate with the original superhero, 1938's Superman, whom Umberto Eco (1998) famously read as an iconic, unchanging representation of social ("civic") and gender normativity. However, Rogue's mutant power of absorption and transformation, which makes her physical and psychological makeup a dynamic and fluid amalgam of traits from disparate identities (in terms of gender, age, powers, etc.), is representative of Ramzi Fawaz's (2016) conceptualization of postwar superheroes—derived from the X-Men themselves—as "new mutants." Postwar superheroes, Fawaz explains, are possessed of "monstrous powers and bodies," which, instead of representing unchanging normative ideals, exhibit "a form of . . . material and psychic becoming characterized by constant transition and change" that defies the narrow dictates of heteronormativity and gender conformity.

Thus, Fawaz positions postwar superheroes as "distinctly 'queer' figure[s] . . . [whose] mutated bodies . . . cultivated an affective orientation toward otherness and difference that made so-called deviant modes of bodily expression, erotic attachment, and affiliation both desirable and ethical" (22).

In post–World War II superhero mythoi, this "affective orientation toward otherness and difference" was often given conceptual form as transformative physical contact. In these stories, touch created an access to difference that rendered the human body unrecognizable and wondrous. For instance, in 1956, the first superhero of comic books' so-called silver age, DC Comics' Barry Allen (the Flash), is struck by a lightning bolt that gives him the ability to move at lightning-fast speeds. Similarly, less than a decade later, Marvel Comics' Peter Parker, bitten by a radioactive spider, manifests the proportionate strength, agility, and intuitive senses of that spider to become a superhuman-animal hybrid, Spider-Man. Elements of contact, touch, and bodily susceptibility are central to the origin mythos of the post–World War II superhero.

Rogue, in her own way, restages the quintessential silver age or postwar superhero origin each time she comes into physical contact with another character. In *Uncanny X-Men* #194, for instance, in a desperate effort to make one final stand against the X-Men's robotic archnemesis, Nimrod, who has beaten and left unconscious all her fellow X-Men, Rogue gently grazes her fingertips against the skins of her teammates, the teleporting blue elf Nightcrawler and the metal-skinned strongman Colossus (Claremont and Romita 1985b). On contact, Rogue's body and mind transform; her arms and legs burst out of her sleeves and pants with the added mass of Colossus's steel skin, and her face grows a pelt of Nightcrawler's blue fur (see fig. 1). The result of Rogue's fleeting contact with her teammates is a Frankensteinian composite being, an "amalgam of multiple personas, not all of them human" (Claremont and Romita 1985a), in which she channels the differences of her teammates and yet remains unlike them. Rogue, as a vessel for difference that cannot be pinned down to a single normative identity, stymies Nimrod's computer brain, which allows her to save her fellow X-Men. In scenes like this, Rogue coheres as a metafictional figure not just for the specific heroes she touches but for the superhero genre's general conception of superhuman power as consubstantial with a nonnormative body, which is produced through

Figure 1 Rogue absorbs the powers and abilities of her teammates and becomes an amalgam representing the X-Men as a whole. From Claremont and Romita (1985), *Uncanny X-Men* #194

transformative contact that renders differences mobile across a blurred boundary between subject and object.

Capitalizing on Rogue as a switch point between the superhero figure and queerness, this essay approaches Rogue's touch as a physical materialization and visual enactment of the new mutant superhero's queerness conceptualized in Fawaz's terms as an "affective orientation toward . . . difference." Defined in terms of difference as opposed to identity, queerness, as Annamarie Jagose (1996, 98) writes, "does not assume for itself any specific materiality or positivity"; thus any move to define or identify queerness is, in fact, normalizing, exclusionary, and against the point. This nonidentitarian exigency of queerness as a field has made queerness at once boringly common (anyone and everyone is queer), uselessly utopian (can I be queer at all?), and infuriatingly abstract (what does *queer* mean again?). However, by embodying and exploring an orientation toward difference in specific, discrete, affective forms—in the case of this essay, a stolen kiss and an offered hand—Rogue's power of absorption through flesh-to-flesh contact acts as a focal point for an examination of how queer embodiment and subjectivity constitute themselves in the form of the superhero and how the superhero comments on and interrogates queer modes of being. In short, I argue that Rogue's touch renders queerness as an analyzable process of relationality and subject formation susceptible to close reading and political analysis.[3] More specifically, this essay's close readings of Rogue's touch reveal it as a trope for identification, the "assimilative or appropriative act [of] making the other the same as me, or me the same as the other ... [causing] the I/ego to be transformed by the other" (Diamond 1992, 409–10), a psychoanalytic and political concept that connects theories of reading, the superhero genre, queerness, and feminism.

Rogue Theory: Superheroic, Queer, and Feminist

In Eco's (1998, 873) formulation, the superhero acts as a "pedagogic instrument" of representation and identification; the presumably preadolescent male reader identifies with, can vicariously experience, and subsequently seeks to emulate the superhero's representation of perfected masculinity. Rogue's power of absorption models this reading experience. She, like the reader of the comic book, identifies and "assimilates" into herself the essence—the power—of other superheroes. But Rogue is not a preadolescent male, and her power of identification does not re-entrench her existing identity in terms of gender or race. Instead, Rogue enacts identification as a process that overflows rigid articulations of identity and deterministic conceptions of subjectivity. Rogue does not merely deviate from norms through the power of touch. Flesh-to-flesh contact allows her to cross-identify and empathize with others in ways that go beyond normativity or nonnormativity. Rogue figures and repurposes Eco's theory of superheroic identification to describe how subjectivity might produce itself in queer ways.

In *Uncanny X-Men* #236 (Claremont and Silvestri 1988), Claremont fully illustrates Rogue's consciousness as oriented toward *itself* as different because of her assimilative identification with those whom she touches. While incarcerated by mutant-hunting villains, Rogue "withdraws . . . to the lowest depths of her primal subconscious," a graphic representation of Rogue's consciousness as a space—a mindscape, if you will—she can inhabit and explore. In this mindscape, Rogue is beset by hordes of ghostlike versions of "all the people ah ever absorbed" and asks, "But that effect is only temporary—how can y'all be inside my head?!" A shade of her teammate Nightcrawler answers Rogue's question regarding the composition of her own psyche, saying, "Stolen powers and memories fade, liebchen . . . but there's a psychic residue" (see fig. 2). This scene spatially depicts Rogue's fractured heterogeneous psyche as streaked with otherness, her individuality containing a potential multiplicity of "residues" (Claremont and Silvestri 1988). As Elin Diamond (1992, 409–10) explains, this is because "identification," or in this case, Rogue's absorption, "always works both ways . . . [such that] the borders of identity, the wholeness and consistency of identity, are transgressed by every act of identification." In short, Diamond writes, "To identify is . . . to be radically destabilized" (405). This self-inconsistent, relational conception of subjectivity is one step away from queer theorist Judith Butler's conception of queer identity as continually unmade and remade. She writes, "Indeed, whatever self emerges . . . is always at a temporal remove from its former appearance; it is transformed through its encounter with alterity, not in order to return to itself, but to become a self it never was. Difference casts it forth into an irreversible future. To be a self is . . . not to enjoy the prerogative of self-identity" (2004, 148). In other words, touch shared between Rogue and those whom she absorbs produces a subjectivity that embraces differences, even unto itself, and defies stable homogeneous identity whether in terms of race, gender, or other categories. However, Rogue's reengagement of difference does not occur across identity formations, strictly speaking, in terms of an intersubjectivity that bridges the consciousness of two distinct subjects, each with their own racial, gender, and class

Figure 2 Rogue enters her "mindscape," where she encounters "residues" of those she has absorbed. From Claremont and Silvestri (1988), *Uncanny X-Men* #236

identities. Rather, Rogue's power of transformation through physical contact evolves into what I refer to as a *mutually interpenetrating intrasubjectivity*, where Rogue experiences the differences of those she absorbs as a new hybridized subjectivity arising from the remixing of previously separate sets of traits, experiences, and consciousnesses. This intrasubjectivity bypasses prior designations of self and other to produce a unique experience not comprehensible in terms of existing matrices of identification such as gender, race, and class without occluding or dispensing with those identifications. Rogue acts as a superheroic figure who pushes the psychological and political force of identification along a queer vector that helps us consider subjectivity beyond identity politics.

Even as it figures identification and assimilation, Rogue's power of touch, often applied in terms of specific affective or erotic emotional states (like a stolen kiss), is also a trope for sexual desire. The intermixing of desire and identification is itself a hallmark of queer subjectivity. Queer theorist Michael Warner analyzes Sigmund Freud's separation of identification (what the subject seeks to be like) and desire (what the subject seeks to have sexually) as the root of psychoanalytic gender and sexual normativity. For Freud, the subject identifies with the same (boys identify with their father, girls their mother) and desires what is different (boys their mother, girls their father), to produce a normative gender identity and sexual orientation (see

Warner 1998). Rogue's power of touch, in psychoanalytic terms, merges the registers of desire and identification, producing a nonnormative psychoanalytic formation of subjectivity, gender, and sexuality. Thus, Rogue's power of touch figures a queer erotic imagination of redesigning the self through desire and pleasuring oneself through identification. In effect, physical contact destabilizes the desire for fixed identity by demonstrating and exemplifying the pleasures of identification that are multiple, varied, and productive of ever-changing, unforeclosable possibilities for self-reinvention.

The queer collapse of desire and identification figured in Rogue's absorptive touch is also a primary component of the lesbian erotics of black lesbian theorist Audre Lorde. In an article with a subtitle that could refer to Rogue herself, "The Power of Touch," Sarah Chinn argues that, for Lorde, lesbian sexuality is a mode of the erotic that, in contrast to the patriarchal register of sight, privileges touch. According to Chinn, touch acts as a mode of sharing sensation that allows for a unique sexual intersubjectivity. The "source of connection," Chinn (2003, 184) writes, "is the skin," because touch, as opposed to vision, produces sensation in both the actor and the recipient simultaneously. To touch is also to be touched. As a reflexive and shared sensation, Chinn argues, touch constitutes an intersubjectivity that blurs the strict separation of self and other. Thus, touch allows participants access to one another's differences and facilitates their becoming more similar. In Lorde's lesbian erotic, as in Warner's queer subjectivity, to desire is also to identify. Similarly, when Rogue makes flesh-to-flesh contact with other people, they are acted on, they fall asleep as their consciousness drains into Rogue's, and Rogue gains access to their differences and exhibits their unique personae and superpowers as her own (the trope par excellence for difference in superhero comics). But at the same time Rogue also becomes subject to them: their memories, their will, their subjectivity. For Rogue, like Lorde, contact is never merely skin-deep: touching the other can make the self like the other or the other a part of the self. Given the resonance Lorde's conception of lesbian erotics shares with Rogue's power of absorptive touch, this essay seeks to capitalize on Rogue's touch as a figure for a queer orientation toward difference that is inseparable from its mobilization as a trope for lesbian desire and feminist political identification.

Rogue Politics: The Power of Divergent Feminisms

As my critical reference to Lorde might suggest, I also argue that the queer potential of Rogue's power of touch arises out of Marvel Comics' and writer Claremont's tumultuous but theoretically productive engagement with feminist movements not only of the 1980s, the era of Rogue's creation and development, but also the late 1960s and early 1970s.[4] In the late 1960s feminism began a period of fierce internal division and ideological multiplication.[5] The liberal feminism of Betty Friedan had come under fire by radical feminists, who themselves broke into countless splinter groups along the lines of sexual, race, and class difference (radical feminists, lesbian feminists, lesbian separatists, black lesbian feminists, women of color feminists, and so on). The political strife that fueled the proliferation of feminisms in the 1970s, however, did not hamper various feminisms' social and political growth in the national consciousness. In 1972, Gloria Steinem began publishing the feminist *Ms. Magazine*, and Kate Millett, the feminist author of the best-selling *Sexual Politics*, was a household name. By the 1970s, feminism, in many of its myriad expressions, was a major part of the national political conversation.[6] Despite the seriousness of ideological rifts among feminists, looking back, both feminist historians (like Ruth Rosen) and queer theorists (like Judith Butler) have identified this mutative, multitudinous, agonistic quality of American feminism as a source of social and political power, an unlikely factor in its successes.[7] Rogue's touch-activated absorption—a trope for queer and lesbian sexuality—is simultaneously a trope for feminist political identification, its production of a hybrid or amalgam form containing and synthesizing into superhuman power the agonistic synergy of divergent feminisms. Rogue's relationship to difference so representative of the figure of the superhero's anti-identitarian queerness, I argue, is largely a result of Claremont's attempts to embody the agonism of feminist identity politics, thus suggesting that Claremont's superhero comics constitute their own queer feminism.

I substantiate this claim by performing close readings of particularly representative and pivotal instances of two of Rogue's most common affective forms of touch: the stolen kiss, from Rogue's first appearance as a villain in *Avengers Annual* #10, and the offered hand, from the culmination of her first major character arc as a hero in *Uncanny X-Men* #185. My readings begin by drawing connections between Rogue's use of touch and particular ideological conflicts within feminist politics: liberal feminism's conflict with lesbian and radical feminism; antiporn feminism's "sex wars" with lesbian BDSM feminism and pro-sex feminism; and intersectional feminism's split from radical feminism. In Rogue's story arc, these ideological splits produce affects of sexual violence, betrayal, and identification as well as trust and empathy. The significance of Rogue's touch, and therefore her queerness, is molded by these affective contexts. The way these affects inhabit, inspire, and shape touch into specific forms relates to racial and gender difference in unexpected queer ways. I theorize and analyze how these different affective forms process and metabolize feminist conflicts to produce queer subjectivities. By reading the historical, narrative, and ideological contexts of Rogue's absorption of others through physical contact, I show how each application of Rogue's touch produces a specific queer orientation toward difference that merits its own close analysis in terms of desire, identity, and, most importantly, ethics.

The Stolen Kiss

Rogue's introduction into the Marvel Universe is a flash point in Marvel Comics' evolving relationship to feminism, a direct consequence and critique of the failure of Marvel's first major feminist-themed superheroine, Ms. Marvel.[8] In the early 1970s, as feminist politics gained ascendancy in the United States' national consciousness, Marvel Comics published a slew of female-focused superhero titles, the most significant of which, 1976's *Ms. Marvel*, wove its texture of motifs and themes heavily, if ham-fistedly, from the personalities and politics of second-wave feminism. Ms. Marvel's alter ego, Carol Danvers, the editor-in-chief of *Woman Magazine*, evoked an easy parallelism with famed feminist and editor Steinem and was wont to speak in the political and theoretical idiom of radical feminism ("So much for RAISED CONSCIOUSNESS!") (Claremont and Mooney 1978). For all this feminist signaling, it is arguable whether *Ms. Marvel* faithfully represented any feminist political agenda or theory with any coherence. The title's content peaked under Claremont's authorship, but the comic was canceled in 1979. When Ms. Marvel resurfaced in Marvel's flagship title, *The Avengers*, written by Jim Shooter, her feminist charge was neutralized and then reversed by a series of misogynistic narrative devices; she was mind-controlled, raped, and then written to fall in love with her supervillain rapist, Marcus. When Marcus says he intends to whisk Ms. Marvel off to live with him in another dimension, her fellow Avengers—Marvel icons such as Captain America, Thor, and Iron Man—blithely congratulate her on her "happiness" and provide Marcus and Ms. Marvel with interdimensional transportation for their otherworldly honeymoon. As feminist comic book critic Carol A. Strickland (n.d.) puts it, Marvel Comics' first great feminist superheroine's storyline devolved into a "male fantasy [where] a desirable woman/mother figure is raped and then chooses to be the lover of her rapist/son [because] women love to be raped."

Avengers Annual #10, and Rogue's introduction therein, is Claremont's feminist critique of what Strickland (n.d.) calls "The Rape of Ms. Marvel." In the issue, Rogue brutally attacks the Avengers in a plot to free the incarcerated members of her fellow supervillains, the Brotherhood of Evil Mutants (Claremont and Golden 1981). However, Rogue's role in the brotherhood's plan, neutralizing the Avengers and claiming their powers for use in the brotherhood's jailbreak, can easily be read as "The Revenge of Ms. Marvel." Indeed, Rogue's first utterance—boasting that she has permanently absorbed the identity of Ms. Marvel and thus "possess[es] all Ms. Marvel's mem'ries [and] most importantly . . . her power!"—immediately positions her as a counterintuitive extension of the heroine she has defeated. In absorbing and "possessing," literally introjecting Ms. Marvel's "power" and "mem'ries," Rogue becomes like Ms. Marvel. Thus, Rogue's touch literalizes an identification in the context of feminist political critique.

Rogue's absorption as an identification between dissimilar, even antagonistic women resonates with the political philosophy of late 1960s and early 1970s radical and lesbian feminisms. In "The Woman Identified Woman" (1970) lesbian feminist collective the Radicalesbians invoked the language of identification to define its own brand of feminism against the assimilationist liberal feminist values of earlier second-wave feminisms like that of Betty Friedan and her National Organization for Women. The Radicalesbians (1972, 172) described such feminists as "women . . . [who] try to escape [the hatred of themselves and other women] by identifying with the oppressor, living through him, gaining status and identity from his ego, his power, his accomplishments. And by not identifying with other 'empty vessels' like themselves." Rogue, however, as a mutant terrorist very much akin to Valerie Solanas and members of her Society for Cutting Up Men (SCUM), refuses to be like "passive, rattle-headed Daddy's girls, ever eager for [male] approval" (Solanas 1968). Instead, by enhancing herself through identification with another woman Rogue considers not an "an empty vessel" but a source of "power" she is proud to "possess," the militant female mutant mobilizes her power of absorption as a superheroic trope for political and psychological identification, thus producing herself as a "woman-identified woman."

Rogue's distinctive original character design visually ratifies her engagement with lesbian feminist values as articulated in "The Woman Identified Woman." Her brown hair, streaked with white, is closely cropped, giving her a distinctly masculine appearance. And unlike most superheroines and female supervillains, whose skin-tight and revealing costumes purposefully invite the heterosexual male gaze, Rogue's head-to-toe green jumpsuit, detailed with folds and creases to mark a loose fit, de-emphasizes her breasts and hips, closing her body off from that gaze.[9] Rogue is coded as masculine, even butch, flirting with stereotypes of lesbianism. After her introduction Claremont ingeniously both refuted and confirmed this stereotype. Although Rogue is consistently characterized as heterosexual in her object choice, as the daughter of Mystique and her lesbian partner-in-crime and lover, Destiny, Rogue is, in her own way, lesbian identified. Rogue's mannish and lesbian coding, in the context of the early 1970s radical and lesbian feminist movements from which Claremont seems to be drawing, has strong feminist political connotations.[10] The Radicalesbians (1972, 172) famously defined a lesbian as "the rage of all women condensed to the point of explosion" and lesbianism as the full emotional and political identification with other women, the apotheosis of feminism. Therefore, Rogue's masculinized form and lesbian identification verify her unspoken feminist political identification with Ms. Marvel, evident insofar as Rogue, like the lesbian of "The Woman Identified Woman" acts on the Avengers as the "rage of" Ms. Marvel "condensed to the point of explosion."

If Rogue's visual codes and family ties draw her into association with lesbian feminism, Ms. Marvel's identification with male values and institutions—namely, the Avengers—in the critical context of the "The Woman Identified Woman," evokes a liberal feminist will to assimilate to the power of male dominance. At the end of the *Avengers Annual* #10, however, once woken from her coma, Ms. Marvel confronts the Avengers regarding their complicity in her rape and repudiates her patriarchal identification, telling her former teammates, "My mistake was trusting you!" Claremont's feminist counternarrative not only highlights a conflict between feminism and male supremacy, but it also depicts how differing feminist figures define their feminisms through varied—even opposed—emotional, social, and political identifications. In effect, Claremont raises the question some feminists imply is feminism's central concern: with whom should women identify? (Jagose 2009, 161). This makes Rogue's permanent absorption of Ms. Marvel a feminist identification but also an orientation of women toward other, different women and their different feminisms.

Rogue uses the powers and skills she has permanently purloined from Ms. Marvel to defeat Captain America easily, shattering a park bench with his body and leaving the superhero's red-white-and-blue–garbed form battered and unconscious at her feet amid the wooden bench's rubble. The first on-panel use of Rogue's ability to absorb the powers and personae of others through flesh-to-flesh contact, defined by the revenge of Ms. Marvel, carries a nefarious nonconsensual sexual charge. "Poor li'l Cap," Rogue says, menacingly pulling the green glove off her hand, an ominous gesture toward touch ("when ah touch you") that promises to take from the unconscious superhero his essential essence ("ah'll absorb your power an' mem'ries as well [as Ms. Marvel's]"). Rogue's posture toward Captain America—the slow exposure of her dangerous skin, her stance over his unconscious body—creates a kind of sadistic intimacy, paralleled in the subtle connotations of her speech. Referring to Captain America as "poor" and "li'l" Rogue demonstrates an emasculating empathy and ersatz affection for the superhero she pummels. Referring to Captain America by the nickname (Cap) given to him by his teammates in the Avengers, however, is especially telling, demonstrating that Rogue has not only absorbed Ms. Marvel's memories of how he fights and thinks in order to gain a tactical advantage over him but also the emotional resonances and memories that constitute Ms. Marvel and Captain America's friendly personal relationship. Rogue's sadism in touching and absorbing Captain America is inspired and shaped by Ms. Marvel's betrayed trust in him, monstrously realized in the specific form of Rogue's absorptive touch—flesh-to-flesh contact not limited to her ungloved hands.

Gloating over Captain America's unconscious body as she brandishes her exposed and weaponized flesh, Rogue mentions that "any flesh-to-flesh contact—no matter how slight—will suffice for the transfer" of Captain America's powers and memories into herself, but she chooses to place both her exposed palms on either sides of the sleeping man's face, raise his body off the ground, bring his face to hers, and—in a single, striking close-up panel—press her lips to his, stealing an open-mouthed kiss because, as Rogue says, it "is so much more—FUN." This "fun," of course, is the enjoyment of sexual pleasure, an expression of desire applied to Captain America's nonconsenting body. Still lip-locked, Rogue bends over Captain America's limp, unconscious body, almost appearing to devour him with vampiric intensity, visually registered by a halo of eerie gangrenous green and black Kirby Krackles—a visual technique of linked and overlapping spheres associated with comics legend Jack Kirby to mark states of elevated energy (see fig. 3). Rogue's identification, the urge to be like Captain America, to assimilate his skill and power, is merged with her heterosexual desire for him, and the result is a siphoning of Captain America's essential energies that looks very much like sexual assault. As the instrument for Ms. Marvel's revenge, Rogue's power of touch is formed into the sexual violence of the stolen kiss, forcing Captain America to experience, at least figuratively, a violation akin to the one experienced by Ms. Marvel.

It is perhaps troubling that Rogue's identification with Ms. Marvel is effectuated as a trope for sexual violence. However, Rogue's power of touch, which represents both lesbian sexuality and the politics of women's identification with women, shaped into an affective form of sexual violence, engages directly with the feminist "sex wars" of the late 1970s and early 1980s. In this feminist conflict, "antiporn" feminists like Laura Lederer and, later, power or dominance feminists like Catharine MacKinnon and Andrea Dworkin, who criticized pornography and sadomasochism as the systemic cultural eroticization of sexual violence against women, locked horns with sex-positive feminists like Gayle Rubin and lesbian BDSM feminists like Pat Califia who hailed porn and BDSM as legitimate manifestations of human sexual diversity worthy of responsible exploration.[11] Claremont, especially in *Uncanny X-Men*, probed the ethical dimensions of the feminist sex wars by making BDSM one of his primary themes and motifs in the storylines of some of his most popular characters like Phoenix, the White Queen, and Rachel Summers. In this way, Rogue's power, especially as it is articulated in her assault on Captain America, is a rape trope that represents—if not full-on glamourizes—sexual taking as a source of power, putting Claremont (and Rogue) in the theoretical vicinity of pro-sex and lesbian BDSM feminists.

Figure 3 Rogue's sexualized and vampiric absorption of Captain America via a stolen kiss features a textbook example of Kirby Krackles. From Claremont and Golden (1981), *Avengers Annual* #10

Ultimately, though, with Rogue, Claremont seems to split the difference between antiporn feminists and sex-positive feminists.[12] To wit, in *Uncanny X-Men* #171, Ms. Marvel, or just Carol Danvers, since Rogue has permanently absorbed her powers and ended her career as a superheroine, reflects on her postabsorption recovery. She observes, "I remember pretty much all of who and what I was . . . [but] there are no emotions to go along with them [her memories]." Danvers's loss of her (superheroic) identity and emotional disassociation in the wake of Rogue's absorption mirrors posttraumatic stress experienced by rape survivors (Claremont and Smith 1983a). Rogue's absorption of Danvers's identity and "emotions," at least in a certain sense, doubles the rape of Ms. Marvel. However, in a move of erasure more in line with antiporn feminism, in Claremont's writing, Danvers never again mentions her rape by Marcus. Instead, for many years to come, Danvers reflects on the gravity of the violence done to her by Rogue. In effect, Rogue's absorption of Ms. Marvel's powers, narratively speaking, replaces Marcus's rape as the trauma that ends Ms. Marvel's career. Claremont's replacement of a literal rape by a male with a figurative rape by a female, though not unproblematic in and of itself, is nevertheless an attempt to tackle the feminist conundrum surrounding narrativizing sexual violence. As MacKinnon (1987) famously argues, representations of rape normalize and eroticize sexual violence and male dominance, even when women take on the role of perpetrator, although others might argue that there is a feminist social value in artists addressing the harms of sexual violence and exposing the pervasiveness of rape culture. With Rogue, Claremont attempts to avoid the eroticization of male dominance while addressing the emotional complexities of rape survival. Rogue's doubling of the rape of Ms. Marvel, by replacing Marcus's rape, extinguishes the need to represent (again) and risk inadvertently aestheticizing male sexual violence against women, while at the same time preserving the feminist project of narrativizing and exploring Danvers's gradual but ultimately successful, even triumphant, recovery process.[13] As a result of Rogue's function as a feminist palimpsest for male sexual violence, discussions of Ms. Marvel's trauma do not elicit recapitulations of a male rapist's actions or entrench the social dynamics of rape culture; instead, they recall and continue the textured feminist conversation and critique of *Avengers Annual* #10, which reflects on women's relationships, women's politics, and the vicissitudes of women's identification. By figuring sexualized violence through the affective form of the stolen kiss, even as she occludes multiplied representation of a misogynistic rape narrative, Rogue holds in tension the differing, very much agonistic feminisms of lesbian feminism along the lines of "The Woman Identified Woman" and the liberal feminism it critiques, as well as the adverse theories of antiporn and pro-sex feminisms.

Claremont's positioning of Rogue's power of absorption as a figure for feminist politics concerning identity, desire, and representation of power simultaneously stands as a particular affective orientation toward difference that produces nonnormative states of subjectivity and embodiment contemporary readers would understand as "queer." The surface-level irony essential to understanding Claremont's characterization of Rogue in the 1980s is that Rogue, unable to control her absorption power, cannot embrace, kiss, or hold any partner without putting them in a coma (while she effectively *becomes* them), and so, Rogue cannot engage in sexual contact normatively conceived, irrespective of the hypothetical partner's gender.

In a mode of villainous queer imagination, however, Rogue deploys her mutant touch as a nonnormative sexual pleasure. The sexual

"FUN" Rogue experiences kissing Captain America is at least partly derived by the introjection of Captain America's skills and abilities—his particular differences—into herself. Often, however, the skills, memories, and powers of the men Rogue absorbs are themselves heavily gendered. In *Marvel Team-Up* #150, written by Louise Simonson, for instance, Rogue absorbs the powers of the superstrong, hypertrophic Juggernaut and manifests the gigantic mounds of muscle mass that mark Juggernaut's overblown masculinity (Simonson and LaRocque 1985). In effect, Rogue's power of absorption, scripted to figure feminist identification and holding within Rogue's form multiple antagonistic feminisms, also generates a queer orientation toward sexual difference that allows her to further masculinize and queer her female gender through acts of perverse desire. In Rogue and Captain America's case, the effect of sexual violence and revenge shapes the power of touch into a gender vampirism of the stolen kiss, where Rogue emasculates Captain America by stealing his superpowers, which are linked to his masculine strength, vigor, bodily integrity, and sexual agency. Rogue's feminist critique, then, produces conceptual, imagistic forms that illustrate the production of a queer embodiment and consciousness.

The Offered Hand

In 1983's *Uncanny X-Men* #171, Rogue, now reformed, arrives desperate for help at the X-Men's door. She frantically explains, "Mah powers are out of control. The slightest touch triggers the transfer. It's gettin' so ah don't know which thoughts—or mem'ries, or feelin's—are mine!" Rogue crystallizes her suffering as a kind of self-misrecognition: "Ah look into a mirror an' see a stranger's face!" Rogue's power of absorption, a figure for feminist identification and queer lesbian sexuality, produces a subjectivity no longer structured in terms of self-consistency or the distinction between self and other, and it is "driving [her] crazy!" Rogue's feminist identification with Ms. Marvel is so tight and her identification with others is so uncontrollable that her coherent individuality—her sanity—is rendered painfully precarious. Rogue's psychological dysphoria parallels the costs and pitfalls of queer theory's anti-identitarian politics, whose embrace of difference and refusal to positively define itself in any exclusionary way resists representation and, therefore, political—or in Rogue's case, psychological—cohesion (see Jagose 1996, 101–3). Rogue seeks the X-Men's help in coming to terms with her queer power of touch.

Two years later, in *Uncanny X-Men* #185, now a member of the X-Men but still plagued by her powers, Rogue makes a desperate attempt to reconstitute her racial, gender, and sexual identity in more normative terms through isolation, running away to her hometown of Caldecott, Mississippi. Rogue's intervention on her own identity in terms of space, place, and location evokes and complicates contemporaneous critiques of feminism in terms of race, sexuality, and class. In 1977, the black lesbian feminists who made up the Combahee River Collective (1983, 264) responded to racism found in the women's movement and sexism experienced in black liberation organizations, asserting that "black feminism," as opposed to feminism tout court, was "the logical political movement to combat the manifold and simultaneous oppressions that all women of color face." For the collective, the "major systems of oppression" like gender, race, and class "are interlocking," making the "conditions of [black women's] lives" a "synthesis of these oppressions" (264). The identity category of "black woman," then, the collective argued, was distinct enough from that of white women and black men in shared experience and common interest to necessitate an "identity politics" serving black women specifically (267). In 1984, drawing from Combahee, Adrienne Rich (1994) reintroduced the collective's identity politics in terms of a spatial metaphor, the "politics of location," which conceived of individual identity as a specific coordinate (what would later be called an intersection) of gender, nationality, ethnicity, and class such that generalizations about womanhood or feminism that did not take into account racial, cultural, and national differences were dangerous acts of colonialism and appropriation parading as identification and representation (see Crenshaw 2003). "Isn't there a difficulty of saying 'we'?" Rich (1994, 224) asked, explaining, "You cannot speak for me. I cannot speak for us.... There is no liberation that only knows how to say 'I'; there is no collective movement that speaks for each of us all the way through." The conversation about race and ethnicity in which Combahee and Rich participated is a project of women reconstructing their identities in ways that are both strategically powerful and ethically sound. Rogue's power of absorption presents a similar opportunity for the ethical reformulation of identity.

In *Uncanny X-Men* #185, written the same year as the publication of Rich's "Notes toward a Politics of Location," Rogue explains to Storm, the X-Men's black, female, and recently masculinized leader, why she has run away from the X-Men to Caldecott, citing her powers as problematic in ways that echo Rich's analysis of universalizing, colonizing feminisms. Storm is a major part of Claremont's X-Men mythos, especially its exploration of intersectional feminism. During the period of lesbian-identified Rogue's induction into the X-Men, Storm had gone through her own sexual reawakening and gender reinvention, cutting her long white tresses into a Mohawk and leaving behind her disco-inspired costume for a punk-inflected leather jacket. Thus, the interplay between Rogue and Storm constitutes a major junction for multiple feminism-oriented character arcs within the Marvel Universe. Rogue asks Storm, "How can anyone trust me . . . when the slightest physical contact" can reapportion the powers and experiences of those she touches, effectively appropriating their subjectivity and agency such that Rogue, then, literally "speaks" not just "for" but "as" her victim (Rich 1994, 224) even as she "destroy[s] 'em" (Claremont and Romita 1984).

Rogue's view that her power erases and replaces what it touches, making positive relations with others impossible, takes on added significance in light of the race and gender expression of her interlocutor, Storm. Rogue's white flesh coming into contact with bodies of color and taking those bodies' experiences into itself, leaving those bodies inert, figures a kind of sexualized cultural appropriation.[14] Later in the *Uncanny X-Men* series, on multiple occasions, acting out of some exigent life-or-death necessity, Rogue nonconsensually absorbs the mutant teleportation powers of her silent ally, the Australian Aboriginal Gateway. Gateway's teleportation power is intimately tied to the Aboriginal culture of Australia; he produces "gateways" to faraway places by playing a bullroarer, a musical instrument used in Aboriginal rituals. When Rogue absorbs Gateway's power, her skin darkens; taking the bullroarer off Gateway's unconscious body, she uses the purloined instrument to open a gateway for herself to wherever she pleases, and she leaves Gateway behind, unconscious (Claremont and Lee 1990). In scenes like this, Rogue's power of absorption is an uncanny and very unsettling representation of cultural appropriation. Rogue, by identifying the potential dangers of cultural appropriation inherent in her power of absorption, complicates the Radicalesbians' (1972) call for women to identify with other women in light of the Combahee River Collective's (1983) and Rich's (1994) contentions that such identifications along lines of gender, conditioned by racism and heterosexism, can constitute harm across borders of race and sexuality. In short, Claremont's feminist trope of a touch that identifies with others to produce a nonnormative body empowered by blurring the lines between identity categories has colonialist and white supremacist implications when applied across races and regions.

With these dangers in mind, Rogue refuses to see her power of queer touch as compatible with ethical or happy living. Storm tries to reassure Rogue of her "decency." Rogue responds: "Decency has nothin' t' do with how ah feel—the cruelest sadist in creation couldn'tve thought up a worse punishment. Is it any wonder ah'm so full of anger an' hate?!" Rogue's anger and self-hate stem from her conception of her queer touch as "destruction" and appropriation, and her queer subjectivity as a "punishment." In an attempt to avoid the dangers of appropriating absorptions and escape her own formless, contingent subjectivity, Rogue retreats to Caldecott, where she enacts a kind of reverse "politics of location" intended to normalize and stabilize her identity.

Caldecott, the narrator box says, "is farming country, where once cotton was king and stately mansions lined the river, setting a standard for style and affluent gracious living that was the envy of the world. It was a way of life people believed would last forever." The narrator only subtly veils Caldecott's self-definition in terms of a wistful nostalgia for the institution of slavery. The "cotton" economy that built the "stately mansions" and sustained the region's "affluent gracious living," the narrator fails to mention, was run on black slave labor. This narrative construction of Caldecott is accompanied by lonely, silent landscape images of the Mississippi River that visually confirm the absence of black people amid the narrative erasure of their labor. The narrative and visual economies, then, work together to separate the products of labor from the black bodies that produce them.

The landscape images are populated only when Rogue's bikini-clad form is pictured gracefully jumping off a cliff, diving into the Mississippi. With a rare smile on her face, Rogue gives a carefree, joyous cheer of "Yahhooooooooo!!!" that swirls in bold red letters across the page. The solitude of sunbathing on a secluded riverbank allows Rogue to wear a small black bikini without fear of absorbing the psyches of passersby. In a wide vertical panel, Rogue sunbathes on her back, thinking, "[The] sun feels so good." This reengagement with her flesh, as it is constructed by the narrative and visual sequencing, is inseparable from the racial politics of the region. Caldecott, whose narrative construction erases the black labor that built it, allows Rogue to expose and reexperience her body, her white flesh, as a source of uncomplicated joy. It is ironic but perhaps typical of white supremacy that Rogue's attempt to avoid the appropriation of other bodies' experiences occludes those bodies, even as it depends on their labor, while it also centers (literally, in the panels of the comic book) and magnifies her own.

Rogue's racialization of herself through a politics of location "interlocks," as the Combahee River Collective would say, with the neutralization of Rogue's powers and therefore the normalization of her gender and sexuality. As Rogue swings off a line to perform a flipping dive into the Mississippi, in the distance, slightly out of perspective, a tugboat labeled *M* floats down the river. The boat apparently holds multiple admirers signified by a smattering of overlapping speech bubbles floating over the boat and cheering Rogue's sexualized athleticism: "Beautiful! Way t' go darlin'" one disembodied voice says. "Stop the boat, I wanna get off!" In this case, the desire to get off has a doubled meaning; the presumably male viewer wants to disembark the vessel so he can pursue Rogue, but "getting off" is also sexual gratification. Rogue is pleased by the attention. "Thank you, boys!" she yells back, securing the heterosexuality of the expressions of desire. The *M* on the boat could stand for *mutant* or *Mississippi*, but given how this scene plays out, it would aptly stand for *men*.

Rogue takes the heterosexual flirtation as an opportunity to normalize her gender. "Y'all really know how t' do a girl's heart proud!" she answers. From the long distance between herself and the tugboat, the intimacy of physical contact is replaced by the optical register of male sexuality. As she mentions her "pride," Rogue bows toward the boat in the distance. The perspective of the panel, though, is from behind Rogue and thus centers on Rogue's bottom, jutting toward the reader as she bends forward. Rogue's body is in full view of the male gaze, both from the perspective of the boat and from the reader, while the men's bodies are not visible at all. Rogue plays her part in feminine objectification, even intimating that the men's view of her has informed her own self-conception as a normatively gendered "girl" when she says the men's catcalls make her "*girl*'s heart proud!" (my emphasis). Rogue is no longer the butch power- and masculinity-draining succubus who androgenizes her body in layers of green cloth. Thanks to the powers of distance, she can reimagine herself as a bikini-clad "girl" performing for the male gaze. The feminized

Figure 4 Storm gives of herself "freely, [and] without reservation," challenging Rogue to reconsider the ethical and affective potentials of physical contact. From Claremont and Romita (1984), *Uncanny X-Men* #185

gendering and heterosexualization of Rogue are coeval with her visual racialization, both accomplished by neutralizing her queer power of touch (defined by contact) and restoring her body to the male gaze (projected through distance).

In an effort to prevent Rogue from possibly reverting back to villainy and keeping her impressive array of powers at the X-Men's disposal, Storm follows Rogue to Caldecott, where she challenges Rogue's reliance on the politics of Caldecott's location to neutralize her power by shifting attention to the affective, relational, and ethical context of the use of Rogue's power. "Do you trust no one?!" Storm asks. "Has every exercise of your power been an act of violence? Has no one ever given himself of his own free will?" The language of Storm's queries regarding the circumstances in which Rogue has used her powers—especially that of "giving" oneself and "free will"—reference the narrative contexts of sexual violence and bodily agency that gave rise to Rogue's creation as a feminist palimpsest for both analyzing and representing rape in *Avengers Annual* #10. In effect, Storm questions whether those contexts alone can or should define Rogue's power and by extension her queer relation to others and her own identity.

Then, in a move reminiscent of Rogue's pulling off her green glove in anticipation of absorbing Captain America, Storm rips off her own black glove. Storm's removing her glove, however, reimagines and reinterprets Rogue's first use of her power. Instead of touching Rogue against her will, Storm raises her naked hand palm up between them, offering it to her. Storm invites Rogue to absorb her. "Today," Storm says as she extends her naked hand, "I give of myself freely, without reservation." Whereas Rogue's "stolen kiss" is an affective form of sexual violence, Storm's offered hand is an affective form of "trust," "free will," and intimacy (see fig. 4). It is these affects that constitute Rogue and Storm's touch, reshaping the act of absorption and the two women's orientation toward difference.

Trust and intimacy define Rogue and Storm's renegotiation of individual difference across racial identities. However, the offered hand that distills that trust and intimacy also centers and ratifies the presence and agency of Storm in the very location where the narrative sought to occlude the existence of black bodies and labor. Rogue, at first, rejects Storm's offer in fear of permanently absorbing Storm's powers and persona as she did Ms. Marvel's. Above Storm's offered hand, Storm's speech bubble insists, "I am prepared to take the risk." The image of the offered hand is parallel with dialogue marking informed consent. This parallelism highlights that Storm has no illusion about the negative possibilities that emanate from the renegotiation of difference across identity categories and by giving one's agency and experience over to another who has not lived those experiences. Physical, psychological, and cultural harms are distinct possibilities within the potentials of queer contact and feminist identification across racial boundaries. However, it is Storm, the leader of the X-Men, marginalized and occluded within the politics of location already established by the narrative, who conceives, suggests, and provides the opportunity for that contact. Storm's hand is what is visible, and when Rogue accepts, it is Storm's hand that clasps Rogue's. Storm is in control even as she gives herself to Rogue, suggesting that perhaps when it comes to the ethical queering of race, trust and free will cannot predominate unless the orientation toward difference restores the visibility and centers the agency of those whom white supremacy represses (see hooks 2009, 371).

By shifting the evaluation of erotic and political relations (Rogue's power makes them one) into terms of free will and trust, Storm subtextually injects into her conversation with Rogue (concerning women's sexuality, identity, and race) the language and concepts of prosex and lesbian sadomasochistic feminisms. There is a danger to Rogue's touch that, like sadomasochistic sex, must be managed with trust, awareness, and faith (see Califia 1994). However, Storm, by intimating the possibility of willed absorption, radically suggests that queer contact, not just between identity categories of gender but also of race, is not in and of itself problematic, emphasizing the context of that contact—whether of sexual violence and appropriation or trust and free will—in determining its ethical and psychic quality. Storm uses pro-BDSM concepts to mediate the exchange of difference between Rogue's white body and her own black one, suggesting a conversation between black and lesbian sadomasochistic feminisms.[15]

Indeed, Rogue's touch, activated within the context of trust and affection, takes on a starkly different value. When Rogue takes Storm's offered hand, she says, "Ah'm full of excitement—and joy—nothing seems beyond me! And because Ororo did not resist the transfer . . . her memories have yet to cause me trouble. Perhaps they never will." Instead of feeling "crazy" or dysphoric as she did when she nonconsensually absorbed Ms. Marvel's powers, Rogue's absorption of Storm is a borderline religious experience of "excitement" and "joy."[16]

The discourse regarding Rogue's powers shifts from agonism to cooperation, stealing to sharing, and rape to consent, producing a parallel shift from identity politics to relations of subjectivity. When Storm first offers Rogue her hand, she asks, "Would you like to see the world through my eyes?" Storm's positive emphasis on vision is unusual in Rogue's narrative. It serves to emphasize that this absorption does not result in Storm becoming Rogue's "possession," but rather it allows Rogue an opportunity to feel and negotiate the world in a different way—Storm's way. Rogue sees Caldecott, the location she used to normalize herself, through Storm's "special perceptions." As a mutant with the ability to manipulate the weather, Storm—and now Rogue—sees her surroundings as "patterns of energy resonating within my own being." Rogue came to Caldecott to cut herself off from cross-identification, using the isolation of the riverbank to render her subjectivity self-contained and static. Through Storm's eyes, though, Rogue reapproaches the relationship between place and identity as an ecstatic, fluid "playtime." Using Storm's elemental abilities, Rogue "shape[s] the appropriate natural forces" to produce a miniature rain cloud. The shaping of "natural forces" parallels the way Storm's "special perceptions" teach Rogue that the relationship between environment and self—the politics of location—can also be dynamic and dialectical. In this new interpretation Storm is suggesting, Rogue's absorption is not about appropriating Storm's experiences but instead is about producing with Storm new experiences of a present place and time through a hybrid subjectivity that belongs to both women.

Rogue does not replace Storm through a vampiric, one-way intersubjectivity. Rather, Storm invites Rogue to coexist with her in a mutually interpenetrating intrasubjectivity. Thinking to herself, Rogue observes that the "voice" of her inner monologue "is changing—Hah!—becoming a blend of mine and Ororo's. Ah still have mah accent, but the tone is deeper and my speech more formal, like hers!" Usually, Rogue's distinctive accent is crucial in marking her regional identity. Storm's regal diction is almost equally idiosyncratic, reflecting her transcontinental upbringing in North America, Egypt, and Kenya. However, in this scene, within Rogue's thought bubble, voice stands not for identity, how Rogue and Storm represent themselves or how they identify, but subjectivity, the way in which they view, experience, and interact with the world, including each other. Rogue does not merely "hear" this "hybrid" voice. Rather, the use of the thought bubble renders the perspective decidedly internal. The reader knows that this speech is Rogue's thought, the way Rogue's subjectivity encounters itself. Having absorbed Storm through the offered hand, Rogue "thinks" as a hybridized or "blended" intrasubjectivity that does not represent itself in terms of identity categories because it is felt and experienced as sensation, the sound of Rogue-Storm's voice. Amber Jamilla Musser (2014, 23) theorizes sensation as "connected to politics, bodies, and feelings," but she also conceives of it as "a way to understand structures at a level beyond the discursive . . . without having to appeal to identity; this is about opening paths to difference." Viewing the world through Storm's "special perceptions," sensations arising from Storm's completely singular mutant powers, provides Rogue an access to Storm's unique and personal (rather than racialized and immediately cultural) differences. Rogue is not absorbing experiences of a generalized cultural identity—"experiences" with capital *E*s (see Scott 1992). Rogue is experiencing the subjectivity and physical capabilities of Storm as an individual, which in effect does not appeal to identity formations at all and therefore absorbs without culturally appropriating.

In fact, as Rogue loses control of her weather formations, she realizes the amount of concentration and discipline demanded by Storm's link with the weather. Of a sudden monsoon, she asks, "Am I the cause?!? Is this a reflection of my rage . . . ?!?!" Rogue's experience of Storm's powers results in an intimate and informed empathy with Storm. "No wonder [Storm] has been going squirrelly, if this was what she has to live with . . . her every emotion echoed by the weather around her." Thus, the perennially isolated and self-involved Rogue, by experiencing Storm's differences, develops a sense of Storm's emotional and psychological complexity. Rogue is changed by her experience of Storm's subjectivity in such a way that makes Storm's labor, discipline, and experiences more knowable. Moving from an identity politics of discourse, representation, and intersectionality to affinities of intrasubjectivity composed of sensation, physical contact, and difference, absorption through Storm's offered hand does not allow Rogue to claim what Storm has or to appropriate it culturally, but, rather, it gives rise to experiences of shared Storm-ness that generate Rogue's informed empathy with Storm.

If Rogue's absorption of Storm's powers produces an empathy for Storm's unique situation, it also reflexively reconditions Rogue's view of her own mutant power. When she awakens, Storm notes that Rogue "look[s]—strangely happy." Rogue replies, "Just comin' t' terms with myself—concedin' you may know what you're talkin' about—perhaps ah'm not as rotten as ah liked t' think." Thanks to Storm's intervention, Rogue has learned to embrace her power of absorption as an ethically viable orientation toward difference when defined by trust and free will. In the affective form of the offered hand, physical contact becomes the production of an (intra-)subjectivity that arises out of but cannot be made reducible to identity categories, a queer orientation toward difference that acts as an alternative interpretation of the feminist politics of location. But, of course, as the *M* tugboat sails by, its crewmen, still watching in the distance, hardly able to "b'lieve what we're seein,'" simply write it off as another example of "wimmin's lib."

The tugboat crew is not wholly wrong. Rogue operates as a fantasy figure for a point of contact between queer theory and feminism, where the self-assuredness of identity in terms of gender and race comes under question and moves into an exploration of the possibilities of identification. Rogue's touch presents the idea that who we are cannot be wholly determined in advance by the preordained matrix of classification we have come to know as identity (and, perhaps, as identity politics). Instead, Rogue suggests we might also be conceived as ongoing processes of relationality, empathy, and individual and shared experiences that give rise to subjectivities unforeseeable in terms of established discourses of identity. Consequently, Rogue's touch widens the conversation about "diversity" in superhero comics (and other genres and media) beyond representational inclusion to how media conceptualizes the relationship between difference and consciousness and generates new possibilities for affiliation, solidarity, and recognition that have yet to reveal themselves in the "real world." Crucially, Rogue and Storm suggest what an ethical cross-identification in terms of race might look like. Specifically, they seem to say, it might look like an offered hand. However, this shift from identity and representation to difference and subjectivity is not exclusionary. The access of identification and reconsideration of subjectivity figured by flesh-to-flesh contact that promises new, "mutant" forms of consciousness necessarily arise out of absorbing and negotiating the specificities of identity (and identity politics) and the ineluctable presentness of history, memory, and power.

Anthony Michael D'Agostino received his PhD in English literature from Fordham University. He is a lecturer at Fordham and Marymount Manhattan College, where he teaches writing, Victorian literature, feminist and queer theory, and popular culture. His work has been published in *Victorians: A Journal of Culture and Literature*. He is currently at work on a book that explores representations of feeling at a distance and psychic phenomena in the Victorian novel, American horror films, and superhero comic books as queer modes of desire, affinity, and subjectivity.

Notes

1. Having appeared in countless comic book publications, numerous television programs, and multiple major motion pictures since her 1981 introduction, the readers of *Playboy* magazine in 2005 voted Rogue, a Southern belle hailing from Caldecott, Mississippi, the most popular fictional character ever to be associated with the state of Mississippi. See Threadgill 2016.
2. For a reading of Rogue's power as disability, see Ilea 2009, 173.
3. My methodology draws from Brinkema's (2014, xi–xvi) formal intervention on affect theory.
4. Rogue is, in fact, one heroine in a series of Claremont's feminist superheroines, many of whose storylines connect with and reflect on one another. For a queer feminist reading of Phoenix and Storm, see Fawaz 2016, 144–63. For an African American feminist reading of Storm, see carrington 2016, 90.
5. For more on the fissioning of feminist movements in the latter half of the twentieth century, see Echols 1989, 199; Rosen 2000; and Hesford 2013.
6. For more on the placement of feminism in the United States' national imagination, see Hesford 2013.
7. Ruth Rosen (2000, 88) writes, "At times, ideological or generational differences bitterly divided feminists, but neither branch or the movement, by itself, could have brought about the staggering changes that swept through American culture during the remaining decades of the twentieth century."
8. For a brief but canonical analysis of Marvel's feminist-themed titles in the 1970s, see Strickland n.d.
9. For more on the male gaze, see Mulvey 1989.
10. For more on the centrality of the lesbian and the mannish woman in signifying and cohering a feminist identity, see Hesford 2013.
11. For 1980s early antiporn feminism extant with Rogue's introduction in *Avengers Annual* #10, see Lederer 1980. For a later iteration of antiporn or power feminism, see MacKinnon 1987. For an opposed, sex-positive feminism, see Rubin 1984. For a useful overview of and commentary on the feminist sex wars, see Rubin and Butler 1994.
12. This kind of reading that compromises between multiple and conflicting feminist agendas is very much informed by Janet Halley (2008).
13. For more on the recovery and re-empowerment of Carol Danvers, see Claremont and Cockrum 1982.
14. bell hooks (2009) theorizes this kind of sexualized cultural appropriation.
15. For more on the intersection among African American criticism, feminism, and porn, see Nash 2014.

16   Lorde (1993, 342) makes a similar distinction in *Uses of the Erotic*: "To share the power of each other's feelings is different from using another's feelings as we would use a kleenex. When we look the other way from our experience, erotic or otherwise, we use rather than share the feelings of those others who participate in the experience with us. And use without consent of the used is abuse."

References

Brinkema, Eugenie. 2014. *The Forms of the Affects*. Durham, NC: Duke Univ. Press.

Butler, Judith. 2004. *Undoing Gender*. New York: Routledge.

Califia, Pat. 1994. "A Secret Side of Lesbian Sexuality." In *Public Sex: The Culture of Radical Sex*, 157–64. Pittsburgh: Cleis Press.

Carrington, André M. 2016. *Speculative Blackness: The Future of Race in Science Fiction*. Minneapolis: Univ. of Minnesota Press.

Chinn, Sarah E. 2003. "Feeling Her Way: Audre Lorde and the Power of Touch." *GLQ: A Journal of Lesbian and Gay Studies* 9, no. 1: 181–204.

Claremont, Chris (writer), and Dave Cockrum (penciller). 1982. "Binary Star!" *Uncanny X-Men* 1, no. 164. New York: Marvel Comics.

Claremont, Chris (writer), and Michael Golden (penciller). 1981. "By Friends—Betrayed!" *Avengers Annual* 1, no. 10. New York: Marvel Comics.

Claremont, Chris (writer), and Jim Lee (penciller). 1990. "Rogue Redux." *Uncanny X-Men* 1, no. 269. New York: Marvel Comics.

Claremont, Chris (writer), and Jim Mooney (penciller). 1978. "The Deep Deadly Silence." *Ms. Marvel*, no. 17. New York: Marvel Comics.

Claremont, Chris (writer), and John Romita Jr. (penciller). 1984. "Public Enemy!" *Uncanny X-Men* 1, no. 185. New York: Marvel Comics.

———. 1985a. "It Was a Dark and Stormy Night." *Uncanny X-Men* 1, no. 195. New York: Marvel Comics.

———. 1985b. "The Juggernaut's Back in Town." *Uncanny X-Men* 1, no. 194. New York: Marvel Comics.

Claremont, Chris (writer), and Marc Silvestri (penciller). 1988. "Busting Loose." *Uncanny X-Men* 1, no. 236. New York: Marvel Comics.

Claremont, Chris (writer), and Paul Smith (penciller). 1983a. "Rogue." *Uncanny X-Men* 1, no. 171. New York: Marvel Comics.

———. 1983b. "To Have and to Not." *Uncanny X-Men* 1, no. 173. New York: Marvel Comics.

Combahee River Collective. 1983. "The Combahee River Collective Statement." In *Home Girls: A Black Feminist Anthology*, edited by Barbara Smith, 264–74. New Brunswick, NJ: Rutgers Univ. Press.

Crenshaw, Kimberlé. 2003. "Traffic at the Crossroads: Multiple Oppressions." In *Sisterhood Is Forever: The Women's Anthology for a New Millennium*, edited by Robin Morgan, 43–57. New York: Washington Square Press.

Diamond, Elin. 1992. "The Violence of 'We': Politicizing Identification." In *Critical Theory and Performance*, edited by Janelle G. Reinelt and Joseph R. Roach, 390–98. Ann Arbor: Univ. of Michigan Press.

Echols, Alice. 1989. *Daring to Be Bad: Radical Feminism in America, 1967–1975*. Minneapolis: Univ. of Minnesota Press.

Eco, Umberto. 1998. "The Myth of Superman." In *The Critical Tradition: Classic Texts and Contemporary Trends*, 2nd ed., edited by David H. Richter, 866–76. Boston: Bedford.

Fawaz, Ramzi. 2016. *The New Mutants: Superheroes and the Radical Imagination of American Comics*. New York: New York Univ. Press.

Halley, Janet. 2008. *Split Decisions: How and Why to Take a Break from Feminism*. Princeton, NJ: Princeton Univ. Press.

Hesford, Victoria. 2013. *Feeling Women's Liberation*. Durham, NC: Duke Univ. Press.

hooks, bell. 2009. "Eating the Other: Desire and Resistance." In *Media and Cultural Studies: Keyworks*, edited by Meenakshi Gigi Durham and Douglas M. Kellner, 366–80. Malden, MA: Wiley-Blackwell.

Ilea, Romona. 2009. "The Mutant Cure or Social Change: Debating Disability." In *X-Men and Philosophy: Astonishing Insight and Uncanny Argument in the Mutant X-Verse*, edited by William Irwin, Rebecca Housel, and J. Jeremy Wisnewski, 170–82. Hoboken, NJ: Wiley, 2009.

Jagose, Annamarie. 1996. *Queer Theory: An Introduction*. New York: New York Univ. Press.

———. 2009. "Feminism's Queer Theory." *Feminism and Psychology* 19, no. 2: 157–74.

Lederer, Laura. 1980. *Take Back the Night: Women on Pornography*. New York: William Morrow.

Lorde, Audre. 1982. *Zami: A New Spelling of My Name*. Berkeley, CA: Crossing Press.

———. 1993. "Uses of the Erotic." In *The Lesbian and Gay Studies Reader*, edited by Henry Abelove, Michèle Aina Barale, and David Halperin, 339–43. New York: Routledge.

MacKinnon, Catharine A. 1987. *Feminism Unmodified: Discourses on Life and Law*. Cambridge, MA: Harvard Univ. Press.

Mulvey, Laura. 1989. "Visual Pleasure and Narrative Cinema." In *Visual and Other Pleasures*, 14–26. New York: Palgrave Macmillan.

Musser, Amber Jamilla. 2014. *Sensational Flesh: Race, Power, and Masochism*. New York: New York Univ. Press.

Nash, Jennifer Christine. 2014. *The Black Body in Ecstasy: Reading Race, Reading Pornography*. Durham, NC: Duke Univ. Press.

Radicalesbians. 1972. "The Woman Identified Woman." In *Out of the Closets: Voices of Gay Liberation*, edited by Karla Jay and Allen Young, 172–76. New York: New York Univ. Press.

Rich, Adrienne. 1994. "Notes toward a Politics of Location." In *Blood, Bread, and Poetry: Selected Prose, 1979–1985*, 210–31. New York: Norton.

Rubin, Gayle. 1984. "Thinking Sex: Notes for a Radical Theory of the Politics of Sexuality." In *Social Perspectives in Lesbian and Gay Studies: A Reader*, edited by Peter M. Nardi and Beth E. Schneider, 100–33. New York: Routledge.

Rubin, Gayle, with Judith Butler. 1994. "Sexual Traffic." *differences: A Journal of Feminist Cultural Studies* 6, nos. 2/3: 62–99.

Scott, Joan W. 1992. "'Experience.'" In *Feminists Theorize the Political*, edited by Judith Butler and Joan W. Scott, 22–40. New York: Routledge.

Simonson, Louise (writer), and Greg LaRocque (penciller). 1985. "'Tis Better to Give!" *Marvel Team-Up* 1, no. 150. New York: Marvel Comics.

Solanas, Valerie. 1968. "S.C.U.M. Manifesto (Society for Cutting Up Men)." http://kunsthallezurich.ch/sites/default/files/scum_manifesto.pdf (accessed October 12, 2017).

Strickland, Carol A. n.d. "The Rape of Ms. Marvel." *Carol A. Strickland* (blog). http://carolastrickland.com/comics/msmarvel/ (accessed August 18, 2016).

Threadgill, Jacob. 2016. "X-Men's Rogue: From Mississippi." *Clarion-Ledger*, June 23. www.clarionledger.com/story/magnolia/entertainment/2016/06/23/x-mens-rogue-mississippi-and-proud/86179080/.

Warner, Michael. 1998. "Homo-Narcissism; or, Heterosexuality." In *The Critical Tradition: Classic Texts and Contemporary Trends*, edited by David H. Richter, 1499–512. Boston: Bedford.

Yetta Howard

Unsuitable for Children? Adult-erated Age in Underground Graphic Narratives

Abstract This article explores expressions of eroto-abject desire in two collaborative graphic narratives: Kathy Acker, Diane DiMassa, and Freddie Baer's *Pussycat Fever* (1995) and David Wojnarowicz, James Romberger, and Marguerite Van Cook's *7 Miles a Second* (1996). Reflecting the resistance to heteronormative logics of age categorization, "adult-erated age" names the ways that childhoods in the texts are adult oriented but also characterizes how they, in their respective contexts, revise and reflect notions of impurity and being worsened as singularly queer ways of being and representing. This is accomplished by turning to traumatic memory and ill embodiment via graphic textual form.
Keywords childhood, adulthood, age, underground, queer

One of Keith Haring's most iconic images is the *Radiant Baby*. The baby first appeared in 1980 as a graffiti tag (Arauz 2006, 13) and was spray-painted all over New York's underground—subway tunnels and city streets that served as Haring's primary canvas in addition to tarps, sheet metal, and refrigerator doors. Eventually fabricated as a button in 1983 (Frankel 1997, 58), the baby's characteristic stubby, rounded extremities with several short, thick lines encircling its whole body made it appear to glow or radiate light; these characteristics became a widely recognized feature of the artist's style. In addition to thick lines, Haring's graffiti aesthetic is distinguished by whimsical bodies, chatting animals, and personified objects rendered in chunky, cartoonish outlines often filled in with bright colors. But the *Radiant Baby*, named as such when Rene Ricard (1981) wrote his "Radiant Child" essay on Haring and Jean-Michel Basquiat in *Artforum*, functions as another kind of representation for contemporary viewers. It is one that recasts the image of the crawling baby and of a "childish" aesthetic as symbols of queer art practices that function with more than obliquely political impulses. Haring, who died of AIDS in 1990, continues to be regarded as a radiant child of late twentieth-century American street art. Along with Basquiat's distinctive graffiti style, Haring's queer art beamed incorruptible childlike excitement to the alluring adult danger of the urban landscape, an investment in "play" as erotic spontaneity bound up with artistic craft.

Juxtaposed with the playfulness of smiling facelike images containing multiple eyes and happily yelping dogs in Haring's oeuvre are genitals that appear to be in motion and geometrically shaped bodies erotically dancing in angular poses. On the one hand, the *Radiant Baby* transforms the childhood sensibilities of the adult artist into tangible creative practice. On the other hand, this is less a transformation and more a blend of visual signifiers that inexactly mark the specificities of age. Earlier incarnations of the *Radiant Baby* took the form of an "adult figure on all fours engaged in sex acts" (Arauz 2006, 11), and the "radiance" is not reducible to the eager baby's undeveloped energy but, in Haring's own words, is simultaneously akin to mature sexual energy (Frankel 1997, 58). Indeed, both Haring's queer sexuality and artistic investment in youth iconography should be thought of as a mixed adult-child aesthetics of radiance: in some of his other work the radiating lines appear as ejaculate itself, specifically as the figure of Mickey Mouse clutching a "radiating penis" (Sussman 1997, 18).[1] If Haring's art making invites a ready understanding of comics aesthetics as childhood aesthetics that are not quite for children, then, perhaps more important, his approach also allows viewers to put a tremendous amount of pressure on the boundaries between the suitable age domains associated with adults versus children that the visual-textual qualities of the medium provoke.

I begin with the example of Haring's work because it helps to situate what is at stake in this article: the idea of age suitability but, significantly, the question of age itself in thinking about how the graphic narrative form is particularly positioned to radicalize the definitional borders of adulthood and childhood. To work through this, I turn to examples from underground American graphic narratives of the 1990s because these are textual territories that freely accommodate overt expressions of sexuality and the queering of age coterminous with the reclamation of *queer* in this era of LGBTQ cultural history. Specifically, I explore the interdependence of sexual identity formations and textual aesthetics in two collaborative graphic narratives: Kathy Acker, Diane DiMassa, and Freddie Baer's *Pussycat Fever* (1995) and David Wojnarowicz, James Romberger, and Marguerite Van Cook's *7 Miles a Second* ([1996] 2012). Less categorically stable as a graphic novel, *Pussycat Fever* is a rhetorically distorted pirate tale cast as a coming-of-age sexual narrative that activates traumatic memory and dream states as visual fragmentations. In the stream-of-consciousness experimentation characteristic of Acker's work, the text pairs excerpts from what was published the following year as "The Pirate Girls" section of Acker's full-length *Pussy, King of the Pirates* (1996a) with visually distinctive adult-child–themed illustrations by DiMassa and Baer.

As a semiautobiographical narrative that is also a disruptive coming-of-age story, *7 Miles a Second* chronicles Wojnarowicz's life as a preteen prostitute, teenage hustler, and gay man living with AIDS, doing so in three sections titled "Thirst," "Stray Dogs," and "7 Miles a Second." A collaborative project with artists Romberger and Van Cook, *7 Miles a Second* eschews traditional comics form by drastically disengaging with consistency in its distribution of text boxes, imagery, and coloring alongside an audibly confrontational lettering style. These are less explored projects by cultural producers who were involved in New York's downtown, East Village literary and art scenes during the 1970s and 1980s until their deaths in the 1990s. Their influences have remained on the radar of queer and underground literature and arts. While Acker's and Wojnarowicz's works are more widely recognized within genealogies of radical queer art and transgressive feminist writing, these queer collaborative texts generally have not been read together as a way to rethink the potentials of the medium to harness queer experience as it relates to circumventing dominant perspectives of age. As nonmainstream and lesser known within both of Acker's and Wojnarowicz's bodies of work, *Pussycat Fever* and *7 Miles a Second* were initially published in the mid-1990s, within a year of each other.[2] These collaborations with writers who were terminally ill—*7 Miles* was released posthumously and *Pussycat Fever* presourced its excerpts from Acker's final full-length novel—further underwrite how the texts re-mark the contours of age vis-à-vis their respective forms of terminal textual practice. Initially conceived neither as comics nor as necessarily for children, the queering of these narratives' graphic forms by the artists and writers, I suggest, shows how the categories of "child" and "adult" encounter each other via putatively adult experiences marked as unsuitable for children and, in turn, collapse the adult-child distinction. By "queering," I mean that they resist heteronormative logics of age categorization and, rather than merely offering a comics-focused evaluation of queer childhood or adulthood, demonstrate disobedient age formations that coextend with their graphic textual features.

To do this, I build on Kathryn Bond Stockton's (2009, 11) theory of the queer child, particularly what she describes as the queer child's "ways of growing that are not growing up." "Growing sideways," as Stockton puts it, is a generative way to approach the queer readerly aesthetics that are constitutive of the graphic narrative form. Like growing sideways, graphic texts engender literal ways to read sideways, that is, in non-*straight*forward ways. Even with "standard" reading practices that come with more traditionally executed comics, the Z-directed process—left to right and diagonally downward left, to the next set of panels—queerly and interactively mediates the absorption of textual material beyond the demands of word- or image-exclusive texts. This complexity is certainly at odds with the perspective of comics as a lesser or debased, infantilized form (Groensteen 2000), whose narratives, in such myopic views, are adulterated by images. But the view of comics as inferior or childish is instructive in this regard, especially within the context of LGBTQ identities. Gender nonconformity is often read on the body and perceived as an unsuitable youthfulness or immaturity, just as a second or later "adolescence" is frequently bound up with coming-out narratives or trans autobiography.[3] Thinking about comics and queerness as adulterated textual and identificatory forms, I wish to mobilize the use of *adulterate*—to make impure by adding inferior elements—in excess of the worsening that it denotes and use *adult-erate* to name the ways that childhoods in the texts are adult oriented but also to characterize how their visual-narrative qualities, in their own contexts, revise and reflect notions of impurity and being worsened as singularly queer ways of being and representing.[4] Certainly, then, situating queerness as such requires an embrace of it as an admixture, as a messy grouping of adult-child and text-image. Queerness here is an admixture that corresponds with the graphic narratives' disorderly inconsistencies and unpredictable extremes such as the collagelike and fragmented writing and illustrations in *Pussycat Fever* and in *7 Miles a Second* what Ramzi Fawaz (2017, 357) theorizes as its "deluge aesthetics," "the intentional flooding of readers' sensory experience by an onslaught of visceral language and imagery." As we shall see, this innovative resistance to pure or unadulterated creative vision also migrates to inform the choices that the artists and writers themselves made in their various collaborative practices.

Accordingly, such embodiments of queer comics aesthetics invite a critical meditation on the concept of age itself. When thought alongside *adulterate*, growing old applies to the addition of time as the agent of degradation. Contrastingly, age can also be development, something with which one gets better. Yet age is not reducible to time nor is it conceptually bound to purely temporal designations of bodily or mental growth (think: "it's just a phase"). While connoting an often arbitrary eligibility, qualification, or responsibility, age is more flexible in that it instead characterizes an era or period of life irrespective of chronological time.[5] Placing queerness with comics aesthetics requires this flexibility; hence, rather than consider how age is manifested as getting better or worse, the texts reflect that things get messier rather than better. Dubiously suitable combinations of supposedly age-restricted contexts present themselves as admixtures that define the queerness of the graphic narrative features in question. "Adulterated age" is this developmental hovering, in line with the "elegant, unruly contours of growing," as Stockton (2009, 13) writes, "that don't bespeak continuance." But, significantly, it is also, I contend, a hovering between the derogatory and the sexually libertine, what the undoing of affirmative versus negative valuation means in the reclamation of *queer*—and, by extension, the indefinite status of child and adult. I do not, then, show that children necessarily take the place of adults or that adults simply revert to childhood. Rather, by turning to these underground graphic narratives, I offer some glimpses into where these categories overlap in showing how traumatic memory and ill embodiment yield eroto-abject desires endemic to queerness and comics as admixtures revealing adult-erated age.

Adult-erated age is articulated as ageless memory in *Pussycat Fever* and as disintegrated age in *7 Miles a Second*. Ageless memory refers to the memory-dreams of childhood-focused sexual trauma and adult desire—nonlinear, volatile instances of temporal recollection—that are rhetorically and visually fashioned as fragmentations in the text.

Figure 1 Hustling in front of the aquatics store. From David Wojnarowicz, James Romberger, Marguerite Van Cook, *7 Miles a Second* ([1996] 2012). Used with permission

Disintegrated age borrows its reference from Wojnarowicz's *Close to the Knives: A Memoir of Disintegration* (1991) and refers to the physical, material deterioration of the ill adult body as well as the loosening of childhood distinctions from adult experiences. I want to turn briefly to moments from each text that demonstrate my broader claims albeit via each text's individual aesthetic approaches.[6]

In a section from *Pussycat* described as "Pages Torn Out of My First School Diary," the narrator writes, "After not having sex for years, the pirates came to a land where they could again have sex. Of course, they were girls. . . . Some of them even pissed in their pants. They were remembering their childhoods" (Acker, DiMassa, and Baer 1995, 37). Baer's illustration that introduces this section is an image of a girl in Victorian-era dress clutching a book with a collage of children's book covers behind her, including Edward Eggleston's *Queer Stories for Boys and Girls* (1884). Cast as a distinctively gendered event, the image alongside the narrative situates the play of visual-verbal signification in relationship to an antiquated use of *queer* reflected in the historical despecificity of the pictorial itself. The infantile act of soiling oneself is likewise reimagined as adult sexual excitement. Early in *7 Miles*, linguistic-image play is observable in the first splash page that introduces the "Thirst" section, which shows Wojnarowicz as a boy prostituting himself in front of an aquatics store. Adjacent to the section's title is a partial view of the store's sign, "Aqua-," with another sign that advertises equipment for "water sports" in the window (see fig. 1). The text works with the reading of the sign and the image of the author as a boy standing in front of the store as a simultaneous obfuscation of naïveté and displacement of maturity: "Thirst" signifies the need to hustle for sustenance as much as it implies sexual appetite. The viewer is invited to read the signs' double meanings as urine fetish operating in the same scope as the young Wojnarowicz's guise: "The worst thing about the wait between customers was having to move every five minutes so that the vice wouldn't get wise" (Wojnarowicz, Romberger, and Van Cook 2012, 6). Here, just like an active employment of misreading *queer* and urination's implication in the *Pussycat* example, misreading the signs—the store's in tandem with the image of the young Wojnarowicz in front of the store—forces the reader to confront misreading the signs of age vis-à-vis the ages of those in question. A man accompanying his son to shop for aquatic equipment all at once reads as a john accompanying a hustler to "dive in" to sex.

Epitomized by the opening example of Haring's age-play aesthetics, children's play, wordplay, and their concomitant visual renderings productively reevaluate the age specificities of development through various forms of "play" with sexual autonomy as an aesthetic libertinism within these graphic textual expressions. Moreover, when thinking about underground contexts as the suitable repositories for queerness, we need not look too far to see the appropriation of childhood imagery or elements associated with children within nonheteronormative adult sexual practices. Consider sapiosexual mind *games*, sex *toys*, role-*play*, or even just fore*play*: games, toys, playing—something of childhood is desired that exceeds children themselves. That "something" is the sexual-textual negotiation of adult versus child along with the dehierarchizing of word versus image: age-emphatic frameworks of graphic-queer impurity suitably attuned to underground cultural production and sexual minority difference reaching a productively depictive juncture.

Ageless Memory in *Pussycat Fever*

Perhaps it is unsuitable to think about *Pussycat Fever*, published by radical literary anarchist collective AK Press, as upholding qualities generally recognized of graphic narratives. One of a few mutations of Acker's underground novel *Pussy, King of the Pirates* (1996a), *Pussycat Fever* features excerpts from the novel along with illustrations by collage artist Freddie Baer and multigenre artist Diane DiMassa. Calling *Pussycat* a chapbook, DiMassa, creator of the queer cult classic *Hothead Paisan: Homicidal Lesbian Terrorist* (1991–99) comix, had not read any of Acker's work before agreeing to contribute illustrations (email interview with author, April 16, 2014). According to DiMassa, not having read Acker was "actually a good thing for illustrating it because I had the sublime experience of reading it for the first time." The artists met in San Francisco in the early 1990s, and when DiMassa asked Acker what she wanted illustrated, Acker expressed no preferences, trusting DiMassa to illustrate anything she wanted and opting not to see any of the work in progress.

In a similar spirit of spontaneous art practice, like her collaborations with Riot Grrrl[7] and queercore bands,[8] another mutation of *Pussy, King of the Pirates* is Acker's collaboration with postpunk band the Mekons. Using the same name as the novel and setting some of the content to music, the Mekons and Acker released a quasi-spoken-word album on Chicago's Quarterstick Records, a subsidiary of the underground record label Touch and Go, and performed several live versions of the album together.[9] Featuring a painting by alternative comix artist S. Clay Wilson, the album cover of *Pussy, King of the Pirates* includes two excessively illustrated sentences adapted from the novel version: "Ange and me are innocent. We still don't know that these girls are evil pirates." Partly organized as a set of songs on the album, these sentences are placed in a banner in the top-left corner of Wilson's piece. The significance here lies in the juxtaposition of the text with the image, which depicts two women maniacally engaged in an orgiastic scene of castration, bludgeoning, and stabbing. Blood is forcefully ejected from bodies in the midst of chaotic, crowded carnage, the aesthetic presence of which enters an ecstatic dimension as penetrating, thrusting weapons excessively mark an unbridled indulgence in dark desires. Situated against the insistence of childhood innocence, the cover image's visual narration disassembles the purity expressed in the banner, reconstructing it through the lens of an outlaw adult extremism that activates its violence as an erotic event.

This outlaw status extends to the experimental structure of the novel, which serves as the source text for both the album and *Pussycat Fever*. Incorporating treasure maps, banners, and semipornographic dialogue, both the full-length novel *Pussy, King of the Pirates* and its musical companion position themselves to be read and listened to as subversive pirate tales. Seduced by piracy in all its forms, including plagiarism, the text partially steals from or loots canonical authors such as Herman Melville and Robert Louis Stevenson. In an interview Acker (1996b, 333) stated: "When I was a kid I wanted to be a mermaid, I wanted to be a sailor, I wanted to be Herman Melville, I wanted to be a pirate.... In a way, I feel like a pirate because since I was a child I've never lived anywhere more than a few years, and the way I write has so much to do with piracy." Acker does not leave her pirate aspirations to the memory of being a child but appropriates them ("I feel like a pirate") for an adult understanding of her writerly approach. This approach, surfacing as a radical plagiarism and influenced by William Burroughs and Brion Gysin's cut-up techniques, is heavily critical of the unquestioned praise associated with canonical American and European literature by men. Acker's feminist reappropriation is bound up with understanding how her self-described nomadic childhood translates as a textual practice that has a particularly erratic effect. DiMassa describes her process of selecting which sections of *Pussy, King of the Pirates* to illustrate: "When I read it, I said to myself, 'Holy shit, there's an illustration in every sentence!'" (email interview with author, April 16, 2014). Invoking psychoanalytic notions of female hysteria, "The Pirate *Girls*" that names the section of the source text foregrounds Acker's oppositional method of unpredictability as a gendered "piracy."

As one transfiguration of *Pussy, King of the Pirates*, *Pussycat Fever* departs from a direct emphasis on pirates and piracy and, perhaps justifying its alternate naming, takes on childhood and adolescence, doing so through ageless memory: it is composed of visual fragmentations and discontinuous narratives of memories and dreams based in sexual violence. Acker (1996b, 331) states that she sees the world "through a sexual lens. But that's very different from writing pornography."[10] Yet *Pussycat* embraces pornographic content in the way it reflects explicit material in its constructions of memory. I strategically explore such content alongside the text's innovative structure, expanding how the text's graphic elements express the range of desires that may come with memories of violence enacted on the younger body. Putting pressure on suitable age-specific experiences through its avant-garde visual and narrative features, the text allows for an interrogation of the adult implications of its illustrations as potential access points to how scenes of sexuality and violence are crafted via memories. As Chris Kraus (2017, 58) writes in her literary biography of the author, "Acker worked and reworked her memories until, like the sex she described, they became conduits to something a-personal, until they became myth." These modes of methodological and readerly access are central to understanding the shaping of nonheteronormative perspectives that break down the adult-child distinction in *Pussycat Fever*. *Pussycat Fever* is an adult's story of an often-violent childhood remembered in fragments of memories, an experimental tale of a childhood negotiated with adult desires. *Pussycat* delivers in graphic form the remnants of a past and present indeterminately placed between childhood traumas and the explicit adult recollections of them.

The very first section of *Pussycat Fever* is titled "Before I Was Eight Years Old" but reads as an adult narrating her childhood as a childhood story for adults. Adjacent to this is Baer's realism-inspired, Victorian-style illustration of a girl holding a cat with a collage of cats that fills the entire background (see fig. 2). Acker's genital-animal wordplay with *pussy*, *cat*, and *pussycat* is central. *Pussycat*, as in the title, cannot be uttered without sounding like a childish name for a cat, but even without removing *cat*, which the source novel does in its

Unsuitable for Children? 293

Figure 2 Pussies. Illustration by Freddie Baer. From Kathy Acker, Diane DiMassa, and Freddie Baer, *Pussycat Fever* (1995). Used with permission

title, the *pussy* in *pussycat* to an adult reader resists being thought of as anything other than a somewhat pejorative name for female genitalia, while the word *cunt* is used to name the anatomical referent in the text. Insofar as the adult subject's association of *pussy* with genitalia mismatches the image of the girl alongside depictions of actual cats, the image functions as a graphic analogue for the categorical breakdown of adult and child. Narrated from a memory, a dream, or a memory of a dream, Pussycat instead becomes a character who can be read as many things, especially as the narrator's object of adolescent desire, at times encountered as a receptacle for displaced memories of abuse. Among other things, the narrator, too, becomes a decentered subject of father-daughter abuse and recounts her favorite childhood tale. After explaining a transgendered childhood upbringing and making reference to the abuse, the narrator turns to a childhood story: a girl's heterosexual desire for a boy who plays with snakes and skulls and has uncombed, knotty hair filled with rodents. Reminiscent of the Lunachicks' corrupted Barbie head on the cover of its *Pretty Ugly* album, this trans-Medusa-like image of the boy is not threatening but is desired as "the boy [who] never washes his hair" (Acker, DiMassa, and Baer 1995, 3).[11]

DiMassa provided the illustration for this scene and writes, "I wanted to draw the junk in his hair, and the snake, and the feeling that I got when I read the section was that I couldn't keep up with what she was describing. It spoke to me because my personal experience of life is through an intensely emotionally surreal lens" (email interview with author, April 16, 2014). The inability to keep up, as DiMassa describes, links the changeability associated with memory's unreliability with the instability of the narrative voice in the text. The desiring subject in the children's story is not supposed to be the narrator but a girl who merely looks like the narrator. She states, "A girl who resembled me desired to fuck this boy and wanted him to fuck her. She wanted this so badly that she wanted time to end as soon as they started fucking so that fucking would never stop" (Acker, DiMassa, and Baer 1995, 5). This desire for suspended temporality is one that operates in terms of imagining a space of sexual desire removed from a particularly adultlike or childlike voice. In other words, the bluntness of the statement has the characteristics of a child's straightforward expression but uses adult content and language. Trapped in a childhood tale while in the midst of adult memories of her father, the narrator states, "After fucking, there should be nothing" (5). Accordingly, ageless memory comes through as a simultaneity of time ending and timelessness, a pause both within and as unending desire that maintains an irreconcilable relationship with sexual development.

This experimental structure of time and memory notably comes through when the narrator turns eight (according to the section title, "Becomes Eight Years Old"), when she reads from a letter by a poet about his daughter's death, recounted as a dream before she dies: "The only difference between this present and the present in my memory were three pairs of black leather gloves. The first wasn't mine because they were unlined. The third were almost mine: the only difference between them and the gloves in my memory was a slight change in the color of the lining" (23). This framing of time is coextensive with the graphic elements of the text. Unlike a typical graphic narrative, the text is more often words than images and obliquely calls to mind Phoebe Gloeckner's *The Diary of a Teenage Girl: An Account in Words and Pictures* (2002) in both form and content. In Acker's text, however, the words are framed by alternating patterned borders that, like the fetishistic leather gloves and the narrator's past and present, only slightly change in their different "line-ings" (see fig. 3). The second pair of gloves is not mentioned and because the first pair is not the girl's and the third pair is almost the girl's, the reader is left to assume that the second pair is hers. The second pair, signifying secondariness, points to secondary memory, which processes the effects of raw trauma that exist in primary memory.[12] Graphically narrating this repression, the text functions as a "secondary" personal history and falls in line with understanding memory as compulsively repeating traumatic events (LaCapra 1998, 10), never really getting to the "actual" occurrences in time but nevertheless dependent on them to work through the present. The secondary memory of "becom[ing] eight years old" is therefore routed through an adult recollecting a child's dream state. This recollection formulates sexual subjectivity as an effect of primary associations that become visually expressed as repeated fragmentations of illustrations in *Pussycat*'s textual aesthetic.

As I have been demonstrating, positioning the narrator in childhood memories or experiences of violence and through erotic dreams as an adult, *Pussycat*'s adult-erated age corresponds with an agelessness of memory that relies on its fragmentary qualities. The disjointed elements characteristic of the text as a childhood violence narrative come through in both the semantic and visual contexts of its telling. Rather than introduce new images to accompany the progression of its

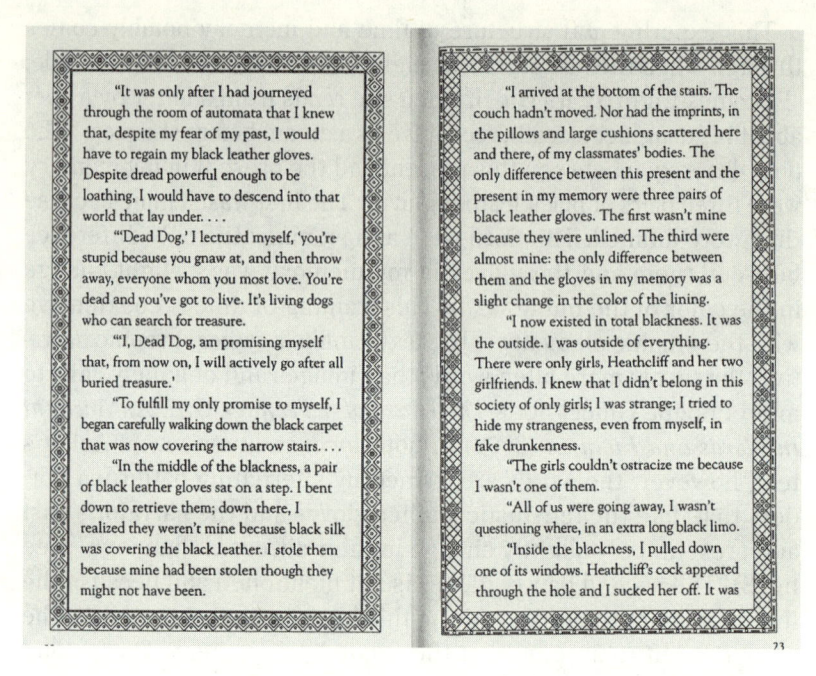

Figure 3 Line-ings. From Kathy Acker, Diane DiMassa, and Freddie Baer, *Pussycat Fever* (1995). Used with permission

experimental narrative, the text often repeats images as fragments of themselves, and in standing for the fragmentary memory, the images visually reflect the narrator's fragmentary account of recollection. One such image is an illustration of menacing-looking girls in a classroom (see fig. 4). "The classroom scene," states DiMassa, "is one of my favorite pieces of any illustration I've done. I think everyone can relate to at least one of those girls and the hell of [nonconsensual] socialization (school) in general" (email interview with author, April 16, 2014). With school rather than sex as the nonconsensual context that DiMassa suggests, the resistance to propriety and to forced rituals of childhood relationality is represented in the image, which features five schoolgirls, all in various modes of disobedience. A girl in the corner wears a dunce cap, flanked by another girl touching herself while another sits provocatively on the teacher's desk with a cigarette in hand. All the girls' eyes are eerily blanked out except for a masculine girl in the front, presumably standing in for the narrator as imagined

Figure 4 Girls' school. Illustration by Diane DiMassa. From Kathy Acker, Diane DiMassa, and Freddie Baer, *Pussycat Fever* (1995). Used with permission

in memory. She clutches an apple in one hand and, in the other, books wrapped in a belt, appropriating while undoing icons associated with school. This illustration appears in a section of the text called "My Dreams Show Me My Sexuality," in which the narrator's father has sent her off to boarding school, where she both inhabits and is alienated by queer female sexuality through her relationship with Pussycat. As mentioned, Pussycat at times functions as an object the narrator uses to work through her past abuses. In one scene, the narrator asks Pussycat to "open her up as wide as she could" (Acker, DiMassa, Baer 1995, 49) but then reconsiders for fear of becoming hurt by being helpless. Pussycat replies, "I'm going to hurt you even more"

Figure 5 The graveyard scene and its fragment. From Kathy Acker, Diane DiMassa, and Freddie Baer, *Pussycat Fever* (1995). Used with permission

(49), explaining that these actions are "natural" (49). While this easily could be read as BDSM-inspired play, more ambivalently, it casts the narrator as unsuitable to consent, a hazardous approach to extreme sexual practices. Along the same lines, as the section progresses and regresses, the classroom illustration is repeated in bits and pieces: first with a cropped shot of the illustration and then just the image of the narrator again who is isolated, possibly from any certain sense of where the childhood abuses end and the budding adult desires begin.

What surfaces, then, is an account of queer sexuality that, through the text's aesthetic, illustrates the violence of a childhood past as a confrontation with memories that cannot be effectively escaped in adulthood. Fittingly, *Pussycat* ends with the narrator:

> My father and his closest friend discussed ways and plans to behead all the unnatural girls who had made this graveyard their home. Girls under the dirt who placed their hands inside each other's cunts and drew them out muddied and bloodied. Put these fingers into their own mouths. Lips left brown and red.

I knew.

I knew what Pussycat wanted to do to me and I knew that my father wanted to kill me, so I left.

Together, Pussycat and I disappeared. (75)

While putting fingers in mouths could be read as childish behavior, it also queerly collapses the distinction between adult and child figures via oral-genital sexualities that are irreducible to the age of the narrator in question. If the "unnatural" girls' hands are bloodied after penetrating each other, then the question of "regressing" to a younger state might be better described as a manifestation of Stockton's "sideways" growth. Put differently, the blood here signifies the girls' menstruation—the marker of a physiological transformation into "woman"—as much as it stands for the non-age-specific effects of violence on the body in light of BDSM blood play. The image that accompanies this is of a graveyard with a zombielike masculine figure wielding an ax and two masculine girls, one escaping out from the page toward the reader while the other sits cradling her legs, lost in thought (see fig. 5). The repeated fragment of the image that is placed below the aforementioned paragraph is just the image of the girl who stays, pondering the moment. The narrator's disappearance, rather than walking away from her traumatic past, reconsiders the expectations about what growing into survival should entail. And even as the image indicates otherwise, she describes herself as departing with Pussycat, standing in for the memory of a sexual or abused self, which shapes queer desire as the internalization of violence that might more suitably end in disappearing in those memories rather than overcoming them.

Disintegrated Age in *7 Miles a Second*

Acker called Wojnarowicz a "saint" at a tribute reading to him in fall 1991 (Carr 2012, 551), a few months before he died of AIDS-related infections in 1992. Acker died of breast cancer just a few years later, in 1997, shortly after *Pussy, King of the Pirates* was published. Acker's and Wojnarowicz's ages at death were early 50s and late 30s, respectively. Just as their deaths retrace the duration of their lives, their texts provide conspicuous revisions of textual-bodily age beyond the effects of disease. Acker's characterization of Wojnarowicz as a "saint," then, is an apt way to think about his posthumous publications as transgressive "resurrections," especially the graphic novel memoir *7 Miles a Second*. In a sense reviving the artist through his work, *7 Miles* was published as a standard comic book–size graphic novel in 1996 by DC Comics' imprint Vertigo Vérité, a subimprint of Vertigo. Vertigo, which focused on darkly violent and sexually explicit topics for a more mature readership, served as a suitable place for Wojnarowicz's story of hustling, homelessness, and living with AIDS. "He wanted it to be a comic book," Cynthia Carr (2012, 361) writes, "so that young gay people would realize that there was someone else who'd survived the things they were going through." Nonetheless catering mostly to an adult audience, Fantagraphics reissued *7 Miles* (using the numeral 7 in the reissued title perhaps to signify its distinction from the original) as a large hardcover art book in 2012, this time correctly crediting coauthor Van Cook as the book's colorist and coauthor Romberger as text editor.[13] Romberger, who began working with Wojnarowicz on the book in 1986, chose its title and largely determined which of Wojnarowicz's writings it would include (email interview with author, May 17, 2011). While Romberger sees the book as an "adult product," he "avoided drawing any sex scenes explicitly," stating that "none of it has any prurient intent" (email interview with author, April 8, 2014).

In a chapter titled "Postcards from America: X Rays from Hell" from *Close to the Knives*, Wojnarowicz (1991, 112) writes: "I am experiencing the X-ray of Civilization. The minimum speed required to break through the earth's gravitational pull is seven miles a second.... We would have to learn to run awful fast to achieve escape from where we are all heading." As part of the aesthetics of poetic rage that characterizes the memoir, this moment suggests the escapelessness of living in a state of physical and psychic disintegration, a death pushed too soon onto the artist who lived a life always close to death. Moreover, *Seven Miles a Second* is also the title of his 1988 mixed-media piece featuring images of dung beetles and felt-tip marker drawings of figures injecting needles and sleeping against the backdrop of a banal supermarket poster. This juxtaposition points to the lived experience of inhabiting a body stricken with AIDS and, as much of his work suggests, allows the viewer to visualize the range of affective responses that accompany the negotiations with sexuality, mortality, and its sooner-rather-than-later inevitability. Living a life debased by AIDS and by what he describes as "contracting a diseased society" (114), Wojnarowicz

Unsuitable for Children?   301

Figure 6   The taboo of watching heterosexuality. From David Wojnarowicz, James Romberger, and Marguerite Van Cook, *7 Miles a Second* ([1996] 2012). Used with permission

revises what "age" means in relationship to life expectancy, a disintegrated age firmly ensconced in queer corporeal temporality.[14]

Similar to *Pussycat Fever*, *7 Miles* is part of a network of textual production that characterizes Wojnarowicz's work as a whole. His artistic output spans photography, writing, performance, and filmmaking, and many themes, images, passages, and clips resurface and repeat across his works. For instance, disks containing images of the artist burning alive and reduced to organs attached to a skeleton are included on the cover of the reissued *7 Miles*. The cover art shows Wojnarowicz as a boy running in the chaotic urban environment of New York and replaces one of the boy's limbs with a tree trunk stuck in the concrete "jungle." Romberger "made the decision to add the disk images to the cover, the intro page, the chapter breaks and the final pages to directly reference David's use of disks in his pieces" (email interview with author, April 8, 2014). The pieces to which Romberger refers are the photomontages in Wojnarowicz's *Sex Series* (1988–89). Executed as photographic negatives, this series features empty landscapes such as the middle of a forest or a panoramic shot of the Brooklyn Bridge. Indeed, the choice to use the negatives positions each depicted scene as a strategic distortion of the visual context. In other words, the uncanny images visually expose the underground spaces of a sexually minoritarian subjectivity and subsequently situate the queerness of the underground as "positive exposures" of the photographic negative.

Influenced by conversations about photographic methods with Van Cook (Romberger email interview with author, April 8, 2014; Carr 2012, 408–12), Wojnarowicz embedded in each piece a circle or groups of circles primarily depicting explicit scenes of gay sex. In writing about the *Sex Series*, Richard Meyer (2002, 252) observes, "The circular insets are not only peepholes giving onto secret sexual exchange but also tears in the fabric of mainstream representation." Accordingly and in addition to the use of circles in the graphic layout of *7 Miles*, a "peephole" appears early in the narrative. In the "Thirst" section of *7 Miles*, which depicts Wojnarowicz as an adolescent sex worker, the text overtly unsettles age distinctions as he is fellated by a grown man while watching a prostitute with a customer through a hole in the door of a seedy hotel room (see fig. 6). For the child Wojnarowicz, the primal scenic view at this moment has him "in awe of the taboo. Them unaware of [the] watching . . . the first time I'd seen men's and women's bodies interact . . . having only had sex with older men since I was nine" (Wojnarowicz, Romberger, and Van Cook 2012, 14). His childhood sexual experience with adult men is deflected to the innocence of watching heterosexual sex for the first time, which culminates not in being repulsed by his own situation as a boy but instead by the revelation of sexual difference and the violence enacted on the grown female body. At this moment in the text, the young Wojnarowicz realizes that the woman has freshly stitched wounds across her abdomen, and he feels physically ill at the thought of her customer's indifference to the wounds. She is also illustrated as menstruating, the bodily signifier par excellence of a girl's transition to "woman" but recast here as Wojnarowicz's own askew coming-of-age via adult female embodiment.

While Wojnarowicz's experiences did not follow standard trajectories associated with childhood, for the adult Wojnarowicz, elements of these experiences inspired the integration of child-themed rebellion in a number of his creative projects and, in turn, can be mapped onto his approach to queer sexuality. These projects included themes of children murdering their parents, burning children attempting to escape, and an installation for "The Missing Children's Show" in Kentucky (Carr 2012, 276, 316). Years before their graphic novel collaboration, Wojnarowicz's friendship with Romberger and Van Cook began in the context of New York's downtown underground art scene. Wanting to avoid the increasing gentrification of the East Village and his uneasy relationship with the art world, Wojnarowicz turned to Ground Zero, a gallery run by Romberger and Van Cook in the mid-1980s that gave much visibility to his work (Carr 2012, 275; Stosuy 2006, 93). Such gallery spaces allowed for a reconsideration of spaces intended for adults or those for children. Invited to curate a show at a gallery in Virginia, Romberger and Van Cook "had come with their four-month-old son [Crosby]. They put a rug down in the middle of the gallery and people took turns playing with him" (Carr 2012, 308). In addition to this collective babysitting among transgressive art practices, Van Cook writes that Wojnarowicz was very fond of Crosby and was invested in "how children fit into an artist's life" (email interview with author, March 23, 2014), even when the children were someone else's. After a barely one-year-old Crosby accidentally walked into an overhanging sign, he was photographed by Wojnarowicz with a bandaged eyebrow. "David found the image of a damaged child interesting," Van Cook recounts, "in terms of his own visual lexicon," and she recalls that Wojnarowicz comforted the young Crosby after the incident.

This moment speaks to but is quite distinct from Wojnarowicz's own childhood relationship with his father, and significantly, it is bound up with how to locate queer erotics vis-à-vis the question of adult-child distinctions in *7 Miles*. In "7 Miles a Second," the final section that illustrates the artist living with AIDS, the adult Wojnarowicz's thoughts are revealed as follows: "The only act of kindness I can remember from my father was one day when he took me into the playroom to beat me as he regularly did and just before starting he asked me what he should do. I replied, 'Don't beat me'" (Wojnarowicz, Romberger, and Van Cook 2012, 54). The very next page has Wojnarowicz desiring a random man he sees with his child at a playground.

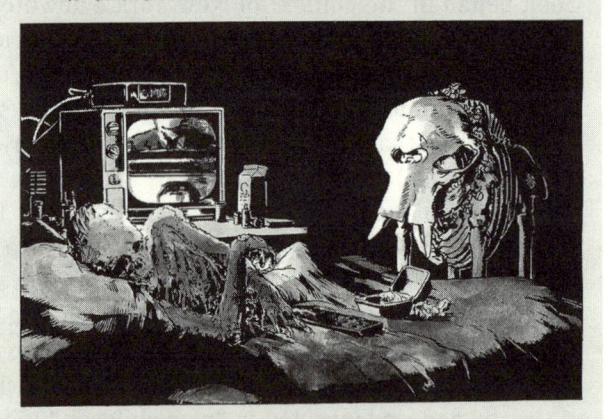

Figure 7 Rotted corpse, dinosaur skeleton, and analog television with abrasive lettering effect. From David Wojnarowicz, James Romberger, and Marguerite Van Cook, *7 Miles a Second* ([1996] 2012). Used with permission

Figure 8 Viral cloud. From David Wojnarowicz, James Romberger, and Marguerite Van Cook, *7 Miles a Second* ([1996] 2012). Used with permission

Wojnarowicz states, "I want to lie naked on the earth and get pummeled into the depths of it with his muscular body the vehicle driving me down" (55). Here, the violence of childhood memory becomes the mode of adult desire within the graphic narrative's execution. As Fawaz (2017, 336) writes, "Comic strip form allows an inarticulable *affective intensity*—Wojnarowicz's conflicting feelings of rage and desire amid the chaos of the AIDS epidemic—to be conveyed through *representational density*." In its erogenous, graphic inhabitations of illness, the text embodies adult-erated age's queerly disinvested duration as modes of being ferociously and negatively propelled in place rather than advanced, consistent with what Fawaz (354) proposes as *7 Miles*' velocity and its accumulative corporeal and aesthetic effects. Exceeding an account of BDSM desire, Wojnarowicz's invocation of an erotic death wish complexly intersects with the violence on the collective queer body with AIDS as darkly stimulating forms of sexual defiance. Romberger and Van Cook's inclusion of visually stunning nightmarish elements such as animal skeletons, entrails, sexual embrace, deathbeds, exploding bodies, and burning cities alongside images of quotidian activities reflects the elements of Wojnarowicz's existence informed by an abject childhood confronted with an adult queer sexuality that operates against the logic of orderly separations associated with age-specific experiences. Indeed, as Van Cook suggests in discussing her use of watercolor for the text, "I'm very resistant to coloring inside the lines, and I thought that was an appropriate metaphor for the depiction of David's life" (quoted in Bello 2013).

Van Cook's use of striking reds, oranges, and pinks figures prominently in the "Thirst" section. This coloring intimates non-age-specific affective states of rage and passion, while somber and serene blues, purples, and black dominate the "Stray Dogs" and especially the "7 Miles" sections, all of which lend to its liminal adult-child affective disposition rather than subscribe to normative realism based on proper color combinations. Accordingly, the text increasingly renegotiates the graphic distribution of text boxes layered on top of images as the figure of the adult Wojnarowicz is represented as coming to terms with his condition and impending mortality. Particularly in the "7 Miles" section, the words take on a visually aggressive dimension in their separation from images rendered in melancholic shades of violet and cornflower with only touches of scarlet. In a fittingly severe separation of the words from the images, Wojnarowicz's human figure is out of the picture, replaced by a rotted corpse and accompanied by a dinosaur skeleton, while an analog television transmits what appears to be a news anchor's broadcast or talking head politician ruthlessly rolling over and over, which is caused by its being out of sync with its signal (see fig. 7). We might extend this to say that being out of sync with the signals of age is not purely a way of being suspended in time but is more about how the visual expressivity—the dinosaur skeleton, rotted corpse, and analog television in this instance—is mediated by its auditory qualities, a radical form of complementarity specific to its graphic properties. In other words, the separation enhances the all-capped lettering's emphatic performative effects: the reader can see and hear Wojnarowicz's voice shouting about the homophobic power structures regulating the body with AIDS (Wojnarowicz, Romberger, and Van Cook 2012, 46–47). The limitations of this politically resistant effort are particularly and audibly pronounced in the final written paragraph. As simultaneously endless and finite, the duration of screaming and the continual rise in volume figure prominently as a queerly negative struggle associated with how the text's disintegrated age figures as ephemeral entrapment: "I am screaming but it comes out like pieces of clear ice. I am signalling that the volume of all this is too high" (64).

Romberger explains that although Wojnarowicz foresaw a more uplifting ending to the book, "there was no piece of text by him that corresponded to that idea and so I opted to show a scene where he is in his apartment alone and isolated, missing his friends and feeling sick" (email interview with author, April 8, 2014). Toward the end of *7 Miles*, the words have completely separated from the image in the text's form, and Wojnarowicz's body is reduced to a viral cloud, with arms that fight in futility (see fig. 8).[15] Just like *Pussycat Fever*, *7 Miles* embraces isolation and culminates in drowning and disappearing: "I am waving. I am waving my hands. I am disappearing. I am disappearing but not fast enough" (Wojnarowicz, Romberger, and Van Cook 2012, 64). Disappearing from memory, from time, from existence is not something to be resisted here. It is a way to see how the pull toward termination is, instead, *irresistible*: an unsuitable way to be as a queerly suitable way to be.

Pussycat Fever and *7 Miles a Second* demonstrate that the value of adult-eration is acutely counterintuitive: it harnesses the medium of comics' remarkable ability to reflect how queerness is articulated as an admixture of adult-child and text-image, communicated in terms of illness, traumatic memory, and their erotic possibilities. But, significantly, these texts make necessary the suitability of the graphic text as a conspicuous analogue for sexual minority difference, especially in their underground contextual intersections. The putative inferiority linked with queer desire and the view of comics as a degraded form function alongside and against the relentless primacy of heteronormativity and the dominance of word- or image-exclusive texts. Destabilizing age specificity is but one potential that the graphic narrative form has for an understanding—and obligatory acknowledgment—of queerness's messiness and the textual domains it requires.

Yetta Howard is associate professor of English and comparative literature at San Diego State University. She is the author of *Ugly Differences: Queer Female Sexuality in the Underground* (Univ. of Illinois Press, 2018) and is editing a photography and essay collection, *Rated RX: Sheree Rose with and after Bob Flanagan* (Ohio State Univ. Press, forthcoming).

Notes

I am grateful to Joseph T. Thomas for inviting me to give an early version of this article as a talk for the National Center for the Study of Children's Literature in 2011. I thank James Romberger, Marguerite Van Cook, and Diane DiMassa for discussing their work with me. The feedback I received from the reviewers and editors, especially Ramzi Fawaz, was indispensable in developing this article.

1. Elisabeth Sussman (1997, 18) also suggests as much in describing Haring's 1982 show at the Tony Shafrazi Gallery, which "included drawings of Smurfs and Mickey Mouses, a frieze of running, falling, tumbling men, a row of radiant babies, a large drawing that includes a flying pair of dice, two running men holding a radiating heart, and a giant Mickey holding his radiating penis."

2. Subcultural space and underground cultural production were pronounced for both Acker and Wojnarowicz, and it is worth noting the vagaries of the adult-child distinction within some of these contexts. Phoebe Gloeckner's *A Child's Life* (1998a) or her more queer-focused "Minnie's 3rd Love or: 'Nightmare on Polk Street'" (1998b) are autobiographically inflected works tackling the breakdown of the adult-child distinction. See Chute 2010 for a reading of Gloeckner along these lines. In music culture, a prominent example is American rave culture during the 1990s, which provided an explicit context for teenagers engaging not so much in the "adult" activities of sex and drinking but in counterintuitively defining cultural resistance through infantilization. In addition to intriguingly disturbing attachments to childhood objects such as stuffed-animal backpacks and pacifiers combined with the heavy use of Ecstasy (MDMA), ravers' attraction to juvenile pleasures and their desire to access primal states via illicit-drug use and dancing found primary articulations in what Simon Reynolds (2012, 130) has described as techno music's "regressive streak" and a childish "heightened sense of here and now."

3. Sigmund Freud famously linked arrested development with nonheterosexuality. See Stockton 2009, 33–36. In the context of queer youth subcultures, see Halberstam 2005, 174–86.

4. Such a notion of worsening in the texts speaks to but complicates what Lee Edelman (2004, 9), in his critique of futurity via the culture of the child, has theorized as queerness's "bringing children and childhood to an end."

5   Relatedly, see Freeman (2010, 3) for a theory of *"chrononormativity* or the use of time to organize individual human bodies toward maximum productivity."

6   Relevant here is Fawaz's (2017, 340) notion of the "queer generosity" of comics: "The fact that the work of these artists could appear so stylistically different yet tackle similar conceptual questions in the same medium suggests the formal elasticity and productivity of the comic strip for queer artists."

7   Expanding the "here and now" to reflect political relevance in the 1990s, Riot Grrrl music culture was important for the disturbance of the child category in the United States. Originating in the Pacific Northwest as an oppositional feminist and queer movement, Riot Grrrl was as much about gender politics as it was about alternative musical performance. This brand of queer and feminist music used underground contexts to account for less digestible aspects of lived childhood and youth experience, often by returning to personal histories of sexual abuse and battery. Spearheaded by Bikini Kill frontwoman Kathleen Hanna, Riot Grrrl started out as the name of a fanzine that merged "girl riot" with "the growling grrrl . . . as a jokey variation on all the tortured spellings of 'womyn'" (Marcus 2010, 80) that second wave feminists employed to avoid using the word *men*. Sometimes appearing on stage wearing a baby doll dress or just a T-shirt and underwear, Hanna, in her early twenties in the early 1990s, disrupted the proper images of both "girl" and "woman." Bikini Kill and other bands falling under the category of Riot Grrrl, such as Bratmobile, the Need, and Sleater-Kinney, crafted a feminism invested in redefining the typical connotations attached to "girls" or to "childish" behaviors and styles. Referring to the fanzine from which the movement took its name, Sara Marcus writes, "A riot grrrl was a revolutionary update of a *Teen* or a *Young Miss* or a *Mademoiselle*: The new zine's title created its audience of girls by naming them, radicalized them by addressing them as already radical" (81). Often incorporating high-pitched screams into their songs as well as shouting out lyrics with a gendered opposition exceeding that of male-fronted punk bands, Bikini Kill's use of illegible screaming as lyrics operates in the same scope as the girlish image's illegibility as child or adult.

8   Queercore and Riot Grrrl shared cultural categories and musical qualities with all-female punk-metal-grunge acts of the era. In addition to Courtney Love's corrupted beauty queen persona in Hole, bands such as L7, Babes in Toyland, and 7 Year Bitch worked with the concept of the girl child as a way to negotiate oppressive pasts and to express a transgressive adult feminism. For Babes in Toyland's Kat Bjelland, "Screaming is a cathartic release from childhood, when she was always told by her parents to shut up and was frequently locked in her room" (Eileraas 1997, 125). Here, Bjelland's approach as a lead vocalist reflects a significant

confrontation between the categories of adult and child: rather than reject what *child* means, the "childish" screams communicate adult female aggression and politically charged hostility. These articulations of unassimilable feminism via putatively masculinist punk and metal styles question the boundaries of adult-child, mobilizing their auditory manifestations with visual and semantic elements of the albums. Indeed, many of the bands' album titles and cover art effectively articulate the movement away from age-specific signifiers. For instance, the cover of Babes in Toyland's *Fontanelle* (1992) features a Cindy Sherman photograph: a startling image of a baby doll placed in a provocative, crotch-focused position with its arms frozen in a needy outward embrace and eyes that look almost blacked out. The album's title, *Fontanelle*, is an unambiguous reference to the soft spot of a baby's head and thus suggests that the child's mind acts as a sponge, susceptible to corruption. Accordingly, the word *fontanelle* signifies a conceptual malleability that takes on a discomfitingly tangible quality in pointing to the literal malleability of the body and its all-too-facile potential for damage—both physical and mental.

9 Acker did a similar spoken word–music collaboration for her novel *My Mother: Demonology* (1993). Posthumously released, it includes music by queercore band Tribe 8; the appropriately named *Redoing Childhood* (1999) collaborative album was released by Riot Grrrl label Kill Rock Stars.

10 As Acker suggests, this notion of "pornography" is not reducible to representing explicit sex acts but might be understood more as what Robert Mazzola (2004, 30) calls "pseudo-pornographic" or "pornogony," a text that regenerates content through the absorption of pornographic content (33).

11 Like Babes in Toyland's *Fontanelle*, the cover of Lunachicks' *Pretty Ugly* (1997) works with childhood imagery by showing a dismembered Barbie head sloppily wearing too much makeup, adorned with plastic bugs, and appearing to sit in a pile of vomit or other human fluids. Here, the material conditions of abject girlhood experiences translate as a horrific yet somewhat humorous display of the physical materiality of the body. Recasting ideals associated with heteronormative femininity as dreadfully ugly moments of personal development, the album cover exploits typical girlhood crafts of the 1980s and 1990s by displaying the band's logo in sparkling gold glitter that resembles the glitter paint popular among adolescent girls of the era. In resisting standard models of adulthood, these underground and subcultural approaches to the category of "child" were heavily devoted to visual and sonic expressions of negativity. Such expressions maintain a remarkable ability to accommodate negative queer politics and thus crucially inform how Acker's and Wojnarowicz's collaborative underground graphic narratives reconsider the distinctions

between adult and child and ultimately generate alternative forms of queer autonomy.

12   Dominick LaCapra writes (1998, 21): "The participant and the observer-participant meet on the ground of secondary memory, where they may conceivably agree on certain things that constitute accurate memory.... Secondary memory is also what the historian attempts to impart to others who have not themselves lived through the experience or events in question." Primary memory is associated with "lapses relating to forms of denial, repression, suppression, and evasion" (20).

13   My references in this article are to the 2012 edition since that edition correctly recognizes the labor of all the artists and writers involved. In November 2010, after being protested by a religious organization, Wojnarowicz's 1987 video project called *A Fire in My Belly* was pulled from the gay- and lesbian-themed *Hide/Seek* exhibition at the National Portrait Gallery in Washington, DC (Doyle 2013, 140–41). The piece contained images of Jesus on a cross covered with crawling ants and a person's mouth sewn shut. As Jennifer Doyle writes, "The irony of the 'Hide/Seek controversy' was that it had nothing to do with the challenges the piece actually presented to the curators: a silent film featuring a nonnarrative series of gruesome images is, quite simply, hard to work with" (141). Like much of Wojnarowicz's work, the emphasis on the materiality of the body in suffering and pain was deemed beyond the pale as representative of "gay and lesbian art," positioning his work not just as unsuitable for children but, strangely, as unsuitable for adults.

14   It is worth thinking here of female-fronted grunge act Hole's album title *Live through This* (1994) and the way that living through something was, at this moment for many stricken with AIDS, simply the goal. Revising suitable ages to die, AIDS forced new perspectives on living and dying as routed through queer modes of political practice. This was readily apparent in late 1980s and early 1990s activism bound up with performance and artistic practice, particularly in the demonstrations by ACT UP, such as "die-ins" staged in front of pharmaceutical company headquarters responsible for manufacturing AIDS drugs. See Roman 1998, especially the chapter, "'It's My Party and I'll Die If I Want To!,'" named after a line from *Pouf Positive*, a late-1980s play about AIDS. The title of course resignifies Lesley Gore's mid-1960s teen-themed hit, "It's My Party and I'll Cry If I Want To," as a queer anthem that pushes forward the question of suitably reclaiming the AIDS subject's life through death.

15   This image refers to a moment in *Close to the Knives* when Wojnarowicz (1991, 53) discusses a seventeenth-century experiment by a Jesuit friar who peeled away layers of the eye to see what image the eye had captured at the moment of death: "He reported finding one image that was fairly consistent in the eyes he examined: something like a small cloud with two tiny arms waving out from the sides."

References

Acker, Kathy. 1993. *My Mother: Demonology*. New York: Grove.

———. 1996a. *Pussy, King of the Pirates*. New York: Grove.

———. 1996b. "That Expat/Exile Thing." Interview by Noel King. *Meanjin* 55, no. 2: 324–39.

———. 1999. *Redoing Childhood*. Kill Rock Stars KRS349.

Acker, Kathy, Diane DiMassa, and Freddie Baer. 1995. *Pussycat Fever*. Edinburgh: AK Press.

Arauz, M. Rachael. 2006. "Universal Child: The Transformation of the Radiant Baby." In *Keith Haring: Journey of the Radiant Baby*, 11–19. Reading, PA: Reading Public Museum and Bunker Hill Publishing.

Babes in Toyland. 1992. *Fontanelle*. Reprise 9 26998-2.

Bello, Grace. 2013. "Remembering David: A Graphic Tribute: James Romberger and Marguerite Van Cook." *Publishers Weekly*, January 4.

Carr, Cynthia. 2012. *Fire in the Belly: The Life and Times of David Wojnarowicz*. New York: Bloomsbury.

Chute, Hillary L. 2010. *Graphic Women: Life Narrative and Contemporary Comics*. New York: Columbia Univ. Press.

Doyle, Jennifer. 2013. *Hold It against Me: Difficulty and Emotion in Contemporary Art*. Durham, NC: Duke Univ. Press.

Edelman, Lee. 2004. *No Future: Queer Theory and the Death Drive*. Durham, NC: Duke Univ. Press.

Eileraas, Karina. 1997. "Witches, Bitches, and Fluids: Girl Bands Performing Ugliness as Resistance." *TDR: The Drama Review* 41, no. 3: 122–39.

Fawaz, Ramzi. 2017. "Stripped to the Bone: Sequencing Queerness in the Comic Strip Work of Joe Brainard and David Wojnarowicz." *ASAP/Journal* 2, no. 2: 335–67.

Frankel, David. 1997. "Keith Haring's American Beauty." In *Keith Haring*, edited by Elisabeth Sussman, 58–62. New York: Whitney Museum of American Art.

Freeman, Elizabeth. 2010. *Time Binds: Queer Temporalities, Queer Histories*. Durham, NC: Duke Univ. Press.

Gloeckner, Phoebe. 1998a. *A Child's Life and Other Stories*. Berkeley, CA: Frog Ltd.

———. 1998b. "Minnie's Third Love, or, 'Nightmare on Polk Street.'" In Gloeckner 1998a, 70–81. First published 1994.

Groensteen, Thierry. 2000. "Why Are Comics Still in Search of Cultural Legitimization?" In *Comics and Culture: Analytical and Theoretical Approaches to Comics*, edited by Anne Magnussen and Hans-Christian Christiansen, 29–41. Copenhagen: Museum Tusculanum Press, Univ. of Copenhagen.

Halberstam, Judith. 2005. *In a Queer Time and Place: Transgender Bodies, Subcultural Lives*. New York: New York Univ. Press.

Hole. 1994. *Live through This*. Geffen Records B000003TAY.

Kraus, Chris. 2017. *After Kathy Acker: A Literary Biography*. South Pasadena, CA: Semiotext(e).
LaCapra, Dominick. 1998. *History and Memory after Auschwitz*. Ithaca, NY: Cornell Univ. Press.
Lunachicks. 1997. *Pretty Ugly*. Go-Kart Records GKLP024.
Marcus, Sara. 2010. *Girls to the Front: The True Story of the Riot Grrrl Revolution*. New York: Harper Perennial.
Mazzola, Robert L. 2004. "Kathy Acker and Literary Madness: Erecting a Pornographic Shell." In *Devouring Institutions: The Life Work of Kathy Acker*, edited by Michael Hardin, 27–46. San Diego: Hyperbole Books.
Mekons and Kathy Acker. 1996. *Pussy, King of the Pirates*. Quarterstick Records QS36CD.
Meyer, Richard. 2002. *Outlaw Representation: Censorship and Homosexuality in Twentieth-Century American Art*. Boston: Beacon Press.
Reynolds, Simon. 2012. *Energy Flash: A Journey through Rave Culture and Dance Music*. New York: Soft Skull Press.
Ricard, Rene. 1981. "The Radiant Child." *Artforum*, December.
Roman, David. 1998. *Acts of Intervention: Performance, Gay Culture, and AIDS*. Bloomington: Indiana Univ. Press.
Stockton, Kathryn Bond. 2009. *The Queer Child, or Growing Sideways in the Twentieth Century*. Durham, NC: Duke Univ. Press.
Stosuy, Brandon, ed. 2006. *Up Is Up, but So Is Down: New York's Downtown Literary Scene, 1974–1992*. New York: New York Univ. Press.
Sussman, Elisabeth. 1997. "Songs of Innocence at the Nuclear Pyre." In *Keith Haring*, edited by Elisabeth Sussman, 10–24. New York: Whitney Museum of American Art.
Wojnarowicz, David. 1991. *Close to the Knives: A Memoir of Disintegration*. New York: Vintage.
Wojnarowicz, David, James Romberger, and Marguerite Van Cook. 2012. *7 Miles a Second*. Seattle: Fantagraphics Books. First published 1996.

Jessica Q. Stark

Nancy and the Queer Adorable in the Serial Comics Form

Abstract This essay presents in dialogue two renditions of the *Nancy* comics by original creator Ernie Bushmiller and the later poet and visual artist Joe Brainard. Arguing for a generative consideration of these seemingly disparate versions on a continuum, this comparison addresses the ongoing seriality of *Nancy* as offering a complex queer adorability that destabilizes modes of identification in the *Nancy* comics and beyond. Both Brainard's and Bushmiller's *Nancy* texts draw on the controlled miniature and the unwieldy additive catalog, which are characteristic of the long-running serial comics form. As queer texts that oscillate between popular iconographies, these iterations of *Nancy* provide resistance to expectations for normativity, narrative closure, static character performance, and bound space in relation to twentieth-century American collective identities.

Keywords queer theory, Ernie Bushmiller, Joe Brainard, seriality, popular culture

Nancy, the eight-year-old comic icon, has led a long, varied life in the US mainstream. Since her introduction in the *Fritzi Ritz* comic series in 1933, Ernie Bushmiller's Nancy rose to mass popularity through eponymous newspaper strips and several spin-off comics that continue to be published today.[1] Alongside her eighty-plus years of publication, Nancy has been depicted in an Andy Warhol painting, fashioned on a commemorative postage stamp, included in Art Spiegelman's *RAW* comics anthology, adapted for a card game by Scott McCloud, had a brief animation stint for television, and enjoyed marketable success in product sales from vinyl figurines to T-shirts. Reprint anthologies of Bushmiller's original *Nancy* comics endure as well—one of the most recent being an ongoing project by Fantagraphics Books that includes three-year incremental volumes of the original *Nancy* newspaper dailies. As with many long-running serial comics, *Nancy*'s original designs extend beyond Bushmiller's hand. *Nancy* was led by about a half-dozen primary creators after Bushmiller's retirement in 1982, not to mention numerous assistants and secondary collaborators who worked alongside Bushmiller during production.

Several alternative press, fan fiction, and "unofficial" renditions of *Nancy* also permeate its history. Among these contemporary reworkings, New York school poet and illustrator Joe Brainard produced his own version of the Nancy figure for several publications between 1963 and 1978, including the collaborative *C Comics*,[2] which were subsequently excerpted for a collection of his *Nancy* collaborations in *The Nancy Book* (2008). *The Nancy Book*, edited by Lisa Pearson and Ron Padgett, curates a selection of Nancy appropriations that Brainard produced independently and in collaboration with other artists and poets. As a close friend of and poet-collaborator with Brainard, Padgett (2008, 29) recalls the murky origins of Brainard's first attentions to the *Nancy* comic in *The Nancy Book*:

> I don't know if Joe used Nancy for the first time in *S* or in the comic strip called *Personal Nancy Love*, which he did with Ted [Berrigan], or in a handmade book called *Ex-Lax v. Feenamint vs. Ex- Lax v. Feen*, which Joe, Ted, Pat, and I made. All three of these were from 1963, but the exact dates hardly matter, since by then we were freely sharing our energy, ideas, and styles at a prodigious rate.

Collaborating with artists who borrowed frequently from mass media, Brainard began cultivating an attention to popular culture in his work during the first years of his relocation to New York.[3] According to Padgett, the Nancy figure "quickly emerged as his clear favorite, culminating in the 'If Nancy Was . . .' series of 1972 and the large *Nancy Diptych* of 1974" (28). Much like the hazy origins of Brainard's first appropriations of *Nancy*, however, his attraction to *Nancy* remains open to interpretation from close friends and co-collaborators. Ann Lauterbach (2008, 14) connects Brainard's use of *Nancy* as an easy "pivot between subjective and objective states" and as an "at once found object and phantom projection of inner imaginings." Padgett (2008, 30), as well as Brainard's brothers, Jim and John, gestures more simply toward Joe Brainard's attraction to Bushmiller's clean, bold line and *Nancy*'s "dopey sense of humor." Whatever Brainard's likely varied investments in the Nancy figure, *The Nancy Book* hosts a unique distillation of Brainard's scattered one-offs and collaborations that are testament to his ongoing captivation with Bushmiller's creation. Analyzing the original Nancy figure in light of Brainard's compiled work in *The Nancy Book* offers another perspective on the provocative, queer affordances of the comic writ large and highlights Brainard's sustained attention to the potential for comics to simultaneously inhabit, subvert, and reposition modes of mainstream culture on the page.

This essay follows *Nancy* in two specific iterations: the original Bushmiller newspaper dailies and the appropriated Nancy figure in Brainard's compiled pieces from *The Nancy Book*. A figure both malleable and instantly recognizable, Bushmiller's *Nancy* provides a compelling basis from which to view Brainard's appropriations and how they address mainstream popular culture and its representations. Superficially, it may seem like a newspaper cartoonist and an avant-garde visual artist would have little in common when converging on the same comic figure. However, restricting Bushmiller's and Brainard's intentions to their individual historical contexts and intended audiences limits the potential for their works to be interpreted in continuity. Recent Amazon.com reviews of *The Nancy Book* reveal how far Brainard's more contemporary renditions fall from the *Nancy* canon to the unprepared eye (see fig. 1). Some of Brainard's most incendiary frames for readers are unabashedly pornographic; for example, Nancy reveals a penis under her skirt in one episode (Brainard 2008, 33) and engages in explicit sexual activity in another (101–7). Although the public comment section of any Internet feed is unlikely to provide the deepest resonances of human inquiry, the array of these responses— from livid outrage to stumbling confusion—raises questions about an impulse to detach Bushmiller's and Brainard's characters from each other. In contrast, how may analyzing these characters together complicate this distance? How can a popular comic strip written for mass audiences also suit Brainard's particularized queer poetics? Where might the artists' worlds unexpectedly converge? Rather than approach these works separately, I resist the compartmentalization of these authors' separate designations (e.g., journalist, comics artist, poet, avant-gardist, homosexual, pulp creator) to highlight the potential for both connection and provocative disrepair in comparing their Nancy figures. Although much is to be said about Brainard's *Nancy* comics as specifically reflecting and celebrating gay male liberation from the 1970s,[4] his precarious engagement with *Nancy* challenges the fixity of this temporal contextualization in its playfulness with "normativity" as persistently open-ended, troubled, and possibly existing in closer dialogue than one might imagine with Bushmiller's original adorable comic creation. Attending to Sianne Ngai's (2012) concept of "cuteness" and Lauren Berlant and Lee Edelman's (2014) engagement with adorability, Brainard's subversive homage to Bushmiller's *Nancy* extends rather than diverges from the destabilizing humor of the original canon and its (a)cute destruction of normative expectations for gender, sexuality, performances of nationalism, and artistic taste. I argue that Brainard recognizes the potential for an already-existing queer locus in Bushmiller's original *Nancy*—one that relies on the precarious affect of the Nancy figure's cuteness and adorability to trouble the parameters of convention and question the representational fixity of the long-running comics medium. In this essay, I track the ways in which both renditions of the *Nancy* comics queer familiar forms of identification in dialogue with each other. In so doing, I analyze how Bushmiller and Brainard employ *Nancy* to trouble normative expectations around gender and sexual preference but also to destabilize forms of national identification and interrelated aesthetic categories of taste, the commodity form, and the queer affect of serial adorability. As such, *Nancy* evokes a kind of queerness as both adjective and verb—an ever-unfolding, serial (un)doing of the very structures that attempt to frame its content. Considering these works side by side reveals the paradoxical status of the long-publishing US comics figure writ large as a site for queer knowledge-making that invites revisionary accumulations, serial mobility, playful recombination, and an iconic malleability that underscores the multivoiced site of comics as a characteristically queer medium.

Despite the enunciated one-dimensionality of his stark aesthetic, Bushmiller designed a flexible canvas for the complex figurations of the Nancy character and her personality throughout the series. Among her varying roles, she is an opportunistic businesswoman, a fawning femme, a brawny counterpart to and love interest for Sluggo, a public nuisance, a schoolgirl, a dutiful daughter, an American patriot, and a town trickster. In contrast to her changing personae, her appearance endures across the generations of her publication: her chubby cheeks, plump stature, and the iconic rounded silhouette of her hair

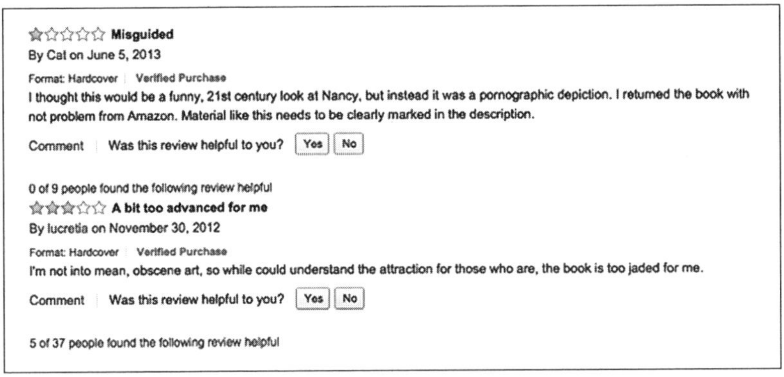

Figure 1 Amazon reviews of Joe Brainard's *The Nancy Book*, www.amazon.com /Joe-Brainard-The-Nancy-Book/dp/097995620X

lend a predictable visual uniformity across generations of publications. Her simultaneous pictorial flatness and flexibility draw attention to a repetitious one-dimensionality in the series that complicates rather than clearly discerns between projected binaries that inform interwoven cultural narratives: femininity and masculinity, American nationalism and iconoclasm, childhood and adulthood, and mass culture and highbrow categories of taste. Newspaper comics like *Nancy* rely on a reproducibility of narrative formula that does not, moreover, confuse character recognition with predictable character performance. On the contrary, *Nancy* breaks down the parameters of fixed characterization by virtue of perpetual narrative seriality and, thus, a constant revision of former *Nancy* renditions. There must always be another episode, another generation of audiences, another Nancy. *Nancy*'s resilience across generations emphasizes the plasticity and queerness inherent in her original design, which hinges on a type of camp humor that aids in complicating the so-called rigid structures within the medium of serial comics.[5] Queerness in *Nancy* invites a complex challenge to the limitations of fixed performance, incorporating (while questioning) gender and sexual norms as well as maintaining the capacity to adapt serially to varying contexts within a wider range of so-called restraining structures. *Nancy*'s camp framework, or an attention to both the artifice and the exaggeration of its humor, invites a deeply subversive yet tongue-in-cheek deflation of the constraining standards that specifically pertain to gender, sexual identity, national identification, and aesthetic taste. The comic's humorous challenge to normativity and structure, predicated on Nancy's characteristically innocuous, cute, and adorabilized figure, employs a queer perspective that continually destabilizes *Nancy*'s canned and predictable content. As both adorable and a trickster figure, Nancy pushes the boundaries of her own bound frame, employing what Susan Sontag (1982, 115) calls a celebration of "failed seriousness" inherent to camp humor that places pressure on structures of constraint.

In dialogue with a type of camp deployment, Nancy's "queer adorability" challenges fixed forms of identification through a humorous oscillation between sustained homage and brutal irony. In understanding both versions of *Nancy* on a continuum rather than in opposition to each other, Brainard engages with what Muñoz (1999, 31) calls a "queer disidentification" with popular culture or the "recycling and rethinking encoded meaning" that we may associate with the original Nancy figure. In *Disidentifications: Queers of Color and the Performance of Politics*, Muñoz refers to a wide range of examples from contemporary queer performance art in investigating the ways in which those positioned outside the mainstream appropriate majority culture for their own cultural purposes. Instead of distinctly aligning with or negating modes of mainstream culture, he argues, queer artists transform these works to suit the demands of a more nonnormative perspective. In a parallel process of queer disidentification, Brainard similarly "scrambles and reconstructs the encoded message of a cultural text in a fashion that both exposes the encoded message's universalizing and exclusionary machinations and recircuits its workings to account for, include, and empower minority identities and identifications" (Muñoz 1999, 31).[6] A key aspect of this complex process counterintuitively involves preservation of the original cultural text.[7] In his critical analyses Muñoz cites queer modes of interaction with mainstream film and television; similarly, Brainard engages with Bushmiller's comic in a way that both undermines the stability of *Nancy*'s so-called universalized machinations for normativity and underscores the ways in which *Nancy* was always already a paradoxical medium for queer rethinking in its original manifestations. In this way, as Muñoz writes, "Disidentification is a step further than cracking open the code of the majority; it proceeds to use this code as raw material for representing a disempowered politics or positionality that

Figure 2 "Ladylike" Nancy slides down the banister. From Bushmiller, *Nancy*, January 2, 1947

has been rendered unthinkable by the dominant culture" (31). Brainard's appropriation of the Nancy figure therefore does not work to *erase* the normativity inherent within the dominant structure of the original *Nancy* comics but rather to manipulate the script of those very structures for new ways of looking at and engaging with mainstream culture through a queer lens.

On the surface, one might claim that Bushmiller's early *Nancy* more strongly mimes and therefore reinforces the heteronormative domestic structures typical of American mid-twentieth-century culture. However, much of the "adorable" camp humor in Bushmiller's work reveals the discordant fringes in Nancy's characteristic misunderstandings of limiting behavioral codes. For example, in one episode with Aunt Fritzi (see fig. 2), Nancy assumes a "ladylike" posture that defies Fritzi's ideas of female gender restrictions. In a corrected "feminine" posture, while rebelliously sliding down the banister again, Nancy performs the lady in a typically rambunctious or "unladylike" action. The humor in this posture lies in Nancy's immediate correction of her posture to obey femininity, while remaining disobedient to the expectations from the authority figure of Aunt Fritzi. Nancy understands some gender conventions but opts to deny others. She wants to slide down the banister again, and she manipulates the gendered script in order to do so, while still submitting to the correction. As a precocious young girl—adorable in her tenacious misinterpretations—Nancy accesses a subtle defiance of gender normativity, which mocks behavioral codes strip after strip for a humorous gag, while precluding direct punishment. As well, Nancy's aesthetic roundness stands in sharp contrast to Aunt Fritzi's more detailed pictorial representation on the page. In contrast to Aunt Fritzi's specifically "feminized," more three-dimensional visual depiction, Nancy's body exists as an illustrated, flattened abstraction: imprecise, not quite fully formed, and characteristically bearing cute, indefinite features. "Cuteness," as Ngai (2012, 87–88) describes, operates as "the name of an encounter with difference—a perceived difference in the power of the subject and the object." Ngai notes the origins of the word *cute* itself, which in many respects mirror Nancy's innocuously cute rebellion against Aunt Fritzi. Because the word *cute* "derives from the older 'acute' in a process linguists call aphaeresis (the process by which words lose initial unstressed syllables to generate shorter and 'cuter' versions of themselves; 'alone' becomes 'lone,' 'until' becomes 'til'), its etymology strikingly replicates the logic of the aesthetic it has come to name" (87). In this way, "Cute thus exemplifies a situation in which making a word smaller—or, if you like, cuter—results in an uncanny reversal, changing its meaning into its exact opposite" (87). In the banister scene, Nancy cutely (and acutely) feigns ignorance about gendered expectations, while devoiding meaning from the word *ladylike* in her disordered interpretation of Fritzi's request. This action, both shocking and acceptable due to Nancy's precocious brand of aesthetic and behavioral cuteness, defies normativity while simultaneously fulfilling Bushmiller's comedic gag. The result is a subversive derision of gendered expectations of the body acting in camp defiance. Her sustained access to the affect of cuteness not only facilitates but also enables her to pose as harmless, while subversively threatening the construct of gender performance.

Parallel to Bushmiller's playfulness with gender, Brainard most directly complicates Nancy's category of gender in his piece titled *If Nancy Was a Boy* (Brainard 2008, 33) from *The Nancy Book*. Illustrating Nancy proudly exposing a penis under her skirts (see fig. 3), Brainard confronts audience assumptions of Nancy as a familiar representational girl figure. Using an understated aesthetic, Brainard features an illustrated penis in a small portion of the frame, drawing attention to the discordance between the seemingly innocuous (adorable) scale of the pictorial penis and the enormous normative scripts that it disrupts. This tongue-in-cheek exposé reveals the ways that Brainard's Nancy "transforms, destabilizes, and subverts the existing balance of acceptance of sexual identity and sexual roles" (Ross 1999, 324). A camp destruction of normativity in this scene disrupts "the relation

Figure 3 *If Nancy Was a Boy* (1972) is used by permission of the Kenward Gray Elmslie Revocable Trust

between 'artifice' and 'nature' in the construction of sexuality and gender identity" (325). Brainard's accompanying tagline, "If Nancy was a boy," places pressure on fixed expectations of gender, as Nancy (other than wielding an anatomical penis) still appears every bit like her girl self in this illustration. In this way, Brainard pokes fun at the compulsory anatomical alignment with perceived "maleness" when, according to this definition, Bushmiller's Nancy could very well have always been a boy under her skirts and unbeknownst to her audiences. As Ramzi Fawaz (2017, 343) argues, "We could not say that Nancy is necessarily (or only) transgender, since the mere fact of her having a penis could have countless meanings including, but not limited to, transgender embodiment." Brainard queers anatomical assumptions of the Nancy figure in this piece, revealing the requisite visual guesswork that audiences fashion onto even highly fictional "sexless" character-commodities like Nancy. This confrontation challenges the ways in which we assign earnest expectations to shared popular narratives like comics and their figures, regardless of how trivial or inconsequential their cultural value might seem.

However extreme Brainard's *Nancy* appears in contrast to earlier versions, a closer examination of the original *Nancy* reveals provocative relationships between its characters that similarly question, refute, and trouble fixed modes of identification. The flexible behavioral scripts between Nancy and Sluggo, for example, more frequently trouble rather than reinforce fixed ideas around their assumed heteronormative coupling. Their relationship plays on an ongoing gag of swapping expected (and specifically gendered) roles. For example, while Sluggo performs macho masculinity in the series, Nancy often compensates for his lack of courage and brawn in ways that question her adherence to conventional gender expectations (Bushmiller 2012a, 77). When it comes to business, Nancy also ignores gender restrictions if they do not provide a pragmatic advantage within her schemes, and as a result, she often surpasses Sluggo in their competitive entrepreneurial attempts. She is a tenacious businesswoman, frequently challenging Sluggo's underestimations of her skills because of her female gender (64).

In conversation with Nancy's opportunistic gender-bending, Sluggo's subtle mistranslations of masculinity routinely pepper Bushmiller's pages in ways that also cast doubt on the fixity of gendered performances. For example, a particular strip hinges on the gag that Sluggo wears a female face mask in an effort to help "beautify his city" (see fig. 4). The scene involves Sluggo's heterosexual preference of a woman's face as "beautiful," yet his literal interpretation of "wearing" a woman's face disrupts conventional behavioral codes around that heterosexual desire. Sluggo does not sexually desire a beautiful woman; he wants to *be* a beautiful woman—a subversive and queer challenge to Sluggo's usual macho hyperbolic aversion to performing or being perceived as "feminine" throughout the series. However, the comic gag of this scene relates again to the specific cuteness of its application and its interaction with commodity embodiment. As Ngai (2012, 67) argues, the experience of cuteness invites a conflation of desire and identification or confusing "'wanting to have' with 'wanting to be like.'" While it is implied that he heterosexually considers a woman's face more beautiful than his own, Sluggo's cross-dressing as a woman transposes the expected codes of heterosexist desire onto

Figure 4   Sluggo wears a female mask. From Bushmiller, *Nancy*, June 8, 1950

his own body. Viewing himself as a potentially beautiful commodity, Sluggo's queer performance unravels the fixity of gender performance through an unexpected moment of self-actualized commodification. The gap between gazing consumer and projected commodity collapses under Sluggo's cross-dressing shift—a subversive act veiled by the comic's operative gag that relies on Sluggo's bodily misinterpretations. The punchline here invites a playful and humorously abrupt reworking of expectations, calling into question the fixed narrative expectations of gendered performances. Under the guise of an adorabilized misunderstanding, this scene reveals a provocative slippage in the familiar codes of Sluggo's so-called conventional masculinity that relies on the comic medium's frustration of familiarity. The brevity of this narrative and its invitation for swiftly collapsing expectations invoke a queer and playful revision of normativity and fixed performances. Based on the comic medium's ability to thwart convention rapidly with an unexpected gag reversal, Sluggo's performance evokes a humorous (yet violent) affront to fixed characterization and the governing structures of gender and sexuality.

Sexuality and its performances also come under scrutiny upon further examination of the interactions between Nancy and Sluggo. Bushmiller's attention to the machinations of identity performance enables the pair to both conform to and expose the high artifice foregrounding the assumed notions around their gendered relationship. They persistently fail to satisfy expectations, providing playful composite identities in relation to each other; "each alternative implies a different hypothesis of what constitutes the 'whole,' how its parts are articulated, what lies inside that presumed whole and what outside it" (McHale 2004, 17). They are "playing house" with each other throughout these narratives—performing societal expectations in

Figure 5 Nancy mimes heterosexual courtship rituals with Sluggo. From Bushmiller, *Nancy*, February 16, 1951

ways that emphasize, rather than obscure, the derisive caricature at play in their often poor imitations. In figure 5, Nancy and Sluggo mime the repetitious courtship rituals on display via television and mass media in a way that evacuates heteronormative signification. The cuteness of this exchange, which concludes with Sluggo's attraction to the jam on Nancy's hand (and not to Nancy), derides the kind of simplistic mimicry on which certain displays of heteronormativity rely. Through this wordless exchange, Nancy and Sluggo's courtship pivots around iconographic (and reductive) images representing love; Nancy's thought bubble communicates the icon of a heart as an adorable stand-in for the complexities of her interpretation of and desire for romance. It is precisely the mocking, reductive adorability of these visual icons that underscores the queer capabilities in the simplicity of this scene. In Ngai's (2012, 64) words, "The feelings that underpin and traverse cuteness, a sentimental desire for a simpler and more sensuous, more concrete relation to commodities, are thus more multiple and complex than they may initially seem." Although the strip's gag relies on a kind of reinforcement of their heterosexual coupling, it performs a complex jab at the reductive "cuteness" surrounding normative courtship rituals and iconography learned from mass media. The affect of cuteness in this scene mimics the motions of heteronormative performance, while at the same time highlighting its potentially contrived connection to hollow, mainstream forms of advertising. Similar to Sluggo's self-commodification, the camp mimicry in this scene troubles composite normativity through a crass breakdown of the literalized "parts" involved in its instruction and subsequent imitations.

By comparison, in *The Nancy Book* Brainard depicts the courtship in much more explicit terms, while entertaining a parallel attention to the relationship between sexuality and the fraught terrain of its performance. In his most licentious depiction of Nancy, Brainard collaborated with Bill Berkson in the piece titled *Recent Visitors* to superimpose poetry over sequential illustrations of Nancy and a contemporaneous comic strip character, Henry, having sex (Brainard 2008, 103).[8] These scenes, rife with innuendo-imbued wordplay, explore an unexpected juxtaposition of poetic abstraction with explicit sexual intercourse between the two child characters. Brainard and Berkson emphasize the distraction of sexuality in this comic—both in a visual and an abstracted sense in the overlay of poetry with the pornographic image. In a large panel featuring an underwearless Nancy crouched over Henry's erect penis, Brainard and Berkson superimpose the lines, "You're at the edge of the crowd trying to see what's happening. You start moving thru; towards the center, the event, and everyone turns, adjusts—you're the center. Everyone is 'distracted' by your presence" (Brainard 2008, 103). In repurposing the so-called normative mainstream *Nancy* comics, Brainard provides a queer locus for disidentification practices that trouble the reception practices of the original mainstream iteration—etching a space within the existing canon to reshape and lay claim to majority culture for a queer application. As Muñoz (1999, 25) argues with regard to mainstream popular culture, "Disidentification can be understood as a way of shuffling back and forth between reception and production. . . . Disidentification is the hermeneutical performance of decoding mass, high, or any other cultural field from the perspective of a minority subject who is disempowered in such a representational hierarchy." As spectator *and* creator at the edge and inside of a mainstream popular comic, Brainard essentially privileges the space of the queer perspective as front and center, while paying homage to the original canvas of the *Nancy* comics. By decoding and appropriating *Nancy*, Brainard's queer perspective becomes more than just peripherally digressive from Bushmiller's original creation or supposed intentionality. Instead, Brainard's appropriations reveal the queerness as having been always already resident within the mainstream iterations of *Nancy*. Brainard performs an explicit queer identificatory "distraction," as stated in the poetry juxtaposed with a scene of heterosexual intercourse, that an audience cannot unsee or deprivilege in conceptualizing the popular culture object. In other words, Brainard's

Figure 6 Sluggo imagines warfare. From Bushmiller, *Nancy*, March 9, 1943

perspective within *Nancy*'s oeuvre moves from the "edge of the crowd" (a mere distraction) to become a central focus for this version of *Nancy*.

However, the compelling queerness of *Nancy* also extends beyond the scope of nonnormative gender and sexuality performance on the page. I have referred to *queer* thus far in reference to the term that emerged into public consciousness in the 1990s that "challenged the normalizing mechanisms of state power to name its sexual subjects: male or female, married or single, heterosexual or homosexual, natural or perverse" (Eng, Halberstam, and Muñoz 2005, 84), but I also wish to gesture toward the development of queer studies that interrogates larger "social processes that not only produced and recognized but also normalized and sustained identity" (84). In this way, we might approach *Nancy*'s adorable "queer doing" as an expansive critique of "social antagonisms, including race, gender, class, nationality, and religion, in addition to sexuality" (84).

In *Nancy* at the conclusion of World War II, Bushmiller's characters responded to the US nationalistic climate leading up to the 1945 atomic bombings on Hiroshima and Nagasaki (see figs. 6 and 7). Although I have thus far resisted a historical reading of the aforementioned examples of *Nancy*, these scenes' reference to specific events calls for a more precise consideration of their framing historical context. The abruptly dark nature of these wordless serial narratives employs reductive propaganda for the US war effort during World War II and highlights a side of *Nancy*'s adorability in one of its most generatively destructive forms. In addition to performing the motions of courtly love, we witness Nancy and Sluggo blankly deliver their fantasies of bomb warfare over Japan on a map. In these sequences, we receive the cuteness of Nancy and Sluggo in an uncanny reversal of their usually innocuous engagements in mere "child's play." They

Figure 7 Nancy reenacts mass destruction. From Bushmiller, *Nancy*, June 12, 1945

are still adorable, still cute, but they utterly lack compassion for or an acknowledgment of the seriousness of war violence. Cuteness "solicits the violence its pliability lets it withstand, and it invites the performative expression of what she [Ngai] describes as 'ugly feelings'" (Berlant and Edelman 2014, 17). Through a vacant cuteness, Nancy and Sluggo anticipate mass slaughter with the emotionless candor of child sociopaths. As such, they inhabit the precariousness of cuteness and the related danger of its pliable "thingness"; in other words, the object of adorability can also instantaneously embody its opposite affect, often violently so. On the fraught nature of cuteness Ngai (2012, 85–86) asks, "How are we to read the unusual readiness with which cute reverses into its opposite? Is it a sign of the aesthetic's internal instability, or how the experience of cuteness often seems to lead immediately to feelings of manipulation and betrayal?" At its worst, these moments in *Nancy* aid in numbing audiences to a dehumanized concept of Japan—a page ripped out of a textbook. As Edelman and Berlant (2014, 32) caution, perhaps "that's why normativity so often insists on the adorable: to underscore the familiar forms of emotional attachment and domesticate the violence by which attachment to the familiar is enforced." However, a more generous (albeit more uncomfortable) reading contemplates the potentially queer move away from the domestication of violence in these scenes and toward an embrace of the discomfort of violence made adorable. In its adorabilized artifice, the comic provokes (rather than buries) unease and underscores the potentially subversive seriality of Bushmiller's repetitive gags.

In one of the first essays to analyze Bushmiller's *Nancy*, "How to Read Nancy," Mark Newgarden and Paul Karasik (1988, 100) claim, "There is little that is beneath Bushmiller in his quest for a gag. A kind of sublime dumbness became Bushmiller's personal territory and he mined it brilliantly." Newgarden and Karasik outline a handful of Bushmiller's predictable gags that repeat throughout *Nancy*, which indulge in near-programmatic visual puns, slapstick, misunderstanding, incongruity, and simple inversion (100). According to Newgarden and Karasik, Bushmiller relies on this operative predictability to deliver the swiftest and sharpest gag for easy laughs in the fewest panels allotted. However, Nancy's and Sluggo's actions bring multiple resonances to the word *gag*. Reading these wordless scenes in light of World War II, for example, feels abrupt and mirrors the hasty temporality of catastrophic actions undertaken in times of war. The cuteness of these scenes relays an acute reflection on wartime violence, inviting its readers to participate in tandem with the swift actions of its characters on the page without much thought. Beyond a "sublime dumbness," however, these episodes demonstrate what Ngai (2012, 92) assigns as the "latent threat" of cuteness: "by making the dead or inanimate or inhuman speak . . . the living human speaker who personifies or throws voice into the nonhuman object can be 'struck dumb.' In other words, if things can be personified, persons can be made things." In fashioning Nancy and Sluggo as programmatic, cute child accomplices to mass violence, Bushmiller casts an unsettling parallel with a type of American "sublime dumbness" in the charge for collective patriotic war complicity. The effect provides a queer oscillation in *Nancy* as part flattened propaganda, part animate (animating) gaze. Bushmiller captures in these short strips an essence of the banality surrounding evil, operating in parallel to the algorithm of his own comic strip gags. The articulation of Nancy and Sluggo as toylike, malleable "things" emphasizes the participation of their audiences as potential accomplices to the violence that sustains a US nationalistic narrative toward linear-progressive conclusions, particularly during times of war. These scenes partly undo the very scripts they superficially promote regarding US involvement in World War II, destabilizing binaries of war as they are presented with the striking, incomplete, and reductive nature that is particular to the abbreviated comic strip medium. Delivered with the brevity of Bushmiller's comedic gag, these scenes carry evocative potential for a subversive derision of the collective hasty narratives around US war violence. In other words, *Nancy* presents provocatively reductive representations of the US war effort and accentuates the potentially childish, adorable dumbness surrounding wartime nationalistic narratives.

Figure 8 Joe Brainard, *If Nancy Was President Rosevelt* (1972), mixed media on paper, 12 by 9 inches, Colby College Museum of Art, gift of the Alex Katz Foundation, 2008.189. Used by permission of the Estate of Joe Brainard and courtesy of Tibor de Nagy Gallery, New York

Brainard's *Nancy* also sheds light on the ways in which we approach nationalistic identity and the objects that help shape narratives of US history. Intruding within the frame of both gigantic and miniature US monuments, Brainard's Nancy figure disrupts familiar emblems by inserting her own hypercommodified presence in otherwise "sacred" nationalistic territories. In one instance (see fig. 8), Brainard configures Nancy as Theodore Roosevelt on the Mount Rushmore National Memorial. In *If Nancy Was President Rosevelt*, Brainard misspells the

Figure 9 *If Nancy Was Abraham Lincoln* (1972), mixed media on paper, 12 by 9 inches, Colby College Museum of Art, gift of the Alex Katz Foundation, 2008.190. Used by permission of the Estate of Joe Brainard and courtesy of Tibor de Nagy Gallery, New York

president's name and superimposes Nancy's smiling face on top of the familiar monument, accompanied by a conventional blurb about the landmark. However potentially inadvertent Brainard's misspelling may have been, much can be surmised from its provocative gesture. In this piece, the misspelling—a glaring accident—leaks into this playfully "official" account of President Roosevelt at Mount Rushmore. In another instance, Brainard poses Nancy as Abraham Lincoln on a tiny commemorative stamp (see fig. 9). The scale of the postage stamp, minuscule on the blank page and placed far from its caption, "If Nancy was Abraham Lincoln," emphasizes the cuteness, again, of her unexpected image.

Notice that Brainard does not propose Nancy to be a postage stamp in this piece. Instead, "to be" Lincoln in this context means to become a tiny postage stamp. Brainard subverts US folklore around the immense figure of Lincoln—creating a discordant perspective on how significant US historical figures are narrated and the seemingly trivial modes of collective commemoration. Brainard's *If Nancy Was President Rosevelt*, in contrast, superimposes Nancy's figure on what resembles a page from a textbook or an "official" informative historical text. Her face willfully distorts an emblem from the US historical archive, looming in the frame of what would otherwise be an ordinary text communicating "objective" information. In both images, Brainard draws attention to the role of commemorative commodification that supposedly solidifies the temporal and spatial narratives that compose US history. From monuments like Mt. Rushmore that employ grandiose gigantism to small everyday objects like the postage stamp, US commemorative objects aid in circulating established chronicles of an inherited (and fixed) form of US identity. Erika Doss (2010, 46), who writes on the complexity of memorialization in the United States, argues, "Commemoration has been customarily viewed as the product of shared national beliefs." But as her work reveals, memorialization is almost always fraught with contradiction, historical traumas, and the dialectical exchange between events and a nation's sometimes selective memory. Although memorialization and commemoration attempt to crystallize historical events or actions within a single stable object or place, there is almost always a carefully crafted narrative of shining heroism, nobility, and progress behind these US tokens—narratives so shining you might even call them adorable. Brainard's superimposition of the adorabilized figure of Nancy, one partly associated with childlike naïveté and commodified hollowness, violently subverts the gaze on these familiar US emblems as characteristically stable. Nancy's presence in these scenes forces these Panoptimistic objects to move—troubling again the adorable object's supposed "promise of consistency, stability, and normalization" (Berlant and Edelman 2014, 19). As a result, we are left with an encounter with negativity—images that derive subversion from the misleading simplicity of Nancy's adorability and the pervasiveness of this affect in national emblems that wish to appear anything but. In the work of both Bushmiller and Brainard, the figure of Nancy invites us toward unsettling encounters with an unreliable individualized and collective body. In this case, the queerness of Nancy's adorability extends beyond gender performance or sexuality to address a messy composite of national (dis)identifications. In doing so, both Brainard's and Bushmiller's *Nancy*s underscore the subtle yet highly influential role of the commodity form in reflecting and shaping the metanarratives of cultural history.

Inherent in this subversive attention to cultural narratives is an emphasis on Nancy as a powerful commodity figure that speaks to the strata of cultural taste. Playing with the comic medium's pulp status in mainstream culture, both Brainard and Bushmiller explore the adorabilized commodity object and its potential for disrupting the very aesthetic codes that attempt to circumscribe the appropriate territory of mainstream comics. Pushing his Nancy figure into recognizable art styles, for example, Brainard questions the ways in which we compartmentalize highbrow artist-"characters" and their associated categories of taste. *If Nancy Was a Drawing by Larry Rivers* (Brainard 2008, 50) and *If Nancy Was a Painting by de Kooning* (51) hinge on the repetitious conditional clause ("if") with regard to Nancy's representational posture throughout Brainard's text. The "if" in many of Brainard's Nancy iterations emphasizes, again, Nancy's malleability and the threat that her iconic intrusion wields in various so-called fixed contexts. Similar to Bushmiller's Nancy figure, Brainard appeals to "less an identity than an ongoing effort of divestiture, a practice of undoing" (Berlant and Edelman 2014, 19) by playfully coopting highbrow cultural narratives in conversation with his Nancy appropriations. Brainard's infusion of mass media and the pictorial comic form into his work challenges the hierarchies of taste in avant-garde poetics and art, both inside and outside the New York school coterie. Brainard's *Nancy* muddies the delineations between so-called highbrow versus lowbrow cultural materials and interrogates the antithetical impulse in their too-tidy separation. His interpretation of Willem de Kooning and Larry Rivers engages with a playful misunderstanding of their artistic styles by inserting the unexpected figure of Nancy into their frames. This humorous disruption speaks to the resident thread in Brainard's work that, like pop art, "refuses to secure a fixed place for itself *outside* of the everyday ephemera it celebrates" (Fitch 2012, 140). His Nancy not only compares but conflates the avant-garde with materials of the disposable everyday.

In conversation with Ngai's attention to the role of cuteness in avant-garde poetry, the adorability of Nancy's figure in these imitated artistic forms of high taste draws attention to the unavoidable relationship between American artistry and the commodity, commodification, or both. As Ngai (2012, 4) argues, "The cuteness that avant-garde poetry finds itself grappling with thus gives us surprising leverage on the ambiguous status of the contemporary avant-garde in general, and on the closeness between the artwork and the commodity." Brainard unsettles an orderly idea of art and its categorizations, drawing attention to the potentially complex and disruptive work of its commodity forms. The comics medium, designed for reproducibility and disposability, stands as an affront to the reductive perception of art as static (timeless), framed (permanent), and untouched by market pressures, demands, or indulgent pleasures (beautiful).

As a pulp creation that changed several hands, *Nancy* must shift to the topical demands of her creators and an ever-changing American audience. Brainard's *Nancy*, featured in reference to a dizzying range of both popular culture references and the New York school avant-garde, also operates as an adaptive emblem in a "retroactive coherence to the poet's (additive) catalogue" (Fitch 2012, 90). As mass product, *Nancy* provides a complicated locus between the author and a larger social body of consumers. Parallel to his long poem, "I Remember," Brainard's accumulative catalog of Nancy renditions from *The Nancy Book* relays the ongoing trajectory of a cohesive (yet closure-resistant) and personal (although not confessional) serial pastiche that relates to how Bushmiller's newspaper dailies function as both deeply personal and detached from their artistic creator(s). The multitude of *Nancy*'s creators and audiences—coupled with its irresolute seriality—contributes to what Edelman highlights as possible through the affect of the queer adorable in *Nancy*: the rictus of smiley stability (Berlant and Edelman 2014, 19) in juxtaposition to a medium characterized by constant flux. The history of *Nancy* as a long-running comic complicates a unified authorial presence in the work of both Brainard and Bushmiller and dissolves a narrative of fixed identities in the wide scope of *Nancy*'s world—a world in which Nancy and her cohorts may similarly refract under the weight of accumulative seriality. However, it is the engagement with *Nancy*'s adorability throughout this comic that ultimately allows for a radical queer engagement with the recognizable site of mainstream popular culture.

Berlant and Edelman's discursive text, *Sex, or the Unbearable*, briefly unpacks the function of "adorability" in approaching how we attempt to contain sexual anxieties with objects that employ anesthetized adorability. With reference to a specific object of the adorable, *Untitled (Ass)* by Larry Johnson (Berlant and Edelman 2014, 17), Edelman argues that adorability in this image functions in part as an anesthetic to shared anxieties around sex. Edelman qualifies his statement and choice of object, stating, "The very disturbance that the negativity of sex can induce makes it logical that sex without optimism would seek the shelter of adorability, invoking the familiarity, the recognizability of the aesthetic" (Berlant and Edelman 2014, 15). I agree with Edelman's attention to the paradoxical potential for the adorabilized cartoon figure; the overlapping aspects of cartoon and caricature present in Bushmiller's *Nancy* reveal the potentially complex multiplicities of affect available to the medium of comics. However, pushing Edelman's stance even further, we might view comics' potential, as exemplified in *Nancy* (in both its contemporary and original iterations), to refuse the very anesthetic optimism that it offers by a near-consistent comedic deflation of narrative (and normative) expectations. The operative "gag" in *Nancy* relies on the repetitiousness of this frustration. Despite the suggestive work he evokes, Edelman reduces characterizations of the adorable as stable emblems for anesthetic positivity. In these more flattening instances of his argument, Edelman falls closer to distinguishing "functions" of the adorable in suggesting that "the adorable might be a treasure trove of negated encounters with the forms of negativity" or that the adorable merely "domesticate[s] the riskiness that inhabits sexual encounter" (17). I draw attention to these moments not to downplay the complexity of Edelman's dialectic argument but to highlight the suggestive precariousness of his specific encounter with the adorable—and the limitations of that precariousness when it enacts the very binaries it wishes to problematize. Moreover, Edelman chooses a particular image that hosts similarities to as well as salient differences from the genre of comics. The illustration is a still image—a single cartoon and not a serial comic. Both Edelman and Berlant imbue the concept of "stillness" throughout their text with "the smiley-faced representation of Panoptimism's investment in relations . . . that smooth negativity's rough edges by means of a violence" (17). What of a comic, then? What can seriality lend to the task of the adorable? What might it undo? Approaching the

Nancy comic as queer corpus, inhabiting both stasis and temporal mobility at once, resists the boundaries of its frames and invites an interpretive disruption of fixed forms of normativity.

Like other long-running comics publications, *Nancy*'s resilience as a narrative and a commodity relies on a consistency for the potential of ongoing production. In other words, at the root of *Nancy* lies the necessity to move and continue. The comics medium in this sense adheres to an irresolution of seriality or the "continuous starting over, not out of optimism for projected out futures but for being in the world whose pressures are continuous and demand all of the resources they can scrape up and offer" (Berlant and Edelman 2014, 25). As a commodity, comics rely on the perpetuation of narrative; comics (particularly newspaper dailies) thrive on the pressure of topicality, generational relevance, and a persistent ability to respond to audiences. Likewise, Bushmiller's *Nancy* shape-shifted across the twentieth century in response to its readership. This tension between maintaining a recognizable product and adapting to shifting market needs speaks to the queerness of *Nancy* as a serial text. As Muñoz (1999, 141) argues in *Disidentifications*, queer engagements with mainstream objects afford "a politics of hybridity that works within and outside the dominant public sphere, and in doing so contests the ascendant racial, sexual, and class strictures" assigned by the mainstream. By the very projection of her ongoing narrative, *Nancy* resists allegorical or anesthetic closure to the bound frame. On the contrary, the seriality of the *Nancy* canon—always hinging on another episode, another scheme, another position of her recognizable figure in a familiar temporal sequence—engages with the border between narrative closure and the (erotic) perpetuation of an unending narrative. Content continuation without closure subsequently both affirms and expands Edelman's proposed reduction of the cartoon adorable. In evading finality, a comic like *Nancy* does not always temper against sexuality (most brazenly demonstrated in Brainard's pornographic depictions) but, rather, "inhabits an interminable oscillation as [sexuality] comes into focus and then retreats from view" (Berlant and Edelman 2014, 33). As Edelman argues, the donkey cartoon image enables a touch-and-go engagement with sexuality that is suggested but is perpetually obscured within the comics medium as a nonhuman, nonrealist representation.

Figure 10 The artist's physical state as character extension. From Bushmiller, *Nancy*, September 23, 1949

As Edelman describes, there are several disruptive interactions between the image of the ass, its implied creator, and the erotic within the photograph of the pencil and the donkey. Troubled boundaries between author and *Nancy* similarly destabilize a conceptual wholeness in renditions by Brainard and Bushmiller. In the earlier versions of *Nancy*, for example, Bushmiller exposes his persona as a running gag. For instance, he might drastically alter the appearance of his characters to reflect a personal event (see fig. 10) or explain topical circumstances to justify artistic deviations from his usual blueprint approach (see fig. 11). These types of dailies are not all that rare throughout Bushmiller's canon; he frequently employs Nancy's hyperflexibility and performative artifice as a humorous punchline. In these self-exposing moments, Bushmiller underscores an arbitrary plasticity of his characters and inserts his own individual and subjective experiences in *Nancy*. These momentary suspensions of narrative fantasy call into question binary separations between puppet and puppeteer, content and audience, fixed commodity and imagination. In other words, Nancy is at once the epitome of girlhood never aging out of adorability and an intimate reflection of a multitude of creators, generations, and individual readers. Consider again Edelman's attention to the photographed cartoon figure of the donkey and its interacting pencil. As Edelman notes, the figure of the ass dons an expression of (erotic) pleasure, derived possibly from its interaction to its maker's pencil. In the image, Edelman observes:

> The donkey's expression of enjoyment may merely express the artist's, reflecting within the image itself what the photograph frames as outside it. Does this rendering of a sexual encounter then, represent one subject's presence or two? It depends not only

Nancy and the Queer Adorable 339

Figure 11 Bushmiller's New Year's Eve *Nancy*. From Bushmiller, *Nancy*, January 1, 1949

on whether or not we view the ass as animate but also on whether that animation makes it other than the artist or the same. As Paul de Man notes in a different context, Pygmalion may want to escape his own consciousness by encountering in his statue another subject, but he also may want to impose on the statue's otherness his own subjectivity. (Berlant and Edelman 2014, 31)

Reflective of the exchange between pencil and cartoon in Johnson's *Untitled (Ass)*, we witness again a slippage between the Nancy figure and her creator within these gags—a series of winking gestures toward *Nancy*'s self-conscious artifice and by implication the artifice of Bushmiller's own performances of selfhood on the page. These gags highlight the indistinct boundaries between author and artistic object within the comics frame, troubling the parameters of character and the associated markers that converse with identities on and off the page. To delineate one character from another in this conversation between Bushmiller and his creation is to miss the unstable essence of *Nancy* in totality—one that is always (comically) refracted and serial, both an extension of and a departure from the personal life of her creator. The result lends a queer view of both the conceptual stability of Bushmiller and his Nancy. Nancy's creator inhabits the character, he can enter her persona at his whim, and he can erase her while narrating her (see fig. 11). Although not explicitly erotic in this rendition, Bushmiller positions Nancy's figure in a way that conveys her as the ultimate submissive to the dominant hand of her creator.

Through a parallel approach, Brainard's Nancy figure repetitiously literalizes this discursive pliability in *The Nancy Book*. By fashioning Nancy as a material object in several instances—for example, emerging from a Tareyton cigarette package (Brainard 2008, 71) or functioning as an ashtray (38)—Brainard reveals Nancy as an imaginative commodity that lives by extension of and in response to her master manipulator. Brainard positions Nancy, like Bushmiller's Nancy, in mediation of his daily personal experiences. She becomes his preferred brand of cigarette. She inhabits the artistic styles of his close friends. As Lauterbach's (2008, 13) essay in *The Nancy Book* states, for Brainard, "Nancy could be the agent of an accommodating, domestic nearness and hereness. Both the troubled, earnest pathos of the times and the overwhelming grandeur of 'high art' might be resisted, or converted, by Nancy's ubiquitous smile." Nancy's function for Brainard remains distant from Edelman's proposed "regime of the smiley face whose rictus carries the promise of consistency, stability, and normalization" (Berlant and Edelman 2014, 19). Instead, *Nancy* continually disrupts the stability of her own subjectivity, while persisting as a recognizable commodity to mass audiences. For both Bushmiller and Brainard, *Nancy* resides in the abject space between the authors' first-person transparency and a kind of algorithmic artifice of her familiar appearance. Her figure provides an agent of transposition on display that is simultaneously self and other, providing "a constant engagement with negativity, with what opens us to an otherness that undoes our image of the self" (33–34). She exists within the authors' day-to-day and (as we witnessed previously) in exceptional reference to larger historical events. By fashioning the Nancy figure as a literal object, Brainard pushes farther along the trajectory of comic figurations with which Bushmiller was always initially playful: Nancy as commodity emblem, Nancy as ordinary, Nancy as functional plaything.

An apt approach toward this oscillation between author and creation borrows less from the current vocabulary available in comics scholarship and more from one that might suit Brainard's endeavors as a long-form poet. Brian McHale (2004, 15), attending to the contradictions and difficulty of analyzing long-form poetry, describes the particularity of the long-form poem as "hovering" over direct meaning within accumulative texts. With regard to his analysis of Ed Dorn's long poem *Gunslinger*, for example, he underscores the use of pop and a related "flatness" in Dorn's work. Referencing interpretations of Roy Lichtenstein's and Andy Warhol's techniques, McHale cites a kind of pop art flatness in Dorn's poem (parallel to the potential of Nancy's flatness) that "exploit[s] exactly the same tension between ontological fullness and emptiness" (95). Both Brainard's and Bushmiller's *Nancy*s similarly move in contradictory directions and act "one moment, [as] a masque, in which personifications spring into three-dimensional life; the next moment, a tapestry, in which living realities are reduced to patterns in fabric" (82). Parallel to Edelman's attention to the paradoxical inanimate animation between the image of the donkey and the pencil, Nancy interacts with and remains separated from her current creator. So rather than quell anxiety, as Edelman partly proposes for adorability's function, Nancy operates more closely within what Susan Stewart (1992) distinguishes as the abject plastic toy. The malleability of the toy, like Nancy's character, allows for human fantasy, manipulation, and momentary enclosure in (re)imagining manifestations of the everyday. According to Stewart, "The toy is the physical embodiment of the fiction: it is a device for fantasy, a point of beginning for narrative. The toy opens an interior world" (56). As flexible toy for Bushmiller, Brainard, and their consuming audiences, Nancy is both inanimate and able to come to life. She caters to both the individual imagination and public contexts. Her hollowed presence, a specifically queer figuration, "is essentially about the rejection of a here and now and an insistence on potentiality or concrete possibility for another world" (Muñoz 2009, 1). In its essential mutability, the pliable queerness of the *Nancy* comic actually procures, rather than obscures, both the underlying refractions of *and* the imaginative potential for fraught representations of American identity.

As scholarly interest in the work of comics continues to develop, there has been increasing critical attention to the numerous ways in which this medium can underscore, bolster, bastardize, manipulate, and significantly belittle culturally shared modes of representation. As demonstrated by the plentiful literary scholarship on more contemporary "graphic novels," such as critical works on Art Spiegelman's *Maus* (1986) or Alison Bechdel's *Fun Home* (2006), the medium of comics continues to garner critical interest not for its ability to anesthetize or miniaturize serious inquiries on cultural identity or representation but for the ways in which the medium attends to how humans subjectively conceive their world. However, the precarious delineation between *graphic novel* and *comic book* in scholarship also accentuates which *types* of comics persistently attract more scholarly attention these days and why. The popularization of the term *graphic novel* in the twenty-first century is a contested neologism among several creators and scholars.[9] Disparaged by comic artists such as Neil Gaiman and Alan Moore, the term *graphic novel* implicitly denigrates a specific kind of comic that might have developed before the more highbrow marketable term became mainstream. Perhaps what fuels this contempt for the term *graphic novel* is the implied denial that a larger canvas of comics, including long-running newspaper serials like *Nancy*, perform something different, specifically something of lesser value, in comparison with the more intellectually weighty, single-authored graphic novel. However, as we witness in the multivalent *Nancy* trajectory, long-running dailies can provide a messy and compelling seriality whose unwieldiness is in fact one of the key elements to the potentially queer fragmentations of fixity, stasis, and the normativity that critical audiences take for granted.

Despite the recent influx of scholarship within the field of comics, long-publishing comics like *Nancy* demand more critical attention for their accumulative serialization and the interwoven, provocative queer modes of representation and (dis)identification. Both Brainard's and Bushmiller's texts extract as much content from the controlled miniature as they do from the unwieldy canvas of the gigantic and the discordance that the long-running serial form offers to the Nancy figure. *Nancy* allows for an oscillation between stable iconography and a pervasive resistance to narrative closure, static character performance, and fixed fidelities to form. In doing so, the Nancy figure's affect of adorability succeeds not in anesthetizing our desires or avoiding difficult categorizations but rather in emphasizing the mobility of ideas on the significant stage of mainstream popular narrative. Brainard and Bushmiller highlight the manner in which a serial subject like Nancy can paradoxically both reiterate *and* trouble the sexual, gendered, and national character performance on the page. Both Brainard and Bushmiller lived during moments in US history characterized by massive transformations in gender relations, political corruption, economic turmoil, and global discontent that left the representation of American modes of identification in question. Whether invoking the turmoil of the recovery period of the Great Depression or a national body still reeling from the Vietnam War, both authors speak to a fissured national consciousness in their imaginatively open texts. Textual breaks from narrative fantasy and agile characterization wink toward our ever-refracted American consciousness, exposing the flimsy illusion of a linear-progressive seriality and the projection of a pictorial adorable flatness that we find in mainstream narratives of US history and by implication in American identities. As a result, we receive a playful glimpse at what long-running comics at their most effective can reveal—the taut seams in a constantly revising, reworking, and ever-becoming imagination for a sum of difficult parts.

Jessica Q. Stark is a doctoral candidate in English at Duke University, where she teaches on modern to contemporary American literature, popular culture, and creative writing. This essay is part of a larger project examining the intersections between American contemporary poetry and comics.

Notes

I am deeply grateful to Ramzi Fawaz, Kimberly Lamm, Darieck Scott, and Priscilla Wald for their meticulous and thoughtful commentary throughout the process of refining this essay. Additionally, I would like to thank Ron Padgett for his invaluable guidance toward its final iteration.

1   Nancy features in the currently published *Nancy and Sluggo* by Guy Gilchrist.
2   Joe Brainard worked with poets John Ashbery, Kenward Elmslie, Frank O'Hara, and Ron Padgett, among others, to create the collaborative two issues of *C Comics*, which were mimeographed anthologies composed of short works, including poetry, and comics from 1964 to 1965 (Vance 2011).
3   In Padgett's (2008, 28) essay in *The Nancy Book*, he also surmises that Brainard's appropriations of popular comics began "soon after his arrival in New York in late 1960." During this period, Brainard used visual materials from a large pool of materials from mass culture, including "consumer goods such as Fab, Tide, Alka Seltzer, Lucky Strike, and 7-Up—and in 1963 he began including comic strip characters such as L'il Abner, Dick Tracy, and Nancy, whose adventures he was following in the New York *Post*" (28).
4   See Ramzi Fawaz (2017) for an evocative consideration of historicity with regard to Brainard's *Nancy*.
5   Using what Andrew Ross (1999) terms *Pop camp*, which expands Susan Sontag's primary definition of *camp* in "Notes on Camp" (1982), the *Nancy* comics invoke the ways in which long-publishing comics provocatively destabilize normativity through derisive humor and their presumed throwaway status. *Pop camp* invites a direct challenge to the boundaries of official taste, while remaining a "non-threatening presence" (Ross

1999, 317) within its assumed marginal presence in popular culture. In consideration of a kind of pop camp in both versions of *Nancy*, Brainard and Bushmiller employ the Nancy figure as a comedic locus for deeply subversive gags against cultural normative expectations for identity and identifications.

6   It should be noted, however, that Brainard's perspective strays from the minoritarian intersectionality that Muñoz focalizes in *Disidentifications*. As a white man working in an artistic genealogy of the mostly white and male New York school and pop art avant-garde, Brainard worked against sexual normativity while simultaneously benefiting from the affordances of his racial privilege. Still, the application of Muñoz's theory aids in revealing how we may reimagine a continuity of exchange between a seemingly normative and "original" *Nancy* to Brainard's subversive rendition. The implication of this connection demands queer revision to a number of representational assumptions, including those perhaps beyond the perspective of *Nancy*'s creators.

7   In a parallel move, Muñoz (1999, 31) notes Wayne Koestenbaum's attention to gay male disidentification with female opera singers, which as he notes "does not erase the fiery females that fuel his identity-making machinery; rather, it lovingly retains their lost presence through imitation, repetition, and admiration."

8   The character Henry, created by Carl Anderson in 1932, invokes a provocative physical likeness to Nancy's usual love interest, Sluggo.

9   Comics creator Will Eisner was one of the first to coin the term *graphic novel* to attract new audiences to his book-length comics, but it wasn't until the late 1980s that the term moved into the mainstream book trade. The publication of the first part of Spiegelman's *Maus* (1986), Frank Miller's *The Dark Knight Returns* (1986), and Alan Moore and Dave Gibbons's *Watchmen* (1986–87) likely contributed to the popularization of the term by the nature of their bound, novel-length series (Hatfield 2005, 29–30). Comics scholars, including Hillary Chute and Marianne DeKoven (2006, 767), take issue with the term *graphic novel* and make astute arguments for other designations (e.g., *graphic narrative*) for single-authored, autobiographical long-form comics.

References

Berlant, Lauren, and Lee Edelman. 2014. *Sex, or the Unbearable*. Durham, NC: Duke Univ. Press.

Brainard, Joe. 2008. *The Nancy Book*, edited by Lisa Pearson and Ron Padgett. Los Angeles: Siglio Press.

Bushmiller, Ernie. 2012a. *Nancy Is Happy: Dailies 1943–1945*. Seattle: Fantagraphics Books.

---. 2012b. *Nancy Likes Christmas: Dailies 1945–1948*. Seattle: Fantagraphics Books.
---. 2014. *Nancy Loves Sluggo: Dailies 1949–1951*. Seattle: Fantagraphics Books.
Chute, Hillary, and Marianne DeKoven. 2006. "Introduction: Graphic Narrative." *Modern Fiction Studies* 52, no. 4: 767–82.
Doss, Erika. 2010. *Memorial Mania: Public Feeling in America*. Chicago: Univ. of Chicago Press.
Eng, David L., Judith Halberstam, and José Esteban Muñoz. 2005. "Introduction: What's Queer about Queer Studies Now?" *Social Text*, vol. 23, nos. 3/4: 1–17.
Fawaz, Ramzi. 2017. "Stripped to the Bone: Sequencing Queerness in the Comic Strip Work of Joe Brainard and David Wojnarowicz." *ASAP/Journal* 2, no. 2: 335–67.
Fitch, Andy. 2012. *Pop Poetics: Reframing Joe Brainard*. Champaign, IL: Dalkey Archive Press.
Hatfield, Charles. 2005. *Alternative Comics: An Emerging Literature*. Jackson: Univ. Press of Mississippi.
Lauterbach, Ann. 2008. "Joe Brainard and Nancy." In Brainard 2008, 7–24.
McHale, Brian. 2004. *The Obligation toward the Difficult Whole: Postmodernist Long Poems*. Tuscaloosa: Univ. of Alabama Press.
Muñoz, José Esteban. 1999. *Disidentifications: Queers of Color and the Performance of Politics*. Minneapolis: Univ. of Minnesota Press.
---. 2009. *Cruising Utopia: The Then and There of Queer Futurity*. New York: New York Univ. Press.
Newgarden, Mark, and Paul Karasik. 1988. "How to Read Nancy." In *The Best of Ernie Bushmiller's Nancy*, edited by Brian Walker, 98–105. New York: Henry Holt/Comicana.
Ngai, Sianne. 2012. *Our Aesthetic Categories: Zany, Cute, Interesting*. Cambridge, MA: Harvard Univ. Press.
Padgett, Ron. 2008. "The Origins of Joe Brainard's Nancy." In Brainard 2008, 27–30.
Ross, Andrew. 1999. "Uses of Camp." In *Camp: Queer Aesthetics and the Performing Subject: A Reader*, edited by Fabio Cleto, 308–29. Ann Arbor: Univ. of Michigan Press.
Sontag, Susan. 1982. "Notes on Camp." In *A Susan Sontag Reader*, 105–19. New York: Farrar, Straus, and Giroux. First published 1964.
Stewart, Susan. 1992. *On Longing: Narratives of the Miniature, the Gigantic, the Souvenir, the Collection*. Durham, NC: Duke Univ. Press.
Vance, James. 2011. "'C' Is for Collaboration." *This Land Press*, November 9. thislandpress.com/2011/11/09/c-is-for-collaboration/.

Rebecca Wanzo

The Normative Broken: Melinda Gebbie, Feminist Comix, and Child Sexuality Temporalities

Abstract *Lost Girls* (2006) is a return to the themes explored by Melinda Gebbie and other underground feminist cartoonists in the 1970s and 1980s. The text, a collaboration between Gebbie and Alan Moore, should be read as reminiscent of feminist cartoonists who intentionally depicted the taboo or obscene in order to address sexual and gender inequalities. These comics suggest that the obscene can push against purity narratives attached to womanhood, narratives that potentially stigmatize all girls and women. *Lost Girls* keeps the taboos of children's sexuality and incest central to the representation in order to reframe possibilities of women's healthy sexual subjectivity. Injurious pasts and irreconcilable desires do not preclude joyous futures. Painful pasts enable the eponymous lost girls' agency, creating the conditions that help them find homosocial and queer belonging with one another. The comic thus models the temporalities of surviving trauma. The feminist temporalities of survivorship here also model utopian futures that are homosocial, queer, often ecstatic, and resistant to normative scripts of what should give women comfort. Undergirded by a radical feminist perspective that sees injury as being embedded in many women's experiences, the creation of community from the wound makes it normal to have been broken.

Keywords underground comix, feminist comics, *Lost Girls*, Alan Moore, child sexual abuse, fantasy

In Alan Moore and Melinda Gebbie's gorgeous graphic narrative homage to a Victorian and Edwardian porn aesthetic, *Lost Girls* (2006), the collaborators reimagine the stories of three legendary lost adolescent girls: Alice of *Alice's Adventures in Wonderland* (1865) and *Through the Looking Glass* (1871), Wendy of *Peter Pan and Wendy* (1911), and Dorothy of *The Wonderful Wizard of Oz* (1900).[1] Moore and Gebbie depict the three having amorous, orgiastic adventures with one another at a hotel prior to World War I; this serves as a frame story as they recast their well-known tales as allegories of erotic awakening (Scarecrow and Lion and Tin Man, oh my!). Contained in three volumes, the graphic narrative is meant to function aesthetically both as art and as a prompt for one-handed reading, but the creators also unsettle attachments to iconographic stories of girlhood.[2] As an elaborate metafictional comic of such well-known texts, it becomes an ineludible part of the archive that readers have of these childhood narratives and how they circulate. While the nastiness of the original Grimm fairy tales and other childhood fables calls attention to how the best-known US adaptations often sanitize regulatory fictions for childhood consumption, their transformation of these iconic lost girls into inquisitive sexual subjects makes childhood purity itself an object, subverting Western cultural attachments to pure (white) girlhood and anxieties about its loss. These revisions are celebratory, but the comic still places child sexual abuse and rape at the center, injuries that, psychological and cultural discourses sometimes suggest, leave girls and women perpetually lost to themselves and others (Sneddon 2013).

This story is hard to tell, and particularly hard to draw, because even fictive representations of child sexual abuse or children's sexuality can be prohibited legally and socially.[3] Children—a more amorphous category than the under-eighteen standard suggests—cannot consent under the law and are treated as lacking the ability to understand sexual acts emotionally. Unlike other forms of pornography, photographs and films depicting children participating in sexual activity make the images evidence of injury (MacKinnon 1993, 35–36). Nevertheless, notions of what counts as a sexual or erotic representation of a child have sometimes been nonsensical, resulting in some parents being charged with trafficking child pornography for photographs of their children taking baths (Levine 2002, 41). People can receive longer sentences for child pornography than for sexual abuse of a child, a punishment based on understanding the injuriousness of circulation and of repeated viewing of the images.[4]

"Virtual" representations have a somewhat different standard. While the Child Pornography Prevention Act of 1996 in the United States treated all virtual pornography created without real children the same as "real" pornography, the US Supreme Court struck down that portion of the act as a violation of the First Amendment in *Ashcroft v. Free Speech Coalition* (535 U.S. 234 [2002]). Convicted sex offenders can still be punished for possession of virtual representations of child sexuality. The absence of "real" bodies nonetheless does not keep creators and distributors from running afoul of community obscenity standards. Many people are understandably offended by violent, sexualized virtual images, particularly of children. The United Nations, for example, has pushed Japan to ban graphic representations of sexual violence in manga, a genre whose characters tend to appear childlike and whose depictions of sexual violence have included sadistic torture (Barder 2016).[5] A concession to such prohibitions in *Lost Girls* is that Moore and Gebbie age up their protagonists, showing a marked difference from how they are described in the original works.

An irony of these prohibitions is that virtual representations are important mechanisms for children to learn about sexuality and talk about sexual abuse. Drawings and other virtual representations of a child's body have been a means of helping children communicate about sex and sexual injury when they struggle to verbalize their feelings or an account of the harm, or do not possess the language to do so (Aldridge et al. 2004). Progressive children's books help children learn about their bodies. The use of the virtual body—like the doll—has been characterized as helping children describe abuse, even as some argue that the use of the virtual body can encourage fictions and false allegations (Everson and Boat 1994). Virtual child bodies clearly enable "speaking" sex—negotiating power relations that can otherwise result in silence and offering an opportunity to push the boundaries of what can and cannot be said about child sexuality (Foucault 1978).

Drawing sex thus may provide a space for adults to address the complicated relationship between child sexuality and abuse. Feminist theorists have constructed a strong divide between rape and sex. But one of the traumas experienced by some children who have been abused is that they may also have experienced some pleasure. The struggle to discuss this can be compounded by the fact that children—despite well-established medical and psychological literature to the contrary—are not seen as possessing a sexuality. *Lost Girls* enters this gap—between what cannot be photographed, filmed, or in many cases even spoken and the lived experience of child sexuality and sexual injury. Moore and Gebbie construct a space for people—an abject, dark space in which things (and sometimes people) are lost and discarded—that is literally and figuratively in the gutter. In the taboo interstices between pleasure and injury, Moore and Gebbie depict a subjectivity fragmented by trauma as a kind of brokenness that can be seen as normal in relationship to other women who have had similar experiences.

The fragmented structure of panels in the comics medium is perhaps uniquely situated to depict divided selves that can remain immobilized by traumatic events. In *Lost Girls*, the ways in which the protagonists are fragmented and doubled shape the basic visual vocabulary Moore and Gebbie use to tell the story of the women's experiences with pleasure and abuse. The standardization of their brokenness is a means by which the characters connect with each other sans judgment. The possibility of pleasure despite trauma suggests that brokenness is a normative subject position and pushes readers to see the quotidian nature of trauma in childhood for so many.

If one of the things that comics does is offer new ways of representing the experience of temporality, *Lost Girls* pushes against scripts about how adults integrate their experiences as abused children. With historical trauma and the present in the same frame, Moore and Gebbie treat history less as something that must be vanquished and more as a doubleness that travels with the adult. Trauma is always present for the survivor because the "body keeps score" (van der Kolk 2015). However, part of the critical work of *Lost Girls* is to imagine integration of trauma with sexual health by using fantasy to imagine how sexual trauma can sometimes be the grounds for building new forms of homosociality that would not otherwise have existed. By blending transgressive representations of sexual fantasy that would be considered antithetical to many feminist frameworks of pleasure, the text creates a space for women who otherwise might be seen as lost—lost to the possibility of pleasure and lost to fulfilling connections with others because of what trauma can sever.

Moore and Gebbie speak to a division that has emerged among scholars addressing discourses of sexual abuse. James Kincaid (1998) and Judith Levine (2002) have compellingly argued against child sex abuse panics and irrational denial of child sexuality as a part of healthy development, with Kincaid (1998, 13) arguing that the discourse of child sexual abuse illustrates the repressive hypothesis—what cannot be spoken is the "sexual appeal" of children, and thus the child is consistently sexualized with the omnipresent discourse of sexual abuse. Kincaid and Levine could be seen as resisting Catharine

MacKinnon's (1991, 1298) "dominance" feminist framework—a theorization of inequality that foregrounds patriarchy's overarching reach in all intimate, political, and social relations. For MacKinnon, the relationships between men and women and between adults and children are foundational hierarchies that shape structural oppression. This is a position that has been criticized for being rigid and not allowing for other complexities that shape power and injury (Fischel 2010, 281). One outcome of the resistance to dominance feminism's insistence on acknowledging a fundamental inequality between children and adults is the claim that child sexual abuse is not particularly widespread or injurious, which can lead to a war of dueling statistics and methodological indictments. *Lost Girls* resists this dichotomy, as it emerges from a feminist tradition of cartooning that emphasizes both injury and pleasure.

Lost Girls is thus a return to the themes explored by Gebbie and other underground feminist cartoonists in the 1970s and 1980s. Moore is the biggest name in the *Lost Girls* collaboration as one of the medium's most respected and celebrated writers, and Gebbie is a secondary figure in many mainstream press discussions of their work.[6] The cartoonist's beautiful artwork nonetheless informs the construction of narrative, and it was a true collaboration, with Gebbie's images often informing the text (Gebbie, Moore, and Green 2012). A glance at her controversial comic *Fresca Zizi* (1977), produced long before the collaboration with Moore, reveals an image of the Scarecrow, Lion, and Tin Man in a sexual encounter in one of her stories, illustrating that she brought content to the conceptualization. Moreover, while Moore's interest in interrogating power relationships—evident in his early work in underground British comics and in his better-known adapted works, such as *Watchmen* (1987), *From Hell* (1999), and *The League of Extraordinary Gentlemen* (1999)—is on full display, reading *Lost Girls* as part of the genealogy of feminist underground comix that produced Gebbie is just as important to framing its textual antecedents and influences.

The text is reminiscent of some feminist comix[7] cartoonists who intentionally depicted the taboo or obscene to address sexual and gender inequalities. *Lost Girls* uses the obscene to contest the Victorian purity discourse attached to the cult of true womanhood and the sentimental child that configures ideal (white) girls and women as asexual and permanently broken if touched by sex or sexual abuse (Bernstein 2011, 39–41). These narratives potentially stigmatize all girls and women who do not conform to the asexual ideal. But by showing how injurious pasts do not preclude the possibility of healthy sexual futures, *Lost Girls* reframes the possibilities for women's healthy sexual subjectivity.

Survivors of child sexual abuse are often marked as perpetually scarred and unable to move forward, but the comic models the temporalities of surviving trauma, often found in graphic memoirs that present, as Hilary Chute (2007, 231) argues of Art Spiegelman's work, an "experimental view of sequence and temporality" that "powerfully—and politically—suggests the enmeshing of the past and the present." I argue that Moore and Gebbie craft a feminist and queer comics temporality of surviving trauma, imagining a utopian futurity that is homosocial, queer, often ecstatic, and resistant to normative scripts of what should give women comfort. Undergirded by a radical feminist comix tradition that sees injury as being embedded in many women's experiences, the creation of community from the wound makes it normal to have been broken. This is a tendentious treatment of desire, but because comics embrace, as Charles Hatfield (2005, 36–37) has explained, "the art of tensions," particularly the tension between image and text, *Lost Girls* is uniquely positioned to articulate what can be created by the seeming irreconcilability between pleasure and trauma.

Reframing the Injury of the Gaze in Feminist Comix

The themes and aesthetics in Moore and Gebbie's work can be understood only by understanding the underground comix that preceded it. The relationship between taboo and liberation was an ongoing theme in underground comix, works mostly associated with legendary male cartoonists such as Robert Crumb, Harvey Kurtzman, and other creators who produced work directly responding to the counterculture of the 1960s and forbidden by the Comics Code Authority in 1954 (Rosenkranz 2008). Sexuality, the autobiographical, and the desecration of beloved mass media narratives were major themes, and many cheaply produced profane comics found an audience. Feminist cartoonists working in the San Francisco underground scene that emerged in the 1960s were sometimes published but found, as cartoonist and feminist comics historian Trina Robbins (2016, vii) recounts, that it was a "boys' club." The first comic book produced only by women, *It Ain't Me Babe*, was published in 1970, and the first issue of the longer-running *Wimmen's Comix*[8] was published in 1972. *Wimmen's Comix* published only seventeen issues in its twenty-year run but included the work of many feminist cartoonists, some of whose work would cross over and be read by non-comics readers, such as Phoebe Gloeckner (*A Child's Life* [1998] and *The Diary of a Teenage Girl* [2002]) and MacArthur-winner Alison Bechdel, whose graphic memoir *Fun Home* (2006) was highly praised by critics in the mainstream press and adapted into a Tony Award–winning musical.

Feminist cartoonists continued to find a home in feminist publications, independent publishing, and online in the twenty-first century, but the most transgressive material appeared in early comics like the first issues of *Wimmen's Comix* (1972–92), *Tits and Clits* (1972–87), *Twisted Sisters* (1976), and the nine-issue run of the French feminist comics magazine *Ah! Nana* (1976–78). These early feminist comix were characterized by the sexual explicitness and taboo content typical of many underground comix, but a notable distinction was the privileging of women's experiences, political struggles, and pleasures. Some feminist critics who looked at the comics did not see a distinction in content, given the emphasis on nudity and ejaculation and, at times, an aesthetic of abjection and the female grotesque (Robbins 2016, x–xi). But the strong emphasis on disrupting gender and sexual scripts and on centering women's pleasure—and not only as part of a masculine subject's fantasies or anxieties—marked a difference. Feminist comics often played with representations attached to a heteronormative male gaze, such as the centerfold and inflatable women's dolls, refusing a binary between the pornographic and the feminist.

Reframing pornographic, objectifying representations extended occasionally to the most taboo content of all—stories that challenged understandings of young girls' sexuality. Cathy Millet's twelve-panel comic in issue #5 of *Wimmen's Comix* is mostly an abstracted image of vaginal walls and female ejaculation, finally revealing a little girl with a slight smile in the last frame, happy with a secret (Millet 1975). Joyce Farmer Sutton's "Doin' It!" appeared in the same issue and was a clear example of how many of these comics pushed readers to rethink a gaze that could be pornographic or injurious (fig. 1). The twenty-two-panel strip begins with two young siblings, Kimmie and Bobbie, almost certainly under the age of seven, watching a couple kiss on television. They mimic what they see and then place their hands on each other's crotches. Kimmie exclaims, "That feels good Bobbie! Do it some more!" Their mother enters the room outraged, with dark speech bubbles: *"What is going on here?? I saw you! You'll go crazy! Go*

Figure 1 Siblings teach each other about their bodies in Joyce Farmer Sutton's "Doin' It!" Originally appeared in *Wimmen's Comix* #5 (1975). Reprinted from Tina Robbins, ed. (2016), *The Complete Wimmen's Comix*, vol. 1, 193

blind! And . . . he'll *hurt* you Kimmie!" Her children's faces are initially relaxed as they greet her with "Oh! Hi Mom!" but the words and her affect terrify them, surrounding the now-anxious children with the knowledge that they have done something wrong. The mother knows she "must calm down" before she causes "damage" to their development, so she places her arms around them and tells them it is "normal to experiment" but that they "must remember not to play like that anymore!" (Sutton 1975).

After she leaves, the bodies of her children suggest shame and anxiety. Kimmie holds her doll with a frown, and Bobbie's head is bowed as he tells his sister that he did not mean to hurt her. They move closer together, and she replies that she did not experience pain. Bobbie replies, "I think Mom was just trying to scare us!" Kimmie returns to her "hole" to "see if it hurts," but finds it feels good, not painful, when she inserts her finger and invites her brother to do the same. They discover that she's "soft inside," and he asks if she wants to feel him, as he feels different—"sort of hard." She rises to turn on cartoons, and he asks if they should tell their mother that their sexual play does not hurt her, but Kimmie nixes the idea because their mother will "get uptight" (Sutton 1975). They return to the television, the normative everyday domestic scene unmarred by the earlier encounter.

The ability to tell this story through comics, with the jarring effects of the visuals and without real children, illustrates how drawing sex can fill in the gaps between what must be discussed and what allegedly cannot be represented. Sutton fills in the gaps of what we should remember and know about childhood but are culturally disciplined to forget. It is hard to imagine where this story could circulate in the twenty-first century without prompting charges of obscenity and child pornography (and indeed, when I teach this story the vast majority of students categorize it as porn but then change their minds after discussion). While "virtual," the representation of young children touching each other's genitalia might prompt rapid state intervention in an era when children—particularly boys—can be marked as showing early signs of sexual predation. The two children are exploring each other, but it is the girl who is understood as at risk for injury. They learn here the prohibition of speaking sex and sexuality as shame, a silencing that can ironically make them more vulnerable to sexual abuse because they have been taught that it should be hidden. Erasing child sexuality provides psychological and narrative closure for adults who do not want to acknowledge child sexuality. An asexual childhood becomes the standard for health, whereas more complete memories become evidence of injury.

"Doin' It!" also illustrates how children—particularly girls—can learn that any sexual feeling must be an injury. The mother recognizes from fragmented memories she may not even be able to recall that this is not true. Readers can recognize her as a good mother because she immediately comforts the children after her outburst and recognizes that her own panic could be the source of injury. She knows she is not only teaching them to hide sex but that speech about sex can be contradictory. This kind of sexual experimentation is extremely common but also prohibited. She is thus either lying in saying that she believes it is normal or affirming the experimentation as a mistake that is a rite of passage. This normal experience may be something she has had but cannot remember. Perhaps, as Sigmund Freud (1995, 549) argues, she is experiencing "the peculiar amnesia which veils [early childhood] from most people" so that they "have nothing left except a few incomprehensible memory fragments." Her relationship to her children's present is influenced by the impressionistic fragments of her past, filtered through regulatory social and sexual scripts.

This example illustrates both the typical fragmented nature of child sexuality and the ways in which subjects close the narrative gap with normative sexual scripts. Closure in comics, as Scott McCloud (1994, 63) explains, is the process by which readers are "observing the part but perceiving the whole." Their imaginations fill in what has happened in the gutter (the space between panels), closing gaps in the narrative. What cartoonists choose to leave undrawn and unsaid in the gutter is part of what animates the meaning. In that sense, comics readers can never step out of an implied reader role, as they are always filling in the gaps, or the ellipses, in the text (Iser 1978). But comics make explicit the relationship between the narrative and narrative (w)holes. Readers are cognizant that filling in the gaps is part of understanding the narrative. Sutton illustrates the gap by drawing what is erased (child sexuality) and scripting the act of erasure (the mother's processing of events). "Doin' It!" is illustrative of the ways in which scripts about child sexuality are always fragmented and filled in by other narratives, which is something that Moore and Gebbie make use of in *Lost Girls*.

Foregrounding the fragmentation of gendered scripts—both individual experiences and idealized representations like those presented by iconographic childhood stories—animates the structure of *Lost Girls*. While the characters seem to have fragmented psyches because of the abuse they experience, the text normativizes the messiness of gendered and sexual histories that people need to reconstruct as they come to terms with their identities as adults. The broken memories and fragmented psyches are not pathological when the women are together. Alice, Wendy, and Dorothy present fragments of their narratives to one another, shaped by what they remember as well as by one another's expectations. At the same time, readers' memories of these texts or of various adaptations function in tension with the stories that are being told and their knowledge of eros in childhood. Readers are also called to recognize the trope of eroticizing children, which takes various masked forms.

Gebbie's work calls attention to the common sexualization of a childlike aesthetic. In the comic strip "Dime Dancer," Gebbie crafts a petite taxi dancer with a Betty Boop–like shape, curvaceous figure, and babylike head. Her cuteness is marred by heavy mascara, angry looks, sweat stains, and poorly fitting clothing. Gebbie revisits the character in issue #6 of *Wimmen's Comix*, where she illustrates the Rodgers and Hart standard, "Ten Cents a Dance." Sung by the taxi dancer, the melancholy song tells the story of a woman fatigued by her work. Large eyes signifying tattered innocence are underlined with heavy black mascara, and the eyes fill with anxiety, discomfort, and emptiness at various moments. The sign of her particular vulnerability is distinctly and troublingly racialized—her petite whiteness poses a contrast to the other women and customers. In one of the last frames, aligned with the famous lyrics, "Sometimes I think I've found my hero / But it's a queer romance," a fairly grotesque dark-skinned man, most likely Latino, bends over her as she looks up with a dead stare. In the last two frames of the comic, her eyes appear wide, with dilated pupils, as she invites customers with the lyric, "All that you need is a ticket." She lifts up her skirt to show her buttocks clad in underwear and a garter, and the mascara seems to be running as she looks over her shoulder and sings, "Come on, big boy! Ten cents a dance!" (Gebbie 1976). The strip ends with her lying prone under the bottom comic frame, a man's head between her legs as she smokes a cigarette, looking bored and tired.

While the song was certainly never a happy one, part of Gebbie's work is to refuse sanitation of the musical standard. If the readers' image of the song evokes previous Hollywood representations of Doris Day singing it in an evening dress or a plucky Barbara Stanwyck marrying her customer, it is a song that refuses the romance exemplified not only by such representations but also by many standards that mask the underbelly of a popular culture that sanitizes those representations. And it is Gebbie's depiction of the babylike face that communicates the injury, a youthfulness that helps communicate the trauma. Cuteness stands in contrast to the lyrics, making readers more uncomfortable with the invitation than they would be with a song that already seems ironic but does not necessarily communicate tragedy.

As opposed to innocence, the child aesthetic facilitates Gebbie's representation of injury and abjection. Abjection does not preclude the possibility of the erotic; it can be part of a practice of sexual and political freedom for many subjects.[9] But the eyes in the strip emphasize that injury is present in a context that some readers might otherwise see as harmlessly erotic. Abjection can sometimes be liberatory in the feminist and queer underground comix traditions, but in this particular context the taxi dancer is clearly not experiencing pleasure. Gebbie continued the practice of subtly showing injury in pornographic contexts in *Lost Girls*.

As comics of women's liberation, these early feminist works often questioned what liberation would look like, rescuing middle-class white women in particular from scripts of who they should be and who they have been. Canonical fantasy narratives are also part of who we were, as narratives that we consume frequently inform our aspirational selves or cultural scripts. We may not think of these lost-girl narratives as having much of a regulatory force, particularly since the allegorical appeal of these books and their adaptation have been profound in the West. The idea of falling through the looking glass, the boy who would never grow up, and Oz have become touchstones to describe many nonnormative experiences. *The Wizard of Oz* alone has had an extraordinary afterlife for varied identity groups, with an African American adaptation of the story into the musical *The Wiz*, Judy Garland's iconographic performance and the character of Dorothy resonating with queer communities, and the stage musical *Wicked* having mass success but particularly appealing to teenage girls who love the theme of finding friendship and power as an outsider.[10] Revisions include these populations in broader cultural narratives while also acknowledging specificity. Much of the allegorical force of these tales focuses on mapping them onto other identities, constructing narratives of inclusion for "others" unimagined by creators of ideal white girls. In contrast, *Lost Girls* frees the girls themselves from narratives of ideal white girlhood. The specific group hailed here is the idealized white girl child, denied agency, positioned only as at risk. They write and draw the sexual child into the children's literature canon, rescripting these fictions by including psychosexual development.

Early underground feminist comix thus have three characteristics that inform the work of *Lost Girls*. These cartoonists took traditional genres of representation that were typically misogynist, taboo, or produced for men and defamiliarized the representations by using the comics to attach a feminist frame to the bodies on display. In so doing, the comics often normalized women's pleasure (and in some cases, the pleasure of girls) in contexts where women would not normally be understood as finding it. The comics also consistently think about how gendered and sexual scripts inform futurity for women, producing obfuscating memories, sanitized stories, and generic narratives that keep women from acquiring self-knowledge and crafting new paths for themselves.

Broken Girls: The Temporality of Mended Subjects

Alice is the most canonical representation of scripts about what happens to sexually abused girls, and Moore and Gebbie's version of her evokes the pathology narrative and disrupts it. Their treatment of Alice's entrance into sexuality is inspired by a fairly popular belief that Charles Dodgson (Lewis Carroll) had a sexual and romantic interest

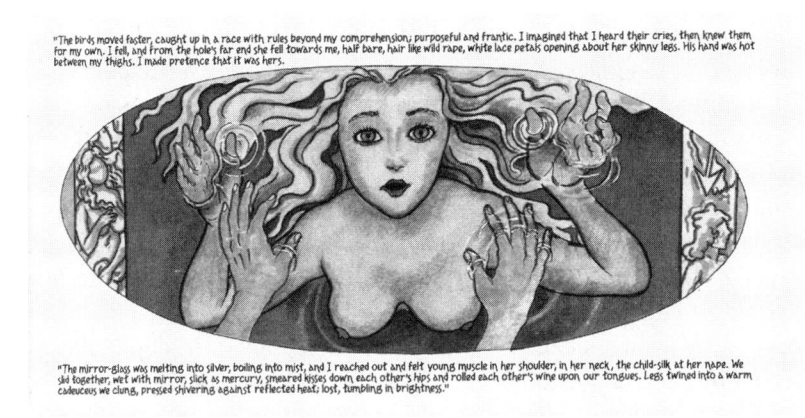

"The birds moved faster, caught up in a race with rules beyond my comprehension; purposeful and frantic. I imagined that I heard their cries, then knew them for my own. I fell, and from the hole's far end she fell towards me, half bare, hair like wild rope, white lace petals opening about her skinny legs. His hand was hot between my thighs. I made pretense that it was hers."

"The mirror-glass was melting into silver, boiling into mist, and I reached out and felt young muscle in her shoulder, in her neck, the child-silk at her nape. We slid together, wet with mirror, slick as mercury, smeared kisses down each other's hips and rolled each other's wine upon our tongues. Legs twined into a warm caduceus we clung, pressed shivering against reflected heat; lost, tumbling in brightness."

Figure 2 Alice experiences dissociation when sexually abused. From Moore and Gebbie (2006), *Lost Girls*, chap. 1, p. 5

in Alice Liddell, the little girl who provided the name (and perhaps inspiration for) *Alice's Adventures in Wonderland* and *Through the Looking Glass*.

Scholars such as Catherine Robson and Kincaid have complicated the readings of Dodgson that fit contemporary understandings of pedophilia in contemporary culture. Robson (2001, 4) notes that girls were particular objects of desire, given the "rampant sentimentality" and "intense valorization of the little girl at the expense of mature femininity" in the Victorian era. In *Lost Girls*, Alice is the paradigmatic blonde and blue-eyed angel of the Victorian imagination, depicted as lost when she is molested. Gebbie's artwork shows Alice fading away into a mirror, dissolving and fragmenting until the reflection/projection of Alice appears more real than Alice herself. In this version of the tale, she remains lost in the looking glass and is transformed into something wholly other than what her Victorian pure girlhood would allegedly guarantee (fig. 2). Alice's reflection is consistently a theme throughout the text, with her childhood double representing the prototypical lost girl who can never be the same after abuse.

She tells her story at the end of volume 1, after Dorothy, who appears the least troubled by her sexual history, tells hers. While Alice encourages Wendy and Dorothy to tell their stories, she shies away from her own memories. "Bunny," her father's oldest friend, is a menacing figure, old and balding, who appears behind young Alice when she is unaware. Gebbie's second frame of him shows Alice being reflected in his glasses, as a bead of sweat runs down the center of his forehead. Alice continues to be represented in a series of fragments in reflections—her young legs and bloomers in a puddle on the ground as he leads her away, a doorknob showing her foregrounded hand as he leads her into her house to molest her, and in a glass of wine that he pours for her (Moore and Gebbie 2006, chap. 9, pp. 2–4). Alice's eyes, as in Gebbie's earlier work, illustrate her anxiety and discomfort. In a fairly classic account of dissociation, she floats away from her body. Moore and Gebbie, however, depict her as coping by becoming another Alice who gives pleasure and comfort.

Alice psychologically escapes by fantasizing that Bunny's "hot hand" between her thighs is "hers," the other Alice's (chap. 9, p. 5). She imagines a sexual encounter with this other self. After Bunny leaves, Alice looks in the mirror. In one frame she is chillingly faceless, and in the next it is unclear which of the two Alices is the "real" one, the one who existed before the trauma (chap 9, p. 7). As she concludes her story, adult Alice says she later struggled to trust men, and her narrative has been condemned as subscribing to a pathological origin story of queer identity—the narrative of lesbianism emerging from abuse and of lesbianism as just a desire for self (Tonik 2016). While this is a fair criticism, one possible complication of this reading is that prior to the incident young Alice looks at her reflection in a stream as adult Alice recalls, "I was thoroughly infatuated with myself; this underwater girl amidst the blonde and drifting weed, her face was mine" (Moore and Gebbie 2006, chap. 9, p. 2). Her "infatuation" with herself *could* be taken as a precursor to discovering how she might give herself pleasure, normal sexual development disrupted by her molester. After her adventures and conversations with the other lost girls, she indicates that she is open to men, after decades of having intimate encounters only with women, suggesting that she needed a talking cure to come to terms with the abuse and embrace the idea of heterosexual encounters. At worst, this conforms to homophobic narratives that lesbians can be cured, but such a reading oddly imagines that expanding one's desires forecloses previous ones. If the text is intentionally baiting the feminist and queer reader, it is similar to some feminist comix that irreverently play with progressive orthodoxies.

One of the clear traditional scripts in Alice's story regards the effect of sexual abuse. Readers recognize that falling through the looking glass is an inversion of what should be, and as an allegory of abuse the trauma has turned her into the reverse of what she should be or could have been. *Lost Girls* begins with her disembodied voice telling a young lover that she cannot quite remember her story—she seems to be constructing sexual scripts from memory fragments—and that she recalls only that "there was something important, very *fragile*. But then a terrible *thing* happened and it got *broken*. Forever. Nobody could ever mend it. But what . . . ? Something about soldiers? The king's horses, the king's men . . . ?" (chap. 1, p. 2, ellipses in original). Readers are invited by the end of part 1 and Alice's tale to see her innocence as lost. Something was lost, but at the same time the text constantly resists innocence as an ideal. The abuse does seem to set Alice on a path of sexual adventure that eventually produces a sexually uninhibited older woman, a representation rarely seen or celebrated in US fictions. The sexual experiences she has with Dorothy and Wendy are treated as both fun and comforting. Same-sex desire is thus not treated as a substitute for the sexuality she should have. Alice's sexuality origin story does not celebrate abuse. She is, after all, "broken." But her story's illustration of how trauma can nonetheless create the conditions for unexpected connections and joy as a *response* to unforgivable and irreparable injury challenges narratives that doom survivors to unhappiness and dysfunction.

"Scared of Grown-Up Women"

To some extent the question of who the women would have become without the abuse haunts all the texts, but Wendy's story most strongly depicts the presence of alternative future selves in the present. Playing with the shadows from the original *Peter Pan* narrative, Moore and Gebbie present them as a manifestation of her unconscious.

Fragmentation is most associated with psychoanalysis in her narrative. The relationship between the child's (taboo, nonexistent) sexuality and the adult she becomes is an ongoing theme, just as it is foundational to psychoanalysis. Moore explicitly references psychoanalysis when Alice speaks to Wendy about her first encounter with Peter Pan, reimagined here as mutual masturbation while her brothers look on and masturbate as well. She fears that she is—and will be seen as—"deranged." "Fiddlesticks!" Alice replies. "Why, there is a notable professor of the mind currently practicing not far from here, in Vienna. He would find your image of flight perfectly acceptable and indeed appropriate" (chap. 8, p. 8). Wendy's account of a flying Peter, his erection, and both of their orgasms maps easily onto Freud's reading of flying as a symbolic representation of the erection moving against the force of gravity (Freud 1995, 358–59). Freud infamously treats women's orgasms as a lesser version of male desire and their dreams as an example of wish fulfillment and their desire to have what men have. But women are at the center of the psychoanalytic paradigm here and not broken for desiring what men possess. Placing Wendy at the center of the story disrupts the centrality of Peter as hero and a psychology that makes men the ideal, longed-for lost object. All these narratives turn to some extent on ideas about possibilities lost for survivors of child sexual abuse. If what Alice loses is herself, the fantasy around loss in *Peter Pan* is that Wendy loses her other half, represented by Peter as a love object and ideal kind of embodiment.

Biographical criticism has questioned J. M. Barrie's relationship to the Davies boys, who served as the inspiration for Peter Pan and whom he eventually adopted in spite of their mother's wishes in her will (Birkin 1979, 194–95). Barrie is as haunted by accusations of pedophilia as Dodgson, though many critics see his work and investment in the orphaned boys as not necessarily mapping onto what we would understand as pathological today because of the Victorian obsession with the child. But the "child" is gendered in both texts, with the ideal child being male in *Peter Pan*. All three of these children's texts have often lent themselves to psychoanalytic readings. Barrie's *Peter and Wendy* consistently references psychoanalytic ideas, and like Freud, it privileges boys as the primary desiring subjects that girls respond to.

Take, for example, Barrie's colorful and elaborate account of the child's mind:

> [It] is not only confused, but keeps going round all the time. There are zigzag lines on it, just like your temperature on a card, and these are probably roads in the island; for the Neverland is always more or less an island, with astonishing splashes of colour here and there, and coral reefs and rakish-looking craft in the offing, and savages and lonely lairs, and gnomes who are mostly tailors, and caves through which a river runs, and princes with six elder brothers, and a hut fast going to decay, and one very small old lady with a hooked nose. It would be an easy map if that were all; but there is

also first day at school, religion, fathers, the round pond, needlework, murderers, hangings, verbs that take the dative, chocolate pudding day, getting into braces, say ninety-nine, three-pence for pulling out your tooth yourself, and so on, and either these are part of the island or they are another map showing through, and it is all rather confusing, especially as nothing will stand still. (2011, 19)

A striking characteristic of this description is that it seems to depict fantasy and real life only in the present. There is little sense of time passing or which events are in the past. Does the child also hold on to the first day of school as a memory, or is it only one affective object among many? Peter Pan does not remember his history and has no sense of time, and this is part of his eternal youth. In contrast, readers are told in the very first paragraph that Wendy learns that she must grow up when she is two. The narrator of *Peter Pan* treats Wendy as a mournful subject—when she becomes an adult, the narrator tells readers not to "be sorry for her," as "she was one of the kind that likes to grow up" (181). And yet when Peter returns and takes her daughter, Jane, away for an adventure in Neverland to be his mother and help him clean, "something inside [Wendy] was crying 'Woman, Woman, let go of me'" (184). Barrie's Wendy and all the girls in her line are doomed to be mothers to the boy who will never grow up, and they mourn the lost girls they were.

Moore and Gebbie's revision of Wendy makes her girlhood something she is still coming to terms with, given sexual scripts that would deem her immoral. But she does not desire to return to her youth. Perpetual girlhood is not idealized. In this emphasis, *Lost Girls* builds on a long history of feminists condemning the construction of the ideal woman as one who has girl-like characteristics. It is a cultural pathology that places adult women in tension, conflict, or competition with their younger selves.[11]

Like Alice, Wendy has doubles, but they manifest as shadows instead of reflections. She and her husband are not sexually free with each other. She desires twin beds, and Gebbie visually depicts their subconscious as sexual shadows—a reference to the independence of shadows in *Peter Pan*. When they are having a mundane conversation as they bend, hold documents, and interact, their shadows depict their exchange as an encounter with fellatio and anal penetration (Moore and Gebbie, chap. 3, pp. 7–8). The tension between the everyday domestic interaction and their desires makes desire as commonplace as their conversation.

The line between the commonplace/open and the pathological/unconscious runs through Wendy's narrative, which references the rise of the "overly affectionate family" in the Victorian and Edwardian eras (Sigel 2005). She is sixteen when Peter, a boy with a "common" and "lower-class" accent (Moore and Gebbie 2006, chap. 8, p. 4), visits the Darlings, teaches her brothers mutual masturbation, and gives her an orgasm. Eventually she has encounters with other "lost boys" she meets in the park when she pretends to be their mother and then begins having a sexual relationship with her siblings. The text suggests that these taboo desires set her on a path for other taboo desires while constantly suppressing her own pathologies. An early sexual encounter between the adult Wendy and Alice is a nonconsent fantasy, with Alice dressed in men's clothing and berating Wendy for being a "prig" and for her middle-class hypocrisy. The older woman tears off Wendy's dress as she protests, but she soon pleasurably submits (chap. 12, p. 5). In her final story, she reveals that she also had rape fantasies about "Captain Hook," a sexual predator who rapes Annabelle/Tinker Bell and leaves her horribly injured.

Because Wendy is the only one of the three who expresses desire for violence, her story is also the most explicit articulation of the fact that women's sexual fantasies that combine pleasure and danger do not necessarily map onto desire for actual sexual practice.[12] While Peter conquers Hook in *Peter Pan and Wendy*—"Wendy, of course, had stood by taking no part in the fight" (Barrie 2011, 165)—it is young Wendy who vanquishes him in *Lost Girls*. Peter is understandably enraged after Annabelle is attacked, "strutting about furiously, blaming the hook-handed man, saying how he'd get revenge. How they'd dig a trap, or leap from ambush with knives. It was *exciting* him." His revenge fantasies seem childish to Wendy and make her angry, and she yells at him to *"grow up"* (Moore and Gebbie 2006, chap. 27, p. 2). This ends up signifying a gendered difference between Peter's fantasies of violence and retaliation and Wendy's fantasies of agency, the latter of which readers are cued to read as more mature. Wendy seeks Hook out, apparently intending to become a victim of sexual violence herself, but in the process comes to terms psychologically with the difference between sexual fantasy and desired sexual practice: "I—If I could *think* such things, then didn't I . . . *deserve* them, in some way? He was right behind me, clutching and cursing and telling me I knew I wanted it, I knew I wanted it. And though I kept running through the rain, heart hammering, I thought that he was *right*" (chap. 27, p. 4, ellipses in original). But after a number of fantasies of gang rape and incest run through her imagination, she realizes, "I could think about what I *liked*. That didn't mean I wanted it to *really* happen to me. That didn't mean that anyone could force it on me" (chap. 27, p. 5). As Gebbie draws this chase, Hook mirrors Wendy, an aesthetic choice that suggests her complicity with injuries she might experience in such fantasies. In reality, "Hook" is a business acquaintance of her father's and has short hair, but in the fantasy he looks like a pirate. In this fantasy, he encircles her from behind with his hook and hand, her breast bare and her vulva fantastically enlarged; Gebbie renders Hook's and Wendy's hair identical in style and blue-black color. By the time young Wendy turns the tables on Hook, she is a mature woman and appears to be the age of the adult Wendy who is narrating the story (chap. 27, p. 5). She stares Hook down, and her confrontation is a woman's fantasy far from the pirate vanquishing at the center of Barrie's fable (fig. 3):

> I—I pushed my bare cunt at him and asked if he didn't think it was too hairy, too old for him? Weren't my tits too much for someone who preferred flat little chests and bald little quims? Someone who was *scared* of grown-up women, thought they'd overwhelm him, swallow him? I worked my hips, spreading my furry vagina with my fingers, bellowing at him. "Children won't realize you're *inadequate*. You can pretend you're still young, like them, that the clock isn't *ticking. That's* why you fuck children, why you dye your hair. You're afraid of *women*. And you're afraid of getting *old*." (chap. 27, p. 5)

This evokes feminist comix that relished a feminist grotesque and gleefully embraced fantasies of emasculating feminists. In the page's final frame she is a barely clad Medusa in Hook's eye, clutching her vagina, her hair streaming behind her as she stands against a tree. Her righteous diatribe breaks him, and she leaves as he falls to the ground a broken man, rocking in the rain. The next day, she thinks it "might as well have been a dream" (chap. 27, p. 7).

Wendy's annihilation of a violent rapist is as much a fantasy as Peter's but is nonetheless particularly feminist and requires an adult, woman-presenting subject. Key to the narrative are the ways in which

366 American Literature

Figure 3 Wendy confronts Hook. From Moore and Gebbie (2006), *Lost Girls*, chap. 27, p. 5

the adult Wendy, the teenage Wendy, and the desiring Wendy (often signified by Wendy's shadow) are conterminous and not the same. Some of her desires are part of her but do not reflect what she wants to happen to her physical body. She moves into her adult self in the memory, making it uncertain when, or if, the resistance occurred. But this negotiation of multiple selves that remain in tension with one another is still part of her path to health. The summer of sexual exploration and the force of her desires have frightened her. Perhaps the fear has emerged because Peter is actually a young sexual predator or because she has crossed a line with her brothers that leaves her unable to differentiate between sexual fantasy and unhealthy sexual practices.

Wendy's fantasies are the most suspect, as they are presented as real. Alice has become an addict, and we are often invited to read her stories through a haze produced by substance abuse. The fantasy in Dorothy's story is allegorical. Given the strange appearance of Peter, the line between real and fantasy is most obscured in Wendy's story. She nonetheless suggests that she achieved some emotional maturity either that summer or in the story as she reflects back on it. But despite her evolution in parsing out the role of fantasies in her sexual life, Wendy seems unable to escape the Victorian restriction against speaking sex with her son, not wanting him to be "taken away by sex, by the wilderness, by the working class. By *shadows*. That will never happen, never. Never." But Gebbie's art suggests the impossibility of repressing sexual desire or holding back the "shadows" (chap. 27, p. 7). While seemingly presenting a respectable picture of a young mother clasping her gown and looking down at her baby, the shadow behind her is an erotic one, nipple protruding, a hand concealed somewhere in the front of her body, its actions covered by the dark.

"Sounds Rather Healthy"

Dorothy's double is the most hidden of all, as she initially seems to be most comfortable with herself and her history. She is the first to tell her story to the group, and for most of *Lost Girls* her sexual experience seems unmarked by taboo. Each part of the narrative suggests a confident young woman discovering her sexuality without abuse, incest, or the threat of sexual violence; as an adult, Dorothy demonstrates a frank and open attitude toward sexuality that, according to Alice, "sounds rather *healthy*" (chap. 14, p. 8). Given the importance of the British class contexts to Alice's and Wendy's stories, the text implies that Dorothy's "healthy" approach to sexuality and her comfort with the older woman's overtures is because of her American difference.

Dorothy's story seems much more mundane and everyday, and comes closest to the unabashed feminist revision of Americana in early feminist comix. The tornado is both "real" and an allegory of young Dorothy's first experience masturbating, with "a tornado inside o' me, and outside too" (chap. 7, p. 4). But afterward, "everthin' was all different," and she feels as if she has "been picked up and twisted around, then put down someplace else in some whole other country." She is elated by the "new ground" she stands on, "where anythin' was like to happen." And she spends the next few years "explorin' all that new territory" (chap. 7, p. 7). Gebbie depicts Dorothy sitting on the floor, disheveled and slightly bemused by the experience of her first orgasm, the image suggestive of a girl struggling to clean up after some random house mishap. The aesthetic choice rejects a binary between innocence and sexuality.

Young Dorothy later admires herself in the mirror as she masturbates, exhibiting a rare sexual confidence for a teenage girl. Compared with this scene, Alice's reflection scene seems less of a depiction of pathological lesbian discourse. Then Dorothy seduces the farmhands. While Alice and Wendy show very little agency in their stories, cast as victims or recipients of the attentions and directions of more knowledgeable sexual partners, Dorothy seeks out sexual adventures. She does not know what to do initially when she pursues a farmhand who bails hay and "smelled *blonde*." This version of the Scarecrow lasts only "a couple o' minutes" (chap. 14, p. 3). During later trysts with the Scarecrow, adult Dorothy recalls, she sometimes "reach[ed] for more an' it weren't there," or wanted to talk, "but it was like he'd squirted all his conversation out his dick" (chap. 14, p. 4). Young Dorothy may be at the center of the first volume of the Oz series, but she is nonetheless a helper figure. Evoking a feminist comix framework that took pleasure in role reversals objectifying male gazes, she sees the farmhand as a "ragdoll, or somethin' you stick out in a field to scare the birds." That is nonetheless an unsatisfactory role for her, as she desires "to be doin' it with somebody who had real thoughts an' feelin's just like I did" (chap. 14, p. 5).

If the Scarecrow is Moore and Gebbie's version of the blonde bimbo, the Lion is their version of a man who talks a great deal about his sexual prowess but has very little experience. He talks about eating "her little pussy" within young Dorothy's hearing, but the wise-beyond-her-years Dorothy knows that he does this only to intimidate her (chap. 18, p. 2). She approaches him, and he is clearly the intimidated and fearful one, which she finds attractive. Adult Dorothy recalls that she "made him scared" and "tame" but that by the end of their encounter she "made him brave" (chap. 18, p. 5). Young Dorothy's attentions make the Lion into a man, one who is better equipped to deal with other women. Dorothy's desire for someone with more "mettle" (chap. 18, p. 5) leads her to the Tin Man, who is "cold and heartless" and "mechanical" and who "handled me like hardware" (chap. 24, p. 2). They do the "dirtiest thing[s]" she has ever heard of, but that is "the road I was headed down, I wanted to follow it as far as it *went*" (chap. 24, p. 5). Despite her youthful promiscuity, her honest expression of her desire for sex, always signified by the removal of her white cotton underwear, makes her introduction to sexuality seem less taboo (and injurious) than that experienced by Alice and Wendy. While the play with objects, bestiality, and robot fetishism is implied by the splash pages that accompany her stories, these desires reside very clearly in the realm of fantasies about consensual sexual acts in which she is an agent.

Dorothy's experiences thus seem sexually precocious but are a healthy counter to the traumatic childhoods of Wendy and Alice. However, Dorothy turns out to be the most unreliable narrator of all. Her last story reveals that her narrative is also marked by sexual taboo and abuse. The man who she said was her uncle and guardian is revealed to be her father, and she discloses incest. The reveal that Dorothy is an unreliable narrator is the culminating moment of rising distrust of all these stories' revisions, with the visuals often cuing the reader into the prevaricating or obfuscating nature of their speech. Dorothy's double is her untraumatized self, a relief from the origin stories and struggles of her companions. That Dorothy also feels shame and that she could not speak abuse until after extensive time with people who had revealed their own trauma demonstrate that trauma can obstruct intimacy and connection even between people who have experienced similar injuries.

These women push through that obstruction by using fantasy to embrace multiple selves. Each narrative suggests an interpretive frame we might use to understand the way fantasy might work for healing. Alice recounts going into her mind when she is sexually abused, and we know that what we see is a fantasy and a mode of escape that distances her from the injury. As Alice recounts later experiences with drug addiction, representations of her world seem most consistently to end in a place of unreality in an attempt to escape pain. Wendy's accounts of incest go far beyond the realistic portrayal of the siblings' sexual play we see in "Doin' It," entering clearly into the realm of inappropriate sexual activity. Young Wendy eventually confronts Peter for his immaturity and vanquishes Hook, and while it is unclear what is "true" in her fantasy, it is clear that aggressively resisting and fighting, as opposed to escaping, is the fantasy that proves cathartic for her.

In the end, the fantasy that allows Dorothy to deal with her history is the story that provides an adult moral for the stories told about child sexual abuse. Young Dorothy's father takes her to the city, ostensibly for therapy mandated by her stepmother after she learns that Dorothy had a group sexual encounter with the young men on the farm. But he begins having sex with his daughter during this trip and continues it afterward. Dorothy's eyes, previously filled with pleasure and joy, look empty as her father abuses her sexually at home. Adult Dorothy says that she then saw him "like he really *was*. An' with him *doin'* me, farm life didn't feel the *same* anymore. No place did. There was no place that was like *home*, y'know?" Moore's revision of the famous line, with Gebbie's use of a dead-eyed aesthetic as young Dorothy looks out tragically instead of dreamily into the distance, emphasizes the reality of home as a place of danger and injury for many girls and women (chap. 28, p. 7). No place in Dorothy's house can be a place of safety or joy for her, and she needs to leave home to find freedom. Home is not ideal for any of these women. It is the place where Alice is first abused. It is the site of sexual experiences that cause Wendy shame. And it is the place that Dorothy longs to escape, not the idealized place to which she desires to return. The place that brings her comfort is the hotel, with other women negotiating their own traumas.

The sleight of hand of the reimagined stories is that Moore and Gebbie reframe what these iconic girls lost and in so doing question the normative constructions of these attachments. If Alice loses herself in the topsy-turvy world, Wendy loses her first love, and Dorothy loses the idea of home, then in all the stories they imagine that they can find themselves, intimacy, and a home away from home in the community they find with one another. The normative looks less like integration than constant tension—between word and image, truth and fantasy, and varied selves shaping the future but not requiring an incorporation that conforms to normative scripts of sexual health.

Lost Girls is a controversial text producing polarizing responses, and some people read the violence against girls as symptomatic of misogyny in some of Moore's work.[13] But it has a great deal in common with a tradition of feminist comics of which Gebbie was a part. It is a return to comics that can imagine a comics of women's liberation in which the perverse can be an affective and psychological tool for freedom. By also telling stories about the injuries of sexual abuse, Moore and Gebbie do not gloss over the violence against women or girls. Instead, they treat it as everyday, something touching the ideals of all their idealized protagonists. By making violence omnipresent, they represent it as something that does not irrevocably block the path to sexual health. The recognition of injury and pleasure shapes the utopian imagination of the text, drawing and speaking sexual joy for women despite the ubiquity of violence. And by suggesting that "good" girls and women might have unspeakable fantasies, the isolation engendered by scripts suggesting what they cannot think or imagine is lessened, creating space for women who find community in speaking the unspeakable. It is a generic mash-up of ostensibly dissimilar genres—children's literature, pornography, and feminist tracts—all texts shaped by the wish that, after you experience trauma, a community of women who care about your joy and your stories will be waiting sans judgment or shame. The fantasy of *Lost Girls* is that all survivors of sexual trauma can find such connections, resist normative cultural narratives that cannot acknowledge the complexity of sexual development, and refuse to embrace the label of lost innocence. When brokenness can be the norm for many, we can visualize health and futurity in transformative ways.

Rebecca Wanzo is an associate professor of women, gender, and sexuality studies at Washington University, St. Louis, and a founding board member of the Comics Studies Society. She is the author of *The Suffering Will Not Be Televised: African American Women and Sentimental Political Storytelling* (SUNY Press, 2009). She is currently working on a book manuscript titled *The Content of Our Caricature: African American Comics and Citizenship*.

Notes

1. *Peter Pan and Wendy* was initially a play, *Peter Pan, or, The Boy Who Wouldn't Grow Up* (1904). Famous examples of Victorian and Edwardian pornography include William Lazenby's *The Pearl* (1879–80) and Aubrey Beardsley's work in the *Yellow Book* (1894–97), whose style Gebbie clearly copies in depicting a text the characters are reading. For an overview of the pornographic politics of the period, see Sigel 2002.
2. Parts of *Lost Girls* were originally published in the comic *Taboo* in issues #5 (1991), #6 (1992), and #7 (1992).
3. In US federal law, "any visual depiction of sexually explicit conduct involving a minor (persons less than 18 years old)" counts as child pornography or "child sexual abuse images" (US Department of Justice, 2015).
4. Cortney E. Lollar (2013, 368–69) rejects this justification for heavier sentencing, arguing that while "it is indisputable that there is some ongoing emotional harm to individuals depicted in child pornography, given that their images are being circulated in the public sphere, where they have no ability to control the dissemination of the images," social science literature does not conclude that "the circulation of these images is more damaging than the actual abuse that led to the creation of the pornography."
5. Japan did not ban child pornography until 2014 and had a higher number of child pornography victims than a number of other countries. And while people might perceive that the audience of much of the manga with violence toward girls and women is made up of men, there is unsurprisingly a market for sadism and masochism in women's comics. See Jones 2002. This speaks to the history of scholarship about romance novels and other "women's" genres, in which sexual violence, although not characterized as such by consumers, is part of the pleasure they glean from the texts. See Radway 1991.
6. For examples of discussions of *Lost Girls* that relegate Gebbie to secondary status, see Faber 2008; Gaiman 2006; and Thill 2009; Thill does not even mention Gebbie's name.
7. I use *feminist comix* to reference comics that were part of the movement and production of underground comix. This period is usually understood as beginning in 1968 and ending in the late 1970s. However, *Wimmen's Comix* did continue past this period, and many people use the term *comix* to refer to "alternative" comics in general. Feminist comix should be understood as part of feminist comics and cartooning more broadly.
8. The title for this series had two spellings: For most of its run, the official title was *Wimmen's Comix*, but in 1992 it was changed to *Wimmin's Comix* for the final issue of the series.
9. See, for example, Scott 2010. On jouissance produced by abjection, see Kristeva 1982.

10 See Wolf 2007 and Pugh 2008; Pugh argues that all the building blocks for queer identification can be found in the Oz books.
11 The very first comic story in *Wimmen's Comix* is "Goldie: A Neurotic Woman," by Aline Kominsky. The story maps the psychological development of a girl as she becomes a woman. Kominsky shows the relationship between girlhood and adulthood by mapping the adult face onto the young girl. She is happy as her parents' "princess" and feels loved. As she gets older, she struggles with the relationship between her past and present. Kominsky also provides a mind map, showing Goldie's mental development divided by primary influences. Through age eighteen, her parents direct "praise," "demands," "brainwashing," and "values" to her head, and her husband has an impact on her shaped by "dependence," "paranoia," and "despair" until she is twenty-one. The future of her mind is a "void of fear" and "uncertainty," but she then moves on to the future, not trying to assimilate those influences but imagining, as symbolized through her car ride in the last frame, freedom from "trying to please other people" (Kominsky 1972).
12 See Carol Vance 1984a, especially essays by Vance (1984b), Muriel Dimen (1984), and Paula Webster (1984).
13 Fans have been particularly angry with Moore's infamous treatment of Batgirl in *The Killing Joke* (1988), in which she is shot and paralyzed for life, and with the sexism in *League of Extraordinary Gentlemen*. Moore discusses this controversy over his treatment of women in his work in Flood 2014.

References

Aldridge, Jan, et al. 2004. "Using a Human Figure Drawing to Elicit Information from Alleged Victims of Sexual Abuse." *Journal of Consulting and Clinical Psychology* 72, no. 2: 304–16.
Barder, Ollie. 2016. "Japanese Response to UN Proposed Ban for Media Depicting Sexual Violence is Cogent and Sane." *Forbes*, March 3.
Barrie, J. M. 2011. *The Annotated Peter Pan*. New York: Norton.
Bernstein, Robin. 2011. *Racial Innocence: Performing American Childhood from Slavery to Civil Rights*. New York: New York Univ. Press.
Birkin, Andrew. 2003. *J. M. Barrie and the Lost Boys: The Real Story behind Peter Pan*. New Haven, CT: Yale Univ. Press. First published 1979.
Dimen, Muriel. 1984. "Politically Correct? Politically Incorrect?" In Vance 1984a, 138–64.
Everson, Mark D., and Barbara W. Boat. 1994. "Putting the Anatomical Doll Controversy in Perspective: An Examination of the Major Uses and Criticisms of the Dolls in Child Sexual Abuse Evaluations." *Child Abuse and Neglect* 18, no. 2: 113–29.

Faber, Michael. 2008. "Released at Last." *Guardian*, January 5.
Fischel, Joseph J. 2010. "Per Se or Power: Age and Sexual Consent." *Yale Journal of Law and the Humanities* 22, no. 2: 279–341.
Flood, Allison. 2014. "Superheroes a 'Cultural Catastrophe,' Says Comics Guru Alan Moore." *Guardian*, January 21.
Foucault, Michel. 1978. *An Introduction*. Vol. 1 of *The History of Sexuality*. Translated by Robert Hurley. New York: Vintage.
Freud, Sigmund. 1995. *The Basic Writings of Sigmund Freud*. Translated and edited by A. A. Brill. New York: Modern Library. First published 1938.
Gaiman, Neil. 2006. "Lost Girls Redux." *Neil Gaiman*, June 19. http://journal.neilgaiman.com/2006/06/lost-girls-redux.html.
Gebbie, Melinda. 1975. "Ten Cents a Dance." *Wimmen's Comix*, no. 6. In Robbins 2016, 245–46.
Gebbie, Melinda, Alan Moore, and Matt Green. 2012. "The Critical Currency of Caricature." Panel discussion at the University of Nottingham, Nottingham, UK. Posted June 14. www.youtube.com/watch?v=93sV5XGLmgQ.
Hatfield, Charles. 2005. *Alternative Comics: An Emerging Literature*. Jackson: Univ. Press of Mississippi.
Iser, Wolfgang. 1978. *The Implied Reader: Patterns of Communication in Prose Fiction from Bunyan to Beckett*. Baltimore, MD: Johns Hopkins Univ. Press.
Jones, Gretchen. 2002. "Ladies' Comics: Japan's Not-So-Underground Market in Pornography for Women." *U.S.-Japan Women's Journal (English Supplement)*, no. 22: 3–31.
Kincaid, James. 1998. *Erotic Innocence: The Culture of Child Molesting*. Durham, NC: Duke Univ. Press.
Kominsky, Aline. 1972. "Goldie: A Neurotic Woman." *Wimmen's Comix*, no. 1. In Robbins 2016, 39–43.
Kristeva, Julia. 1982. *Powers of Horror: An Essay on Abjection*. Translated by Leon S. Roudiez. New York: Columbia Univ. Press.
Levine, Judith. 2002. *Harmful to Minors: The Perils of Protecting Parents from Sex*. Minneapolis: Univ. of Minnesota Press.
Lollar, Courtney E. 2013. "Child Pornography and the Restitution Revolution." *Journal of Criminal Law and Criminology* 103, no. 2: 343–406.
MacKinnon, Catharine. 1991. "Reflections on Sex Equality under Law." *Yale Law Journal* 100, no. 5: 1281–328.
———. 1993. *Only Words*. Cambridge, MA: Harvard Univ. Press.
McCloud, Scott. 1994. *Understanding Comics: The Invisible Art*. New York: Harper Perennial.
Millet, Catherine. 1975. "Where Have You Been You Little Pig?" *Wimmen's Comix*, no. 5. In Robbins 2016, 196.
Moore, Alan, and Melinda Gebbie. 2006. *Lost Girls*. Marietta, GA: Top Shelf.
Pugh, Tison. 2008. "'There Lived in the Land of Oz Two Queerly Made Men': Queer Utopianism and Antisocial Eroticism in L. Frank Baum's Oz Series." *Marvels and Tales* 22, no. 2: 217–39.

Radway, Janice. 1991. *Reading the Romance: Women, Patriarchy, and Literature*. Chapel Hill: Univ. of North Carolina Press.

Robbins, Trina, ed. 2016. *The Complete Wimmen's Comix*. 2 vols. Seattle: Fantagraphics.

Robson, Catherine. 2001. *Men in Wonderland: The Lost Girlhood of the Victorian Gentleman*. Princeton, NJ: Princeton Univ. Press.

Rosenkrantz, Patrick. 2008. *Rebel Visions: The Underground Comix Revolution, 1967–1972*. Seattle: Fantagraphics.

Scott, Darieck. 2010. *Extravagant Abjection: Blackness, Power, and Sexuality in the African American Literary Imagination*. New York: New York Univ. Press.

Sigel, Lisa Z. 2002. *Governing Pleasures: Pornography and Social Change in England, 1815–1914*. Piscataway, NJ: Rutgers Univ. Press.

———. 2005. "The Rise of the Overly Affectionate Family: Incestuous Pornography and Displaced Desire in the Edwardian Middle Class." In *International Exposure: Perspectives on Modern European Pornography, 1800–2000*, edited by Lisa Z. Sigel, 100–124. New Brunswick, NJ: Rutgers Univ. Press.

Sneddon, Laura. 2013. "Stripped: Melinda Gebbie—*Lost Girls*, Pornography and Censorship." *The Beat: The News Blog of Comics Culture*, September 9. www.comicsbeat.com/stripped-melinda-gebbie-lost-girls-pornography-censorship/.

Sutton, Joyce Farmer. 1975. "Doin' It!" *Wimmen's Comix*, no. 5. In Robbins 2016, 193–95.

Thill, Scott. 2009. "Seven More Alan Moore Comics That Could Get Librarians Fired." *Wired*, November 13.

Tonik, Ginnis. 2016. "It's Porn, but Is It Art? A *Lost Girls* Retrospective." *Women Write about Comics*, April 4. http://womenwriteaboutcomics.com/2016/04/04/its-porn-but-is-it-art-a-lost-girls-retrospective/.

US Department of Justice. 2017. "Child Pornography." Criminal Division, Child Exploitation and Obscenity Section. July 25. www.justice.gov/criminal-ceos/child-pornography.

Vance, Carol S., ed. 1984a. *Pleasure and Danger: Exploring Female Sexuality*. Boston: Routledge and Kegan Paul.

———. 1984b. "Pleasure and Danger: Toward a Politics of Sexuality" In Vance 1984a, 21–27.

Van der Kolk, Bessel. 2015. *The Body Keeps Score: The Brain, Mind, and Body in the Healing of Trauma*. New York: Penguin.

Webster, Paula. 1984. "The Forbidden: Eroticism and Taboo." In Vance 1984a, 385–98.

Wolf, Stacy. 2007. "Wicked Divas, Musical Theater, and Internet Girl Fans." *Camera Obscura*, no. 65: 39–71.

Kate McCullough "The Complexity of Loss Itself": The Comics Form and *Fun Home*'s Queer Reparative Temporality

Abstract This article assesses the queer world-making potentiality of the comics form as demonstrated in Alison Bechdel's 2006 graphic memoir *Fun Home*. By deploying the temporal openings of the graphic form, *Fun Home* challenges the putative fixity of heteronormative family time and the temporality of kinship lines more broadly. Bechdel represents this queering of generation and kinship as a constituent part of the young Alison's coming-of-age as a queer comics artist; this temporal reworking simultaneously makes possible a queer reparative web of affiliation. Building on Eve Kosofsky Sedgwick's model of reparative reading, I demonstrate how *Fun Home*'s form produces a version of reparation that emerges from a shared artistry and embraces ambivalent affective responses to the past. Ultimately, Bechdel produces a queer feminist reparative reading that understands futurity's potential as complex and grounded in both the pain and pleasure of the queer body.

Keywords comics, queer theory, temporality, affect theory, gender, narrative form

> The desire of a reparative impulse . . . is additive and accretive. Its fear, a realistic one, is that the culture surrounding it is inadequate or inimical to its nurture; it wants to assemble and confer plenitude on an object that will then have resources to offer to an inchoate self.
> —Eve Kosofsky Sedgwick, "Paranoid Reading and Reparative Reading; or, You're So Paranoid, You Probably Think This Introduction Is about You" (1997)

Introduction

In elaborating the concept of the reparative, Eve Kosofsky Sedgwick (1997) makes clear that it is temporally structured; she emphasizes that reparative reading depends on a sense of the future as excavated from an open past, asserting that having "the room to realize that the future may be different from the present" (24) produces the possibility that the past "could have happened differently from the way it actually did" (25) and, reciprocally, that one must remain aware of the "realm of what *might have happened but didn't* . . . otherwise, the entire possibility of things *happening differently* can be lost" (37). Sedgwick's discussion of the specifically temporal aspect of a reparative reading is brief, but it can help us understand why the comics form in particular brings to queer theory a unique and powerful narrative locus for explorations of queer temporality. For the queer temporal openings inherent in the comics form provide a generative medium for queer world making and a potentially reparative one at that; comics' unique combination of the visual and textual allows for the articulation of aspects of a queered temporality that cannot be achieved by other solely visual or textual forms.

Alison Bechdel's 2006 *Fun Home: A Family Tragicomic* offers a particularly acute instance of the way that the queerness of the comics form enables a reparative queer world making for its protagonist. Although Bechdel is only one of the many talented queer feminist cartoonists to appear in the past half century, her memoir is notable in its illumination of the formal potential of the comics form, a potential that renders it a medium from which queer scholars have much to learn.[1] For what is queerest about this memoir is less the sexuality of its protagonist or even the sexuality of her putatively straight father and more the temporalities through which the story is told. Furthermore, in attending to the formal possibilities of comics, we gain a new understanding of temporality's intricate dependence on forms of expression, in both visual and textual structures.

While scholars have productively assessed both the recursive structure of *Fun Home*'s narrative and the thematics of the archive in it, I will focus here on the interplay of form and story, the ways in which the temporal openings inherent in the comic form itself make possible a queer recasting of time.[2] By deploying the temporal openings of the graphic form, *Fun Home* challenges the putative fixity of heteronormative family time and the temporality of kinship lines more broadly. Bechdel represents this queering of generation and kinship as a constituent part of the young Alison's coming-of-age as a comics artist; this temporal reworking simultaneously makes possible a reparative web of affiliation. I see the graphic form itself as the crucial condition for the text's production of a reparative reading of that past: ultimately, the story Bechdel tells of both her father's and her own sexuality relies on the comics form to produce a queerly ambivalent yet healing account of Alison's life and her father's suicide.

Through the potential temporal openings built into the comics form's unique blending of verbal and visual, Bechdel creates a protagonist who is both within generational family time and in excess of it, scrambling the terms of normative generations while simultaneously embodying what Carolyn Dinshaw (Dinshaw et al. 2007, 190) calls "the present's irreducible multiplicity." Although it includes an account of the young Alison's coming-out, this narrative is emphatically not structured as a conventional coming-out story, and its departure from such a narrative structure depends on a representation of a queer temporality that includes simultaneous multiple versions of the past, multiple temporalities within the present, and multiple simultaneous relationships to a given past moment. At the level of the text, this deployment of the graphic form makes possible the production of a reparative relationship between the protagonist and her past, a production that, in recasting the terms of generations, creates a subject who emerges from a past that was never stable and whose version of futurity is also not stable but nonetheless shimmers with potentiality.

More broadly, Bechdel's reparative stance might also be taken as hailing queer theory's attention, reminding us of the queer potentiality of the comics form itself. Comics as a genre might well be the ideal venue for an exploration of queer time, given the fundamental importance of sequence to the form. Comics critic Scott McCloud (1993, 9) refines Will Eisner's oft-cited description of comics as "sequential art" by specifying it as "juxtaposed pictorial and other images in deliberate sequence, intended to convey information and/or to produce an aesthetic response in the viewer." Hillary Chute and Marianne DeKoven (2006, 769) underscore the temporal-spatial comics connection, observing, "The form's fundamental syntactical operation is the representation of time as space on the page."[3] The form itself thus enables a visual representation of the passage of time, but beyond that it also allows for a reshuffling of the chronology of time, as, for example, in its ability to represent past, present, and future as visually coterminous via three sequential panels. Moreover, the relationship between image and text provides a formal opportunity for the scrambling of temporal registers. This temporal play between verbal and visual narrative is perhaps especially acute in the comics form known as the autographic memoir or autobiography. This is partly due to the formal split built into autobiography in general, in the temporal gap between the narrating present subject and the narrated past self. But the visual form of the graphic memoir multiplies that split, for the multiple moments in time and the multiple "I"s who inhabit them are represented both by the split between the verbal and visual narratives and, simultaneously, within the visual narrative.[4]

Employing form to enact a queer hermeneutics centrally concerned with issues of memory, *Fun Home* takes full advantage of the structural potential of the comics form, a nonchronological potential that Eisner (2008, 28) argues "is constructed like memory itself—jumping back and forth in time." *Recursive* is perhaps the most used term to describe *Fun Home*'s form and the ways it reveals central events or pieces of information (Alison's coming-out to her parents and her mother's revelation of her father's affairs with underage boys, in particular) in a partial form, only to return later to those events with more detail. However, Bechdel makes use of a variety of temporal strategies, including prolepsis and analepsis, and deploys them at both the diegetic level of the story and the level of individual images and panels.[5] That the structural asynchrony of the text enables an interpretive mining of the past from the standpoint of the present is apparent from a comment Bechdel made in an interview. Responding to Chris Mautner's inquiry about the "cyclical nature" of the text, Bechdel (quoted in Mautner 2008) observed: "It became clear very early on that I couldn't tell the story chronologically. I tried to put the events in order and there were so many things that I wanted to say about each of them that I kept going off on these tangents and I realized that wasn't going to work. What interested me most about the story was not what happened but my ideas about what had happened." The chronology of "what happened," thus, is secondary to the interpretation of "what happened," a shift in focus that throws the "what happened" itself into question and foregrounds instead a potentiality inherent in the "ideas about what had happened." The method of interpretation itself—the hermeneutic of the text—is thus reflected in the nonchronological narrative form.

These "ideas" enact a certain form of queer hermeneutics at work in *Fun Home*. The young Alison certainly functions as what Kathryn Bond Stockton (2009, 13) identifies as the figure of the queer child, whose temporal potential emphasizes "contours of growing that don't bespeak continuance." Further, Stockton's observation that the "child is precisely who we are not and, in fact, never were. It is the act of adults looking back" provides an apt description of Alison, Bechdel's child protagonist, whose words and images appear within the visually depicted diegesis, and Bechdel (2006, 5), the presumed narrator of the memoir, whose words occur in the voice-over text appearing above the frames.[6] And yet, Alison's temporal queerness goes well beyond the backward birth implied by the out-queer adult narrator's looking back on the not-yet-out child, for the child Alison's queerness inheres not simply in her sexuality but in a certain hermeneutical approach to reading her present; that is, the interpretive method of *Fun Home* is constituted by an attunement to how the present moment—always unstable and never fully knowable—might open onto temporal multiples. In the rendering of the queer child Alison's relations to her multiple temporalities, a rendering that draws (literally and figuratively) on comics' conventions as well as the figure of the comics artist, *Fun Home* recasts the temporality of kinship lines more broadly and consequently enables the production of a queer reparative relationship to the narrator's past. This relationship emerges from an affectively mixed vision of the past, one in which the protagonist recognizes both an identification with and an alienation from her parents and in which she sees both pleasure and pain in the marital bargain her parents made. It is *Fun Home*'s use of the temporal potential of the comics form, ultimately, that allows for the production of this queer reparative temporal vision; as such *Fun Home* stands as a primer on how to read comics queerly, how to see and deploy queerly the form's temporal openings.

Scrambled Time, Scrambled Kinship

Bechdel interrupts the generational lockstep of familial relations by variously repositioning the temporal relationship of parents and child. Through a sophisticated interplay of text and image, panel size and placement, Bechdel figures Alison and her parents coterminously in the past; she represents the same present moment as evoking differing temporalities for parent and child; and she inverts the parent-child relationship and locates it within a narrative temporal pause. All three strategies challenge the temporal fixity of heteronormative kinship configurations, producing openings for a reparative reconfiguring of the queer child's relation to the family. And all three suggest the extent to which heteronormativity relies on temporal norms, what Elizabeth Freeman (2010, 3) terms *chrononormativity*, and thus how disruptive to such normativity comics can be.

That comics call attention to the production of the visual in a way that other visual forms do not and thus that comics foreground temporality's dependence on the visual are made apparent in a brief but powerful sequence of frames concerning the narrator's fantasy of what her own life might have been like had she lived in the 1950s. Indeed, this sequence of frames perfectly exemplifies the reliance of Bechdel's reparative reading of her father on the graphic narrative form. Following a frame in which the adult Alison, now living in New York, reads about the history of the 1950s lesbian scene (a scene coterminous with her parents' courtship in New York), two vertical panels illustrate that 1950s historical moment in a street scene outside Chumley's, a Greenwich Village bar that Bruce and Helen frequented (Bechdel 2006, 108; see fig. 1). The historical reference point of Chumley's, set in and here emblematic of the Village, evokes what Christopher Nealon (2001, 145) elsewhere calls "the set of possibilities Greenwich Village suggests. . . . After World War II . . . a destination for thousands of young people, many of them gay and lesbian." In the first of these two large panels, we look over the shoulders of young Bruce and Helen as they approach the bar and a dyke walks down the sidewalk toward them; in the second panel the dyke, in profile in the foreground, walks by them as Helen enters the bar, back turned, and Bruce, holding the bar door open for Helen, turns to watch the dyke. Taken on their own, these images suggest both Helen's lack of interest in or denial of and Bruce's fascination with the queerness of the Village (represented by the dyke). Chumley's, as a longtime gathering spot for literary figures and journalists, embodies the bohemian atmosphere of the Village, an alluring atmosphere for Alison's parents, given their interest in art, literature, and theater. But if Helen is drawn to the bohemian nature of the Village, Bruce's long look at the passing dyke suggests an equal interest in the place's queer codes. Moreover, the rendering of Helen with her back turned indicates that she either does not notice or is actively ignoring both the queerness of the setting and Bruce's interest. Thus far, this image would seem to position Bruce in a temporality of a pre-Stonewall closet: his desiring look follows the queer object while he overtly enacts heteronormativity. But the temporality of these images exceeds that reading, in part because of the impact of the narrator's comment and in part because of the spatial location of the frames.

Fun Home's Queer Reparative Temporality 383

> WOULD I HAVE HAD THE GUTS TO BE ONE OF THOSE EISENHOWER-ERA BUTCHES? OR WOULD I HAVE MARRIED AND SOUGHT SUCCOR FROM MY HIGH SCHOOL STUDENTS?

Figure 1 From Bechdel (2006), *Fun Home: A Family Tragicomic*, 108

The frames' importance is signaled by their size (together they take up about two-thirds of the page) but also by their location: they occupy the top of a left-hand page in the book, a site of potential visual surprise, as the reader, moving from the previous page's bottom image, turns the page and sees the top left frame. In this case, the previous page's image shows the adult Alison, in 1980s New York, reading about the 1950s lesbian "bar raids and the illegal cross-dressing," wondering in a thought bubble, "If the cops searched me, could I pass the three-articles-of-women's-clothing rule?" (Bechdel 2006, 107; see fig. 2). This question, posed above an image of an androgynously dressed Alison on the subway next to a punk rock couple, can be read in relation to her contemporary sartorial choices, her enactment of a particular 1980s soft butch gendered bodily presentation. But the page turn to the following frames continues this speculation over the images of the young Bruce and Helen at Chumley's; the page turn thus transposes a 1980s textual-visual moment onto a 1950s image, reframing the adult Alison's gender in the context of her parents' youth. Over the image of her parents approaching the oncoming butch, the narrator asks, "Would I have had the guts to be one of those Eisenhower-era butches?" while over the image of her father gazing at the butch behind her mother's back, the text reads, "Or would I have married and sought succor from my high school students?" (108). The text here works in conjunction with the images to identify the narrator with both the butch and her father, respectively.

Here, the dialectic between image and text opens a space for a queer temporality in excess of a pre- and post-Stonewall binary, since in conjunction with the text, the image of the street scene can be read as Bruce gazing at a 1950s Alison, a queerly coterminous father and daughter inhabiting the space of the 1950s Village as imagined by the twenty-first-century Bechdel. And the vehicle of this temporal doubling back and of the reparative compassion with which it allows the narrator to consider both Bruce and Helen is here specifically the materiality of the gendered butch body. For if in the opening image of adult Alison on the subway her thought bubble ("If the cops searched me, could I pass the three-articles-of-women's-clothing rule?") suggests the difference between the 1980s, in which a woman may legally wear either punk fashion or men's clothes in public, and the 1950s, where butch women were subject to police harassment and violence under a law compelling women to wear at least three items of women's clothing, then the page turn's production of the visual shock of the jump back in time identifies the narrator with the 1950's butch who would have been subject to those laws (see fig. 1).

A mobility of desire and identification operates here, a relay between the visual and the textual, as well as a relay among characters; both the narrator and the young Bruce can be read as identifying with the butch across temporal moments, while Helen, remaining (purposely?) blind to the action, protects a fragile heterosexual privilege. At the same time, the mobility of Bruce's desire and its opaque and perhaps multiple objects allow for the mobility of the reader's eye, as well as for a queered erotics of the scene. Temporal mobility serves as a constituent part of the queerness of these erotics (as demonstrated by Alison's identification across time with the butch figure whom her young father can be read as desiring) and also, simultaneously, produces a

Figure 2 From Bechdel (2006), *Fun Home: A Family Tragicomic*, 107

shift in identification. That is, while the 1980s Alison reading on the subway might be seen as identifying with the 1950s butch who is subject to gender policing, the following frames' formal conjunction of the narrator's textual speculation with the images of her parents in the 1950s Village opens the possibility of the narrator's identification with her father: the narrator's questions imply that while the narrator might have found the courage to be a butch, she might also, like her father, have hidden in a heterosexual marriage. These multiple and complex identifications enable a compassionate if ambivalent openness in the narrator's read of her parents; the depiction of Helen as marginal to the scene in conjunction with the representation of the vulnerability of the butch body in the Eisenhower era leads the narrator to a recasting of what might have been and to a consequent reevaluation of what was. This recasting, in turn, produces the possibility of a future relation to the mother that recognizes Helen's ignorance and her loss, and a future relation to the father that is calmer and more accepting of as well as less riven by ambivalence. The narrator's identification across time, produced by the interplay of image and text, produces a sense of the narrator's debt to her father, which comingles with her blaming of him. And the compassion generated by the temporal disruption of the form allows the reader to see that the Chumley's panels depict the vulnerability and danger of 1950s queer life, as well as its cost not simply to queers but also to heterosexual women like Helen. Bechdel's rendering of the porous temporality of the Village thus produces a more complex representation of both Bechdel's parents' choices and her response to them.

A similar moment of temporal scrambling resulting from a queer identification occurs in a powerful series of panels depicting the quite young Alison's first sight of a butch dyke and her father's and her response to this sighting. A panel that occupies two-thirds of the page shows Alison and her father, sitting in a Philadelphia diner, watching a dyke delivery woman. The narrator makes clear the significance of the moment in a comment that underscores the delivery woman's gender: "I didn't know there were women who wore men's clothes and had men's haircuts. But like a traveler in a foreign country who runs into someone from home—someone they've never spoken to, but know by sight—I recognized her with a surge of joy" (118). I will return to this issue of joy but here wish to linger on the temporal note of this sighting. The panel that follows this recognition shows Bruce leaning hostilely toward Alison, the narrator's gloss—"Dad recognized her too"—working in tandem with Bruce asking, "Is *that* what you want to look like?" (118). The cumulative effect of image and words here produces two simultaneous but temporally differentiated relationships to a shared present moment. The bull dyke is understood by Bruce, the narrator, and the reader as a proleptic appearance of Alison's future, as well as an analeptic resurgence of Bruce's past: she is a figure who simultaneously enacts a pre-Stonewall model of female queerness and a utopian promise of Alison's queer futurity. Moreover, the bull dyke becomes a shared past moment that lives on in both Alison's and her father's futures: the narrator notes that although the young Alison, in the moment, disavows her identification with the dyke, "the vision of the truck-driving bulldyke sustained me through the years . . . as perhaps it haunted my father" (119). A multiply signifying image, the bull dyke provokes dissonant affective experiences of a shared present moment, while simultaneously this moment becomes a trace presence of the past in the future. This set of frames might thus be read as scrambling both the putative singularity of the present moment and the reliable sequentiality of heteronormative time.

In a scene between Alison and her father chronicling the visit home in which she last sees him alive, Bechdel similarly exploits the comics form to trouble temporality on multiple narrative levels, inverting the generational time of the family while also producing a disruption in the flow of narrative time. The scene occupies a two-page side-by-side spread and shows headshots of father and daughter sitting in a car, with Bruce driving and Alison in the passenger seat (220–21). As various critics have noted, this scene's use of a traditional comic layout is unique in *Fun Home*; that is, this is the only place in the book where Bechdel employs a page layout of four rows of three uniformly sized horizontal panels. The visual content of the panels is also uniquely consistent; all twenty-four boxes show Alison and her father from the perspective of a viewer looking through the passenger window across the front seat of the car, with very little variation in the two figures' poses. Bearing in mind Eisner's (2008, 30) observation that the "number and size of the panels also contribute to the story rhythm and passage of time," these twenty-four uniform panels must be read as slowing down time, creating a temporal pause in the flow of the diegesis. Here, the formal element of comics works in tandem with the diegetic content, for this is the sole scene in which Alison and her father discuss (in their fashion) their sexuality without mediation of letter or telephone. Deploying the comics form's visual ability to represent the passage of time as space on the page, Bechdel represents the destabilizing of heteronormative time that queer sexuality provokes. Put another way, the queer temporality of this father-daughter relationship here moves beyond a simple demonstration of *Fun Home*'s reverse coming-out narrative to reconfigure the temporality of the parent-child relation more broadly.

On the visual level, this queered temporal interlude is produced by the repetition of highly similar images, which produces a sense of a temporal pause, a hanging in time that is prevented from constituting an absolute stop by the characters' slight shifts in pose (in one panel Bruce puts his hand to his mouth; in several other panels both Bruce and Alison lean their elbows on the car window) and by the sparse dialogue. The two-page spread thus constitutes both a slow sequential moment and, paradoxically, a pause. This doubled temporal status is echoed in the limited conversation between Alison and Bruce, which Alison initiates by asking whether Bruce knew about her sexuality when he gave her Colette's autobiography. Julia Watson (2008, 44) describes this scene as a "breakthrough moment in sexual disclosure shared intergenerationally between father and daughter," but what is striking about this conversation is whose disclosure it entails. For although Bruce notes that "there was some kind of . . . identification" between himself and Alison, the terms of this identification are articulated only from one side; that is, while Bruce tells Alison about his early sexual experiences with boys, Alison never reveals the details of her own sexual emergence. The sole moment of exchange, in fact, hinges not on sexuality but on gender; when Bruce notes, "When I was little, I really wanted to be a girl. I'd dress up in girls' clothes," Alison replies, "I wanted to be a boy! I dressed in boys' clothes!" (Bechdel 2006, 221). The intensity of Alison's desire for connection here can be read in the energy of her outstretched arm, the only indication of motion in the two pages, but even by the next frame she is once again subdued and still as she asks, "Remember?" as if anticipating her father's failure to respond.

This scene scrambles the terms of heteronormative time in two distinct ways. On the diegetic level, the scene reverses the generational line, as the narrator asks in the sequence's final panels, "Which of us was the father? I had felt distinctly parental listening to his shame-faced recitation" (221). Here the daughter stands as parent to her father, producing him retrospectively as the nervous, closeted gay man.[7] Less predictably, the second means by which this scene opens up temporal possibilities operates on the visual level. The reader who encounters the two-page spread of the car scene is confronted with the possibility of two different sequencings simultaneously; one can read each of the two pages individually in a standard Western configuration, reading a left-to-right, top-to-bottom sequence of four rows of three panels, or one can read across the two pages horizontally, reading them as four rows of six panels.[8] Visually, both readings are entirely plausible, given the minute range of the characters' movement between any two panels, while the dialogue is so stilted and riven with silences that there is really only one cross-page jump that might read as strained. While the narrator's voice-over in the last six panels of the second page ultimately suggests that the reader should sequence these two pages separately, the alternate narrative logic of the two-page spread remains a hovering potential, allowing for a sequencing of the dialogue in which Alison's plaintive "Remember?" (221) is followed not by stony silence but by a silence glossed by the narrator as "I kept still, like he was a splendid deer I didn't want to startle" (220), then followed by Bruce's admission, "I guess there was some kind of . . . identification" (220).

Thomas Bredehoft's compelling discussion of the architecture of the comics page can help us better understand this curious formal anomaly. Bredehoft (2006, 885) notes: "The architecture of the comics page—and that of the comic book—opens the door for new configurations of the relationship between chronology, narrative line, and time-sequence. The two-dimensionality of the comics page can be used to allow a single group of panels to be read simultaneously in more than one linear sequence, calling into question the very idea of a single narrative line." The very unfolding of events themselves, then, apart from the sequence in which they are narrated, is rendered potentially nonchronological via the comics page. In this scene, Bechdel takes this very specific formal opportunity provided by the comics form and deploys it to produce two simultaneously possible narrative sequences. In one reading Alison's call to remember and the patience of her waiting evoke a paternal response and identification, while in the other, Bruce remains silent. The juxtaposition of these possibilities produces a glimpse of an affectively mixed queer identification that emerges from both a concurrent critique of and compassion for Alison's father: the narrator is rendered linked to her father both by her disappointment and by her compassion.

Drawing (On) the Reparative

Thus far I have focused on Bechdel's uses of the temporal flexibility of the comics form to interrupt the temporality of conventional family generational time. But having denaturalized heteronormative time, Bechdel goes on to open up new temporal modes, new forms of affiliation that constitute a queer world making. Drawing from scattered elements of her family history, Bechdel produces a reading of that past that is reparative at both the personal and the public level. I will turn now to this reparative narrative and its production from within the comics form, considering its significance to current debates on queer futurity as well as to our understanding of the potential of comics itself.

Sedgwick's influential formulation of paranoid and reparative readings draws on the work of Melanie Klein, specifically Klein's notion of the paranoid and depressive positions. Sedgwick (1997, 15) notes in particular Klein's distinction between a move "toward a sustained *seeking of pleasure* (through the reparative strategies of the depressive position)" and, contrastingly, "the self-reinforcing because self-defeating strategies for *forestalling pain* offered by the paranoid/schizoid position." Borrowing and expanding a psychoanalytic discourse in the service of a literary critical model of analysis, Sedgwick views a paranoid reading practice as "widely understood as a mandatory injunction" in contemporary critical practice but turns, in a search for a more generative critical stance, to what she dubs reparative reading, the product of Klein's depressive position: "The position from which it is possible in turn to use one's own resources to assemble or 'repair' the murderous part-objects into something like a whole—though not, and may I emphasize this, *not necessarily like any preexisting whole*. Once assembled to one's own specifications, the more satisfying object is available both to be identified with and to offer one nourishment and comfort in turn" (8). Sedgwick argues that both the paranoid and depressive critical approaches are strongly temporally structured: paranoia, she contends, displays "a distinctively rigid relation to temporality, at once anticipatory and retroactive, averse above all to surprise," while the reparative position is flexible, viewing surprise as necessary and linked to hope (24).[9]

This open, exploratory sense of the temporal converges with the structural temporal openings of the comics form in *Fun Home*, offering a framework of analysis of Bechdel's reparative heuristic, one that produces a both/and whole that is indeed unlike a heteronormative whole (itself a fantasy) but that emerges out of the protagonist's identity as visual artist and "offer[s] [the narrator] nourishment and comfort in turn" by queerly reconstituting her relation to family and kinship (8). Bechdel accomplishes this reconstitution by employing a version of reparation that embraces an ambivalent affective response to the past and that is represented both on the level of the form of the comic and on the level of the narration of young Alison's becoming a visual artist, linked to her parents less by biological kinship than by their shared status as artists. That is, the comic form itself helps to produce Bechdel's graphic rendition of a past suffused with both anger and compassion, a reparative graphic "family tragicomic." This vision ultimately constitutes Bechdel's contribution to contemporary queer discourse on generations, both the narrowly familial generations of individuals and the more broadly historical generations of queer culture. That Bechdel makes this critical intervention via the comics form is fitting, for as Thierry Groensteen (2007, 22) reminds us, "Comics is not only an art of fragments, of scattering, of distribution; it is also an art of conjunction, of repetition, of linking together." Bechdel employs both versions of comic art in *Fun Home* in a heuristic that, recognizing an asynchronous temporality generated by art, also allows for a compassionate reading of both her parents and herself, a reading that exceeds a conventional queer generational affect of pre-Stonewall shame and post-Stonewall pride by linking them in a queer affiliative web that is stretched across both the past and the future. In a double move that neither fully rejects futurity nor embraces it as a rosy ideal, Bechdel makes use of both the *tragi-* and the *comic* in order to produce a queer futurity that includes ambivalence as a space of potentiality.

Importantly, the queer child Alison's asynchronous relationship to time is inseparable from her development as a comics artist and is linked to the disruption of heteronormative generational lines. In a depiction of a family visit to Greenwich Village, for example, *Fun Home* locates a generative asynchrony as emerging precisely out of art and embodied by the gay friends whom Bruce and Alison visit. In a panel in which Richard, one of the hosts and an illustrator, stands at his drawing board showing Alison his work, Alison's identification with Richard is signaled by a tag pointing to her that reads "marker envy," as Alison takes in his workspace (Bechdel 2006, 191). As he shows Alison his illustrations for a "children's filmstrip about Pinocchio" he observes, "I was getting really bored, but then I realized I didn't have to draw the pictures in order," a comment that condenses the yoking of a queer nonheteronormative temporality and art that is to be the young Alison's future, one enacted in the present of both the narrator and the reader and available to the young Alison as a result of her weekend; the narrator notes that Alison's taking in the queerness of the weekend, "left [her] supple and open to possibility" (191). A sense of futurity hovers here, a not-yet present that is present for Alison and points toward an as-yet-unimagined opening.

This sense of possibility, grounded in the figure of the artist, most fully emerges through the representation of Bruce as Alison's "spiritual father" but applies to Helen as well, for artistry is represented thematically in *Fun Home* both by Bruce's restoration of the house and by Helen's acting and piano playing (210). While Alison identifies more strongly with Bruce than with Helen (in part because of the clear link between the adult Bechdel's cartoon art and her father's interest in visual surface), the narrator quite explicitly recognizes both parents as artists and understands herself as having "an unspoken compact with them that I would ... carry on to live the artist's life they had each abdicated" (73).

This queer artistic bond, however, is explicitly represented as in conflict with paternity and its attendant heteronormative directives and temporality, as, for instance, in a series of panels depicting her mother's use of a family tape recorder to rehearse her lines in a play. In recording lines, her mother discovers she is taping over the voice of her by-then-dead husband, who had recorded a guided tour of the county historical society museum (133). The narrator notes, "The most arresting thing about the tape is its evidence of both my parents at work, intent and separate." Indeed, accompanying these remarks are panels that show Helen and Bruce separately speaking into the recorder, then a panel of the recorder playing Bruce's words accompanied by photo of his younger self, and finally a panel of the recorder playing Helen's words accompanied by a photo of her younger self (132–33). Artistic production is here represented at both the diegetic and the extradiegetic levels as interruptive of chronological time: the analeptic voice of the dead father cohabitates with the still-living mother's recording, the photos represent earlier moments of both parents' lives, and both recording and photos exist in the present tense for the narrator who re-experiences several different moments of the past simultaneously. The following frames set these nonsequential artistic pursuits against the temporal rhythms of parenting; Helen, playing the piano, responds to the child Alison's "I'm hungry" by continuing to focus on the piano, saying, "I'll make lunch in fifteen minutes," after which a frame shows Helen continuing to play in the background while the disgruntled child walks away (133). The narrator concludes, "From their example, I learned quickly to feed myself," a comment located above an image of the young Alison drawing an animal figure on the wall. Taken together, the words and image offer both an indictment of Bruce and Helen's parenting skills (the parent refuses to bow to the imperatives of heteronormative family time; the child remains unfed and draws on a wall) and an acknowledgment of their artistic affiliation (the child learns by example to pursue her own art) (134). Moreover, art's status as interruptive of the temporality of the family is figured in the narrator's use of the present tense: the past occupies the present moment as the narrator comments, "Their rapt immersion evokes a familiar resentment in me. It's childish, perhaps, to grudge them the sustenance of their creative solitude" (133). Here, the resentment pictured on the child Alison's face as she walks away hungry is claimed simultaneously by the adult narrator who looks back on this past, but still not gone, moment, as the narrator's affective response merges with that of the child in begrudging her parents their art. At the same time, however, the narrator recognizes that this pleasure in art, this "rapt immersion," is "all that sustained them, and was thus self-consuming," and in recognizing the contradictory status of art as both gift and loss, solace and isolation, the narrator positions herself as queerly affiliated with these two artists (134).

This affiliation, importantly, emerges from the narrator's reparative reassembling of her past to recognize both the artist identity she shares with her parents and a shared position of affective ambivalence. Her recognition of both her simultaneous anger at and compassion for her parents is accompanied by a recognition of the affective ambivalence of their positions, which works as another bond among them. Bechdel's representation of her mother's pleasure in music, for instance, is accompanied by the depiction of Helen's anger, grief, and loss in the context of her marriage. The narrator notes the "toll" (65) taken by Bruce's behavior, a toll made manifest in the "Arctic climate" (67) of the family and in Bruce's repetitive violence and deceit. The narrator's compassion toward her mother coexists with anger; it also fuels the narrator's anger toward her father, which runs alongside her love for him.

For while these panels (among others) point to the grief and anger that accompany Helen's position as wife and mother, Bechdel's affectively complex approach to the reparative potential of her past is articulated most specifically in terms of her relation to her father. In an online interview with Edward Champion (2006), Bechdel explicitly articulated this relationship, musing, "I've always had very confused feelings about my dad.... It was just always both of these things, really bad and really good.... I had a lot of anger at him, um, but I also have a lot of love for him." Through the interplay of image and text and the temporal possibilities of the comics form, Bechdel fashioned a vocabulary to articulate (in both senses of the word) the mix of love and anger that binds the complex relationship of father and daughter. And this articulation of the complex and contradictory affective bond between Bruce and Alison is crucial to *Fun Home*'s reparative heuristic, a production of a simultaneously traumatizing and empowering past that opens a space for a queer futurity.

Such a rearticulated version of kinship is most fully apparent in *Fun Home*'s use of photographs. Bechdel's use of hand-drawn reproductions of actual family photographs is well known; in addition to serving as chapter heads, these reproductions appear in various places throughout the body of the memoir. The hand-drawn nature of the reproduction of the photograph both evokes the autobiographical sources of this memoir and makes clear the author's shaping representation of those sources. Similarly, these photographs suggest a role as part of a family album, a visual document that shores up heteronormative family time in its representation of generations, but, as Watson (2008, 38) points out, if *Fun Home* "is allied to the family album . . . [it] also marks a distance from its function as official history by reading photos for their transgressive content." Bechdel, one might say, uses family photos both to document the family history and to queer it.

This occurs quite literally with the photograph of Roy, where a heteroreproductive flow of time is interrupted on several narrative levels simultaneously. Bechdel has explicitly identified the importance of photographs to *Fun Home*, and this photograph's importance in particular, commenting, "In many ways photographs really generated the book. In fact the whole story was spawned by a snapshot I found of our old babysitter lying on a hotel bed in his Jockey shorts" (quoted in Chute 2006, 1005).[10] Further, she underscores the erotic nature of the photograph's importance, calling it *Fun Home*'s "centerfold" (1006), an ascription that is materially enacted in the photograph's placement almost exactly halfway through the book on a two-page spread. Formally, the most striking thing about this image is that it breaks the conventional frame of comics structure, appearing across the two pages as a larger-than-life-size photograph held in a hand (presumably the narrator's) that bleeds off the page. This format alone codes Roy and his photograph as an interruption to heteronormative time: this is the only instance in the memoir of such a full-scale departure from the format of the frame. Such a shift in format, as Groensteen (2007, 53) notes, "serves, in principle, to draw attention to a rupture in the level of enunciation regarding the status of the image"; in this case, the shift from Bechdel's typical grid of between two and six panels per page to a single double-page spread interrupts the flow of the narrative and produces a pause as the reader takes in the unusual format. Further, this change in format, along with the fact that these two pages are the only unnumbered pages in the book, indicates a moment out of time, both for the reader and within the diegesis.[11] This effect is heightened by the use of a page bleed (an image that runs off the page due to the lack of a frame), a comics technique through which, as McCloud (1993, 103) explains, "time is no longer contained by the familiar icon of the closed panel but instead hemorrhages and escapes into timeless space." The lack of gutters and frames thus leaves the reader with no means of regulating the narrative passage of time. Further, the image of the unidentified hand holding the photograph troubles the chronological flow of time within the narrative, the undecidability of just whose hand this is collapsing the multiple temporalities of moments in which the photo was taken and viewed by Bruce with the moments in which it is viewed by the narrator and by the reader. All this underscores both Roy's photograph's unique and crucially important status in *Fun Home* and, specifically, its enactment of a queer temporal disruption.

Moreover, the tension within both the image and the tags generates a temporal disruption that casts the photograph as simultaneously *within* heteronormative time and *beyond* it. The photograph is, on the one hand, very specifically located in chrononormative family time both visually and within the narrative, partly by the "Aug 69" stamped on the photograph's border, partly by the narrator's observation in a tag that the photograph "appears to have been taken on a vacation when I was eight, a trip on which Roy accompanied my father, my brothers, and me to the Jersey shore while my mother visited her old roommate in New York City" (Bechdel 2006, 101, 100). In a narratorial comment that grants the photo the status of evidentiary fact, a capturing of a fixed moment in time, the narrator also comments, "I remember the hotel room. My brothers and I slept in one adjoining it," and indeed, the background of the photo shows a door through which another bed is visible (100).

On the other hand, however, both the figure of the sleeping boy and the narrator's description of him take the photo out of conventional family time, locating it instead in a kind of queer sacred time. Mircea Eliade (1959, 104) usefully differentiates between ordinary and sacred time thus, "The one is an evanescent duration, the other a 'succession of eternities,' periodically recoverable during the festivals that made up the sacred calendar."[12] In both religious and secular forms, sacred time marks a temporary departure, a break from the ordinary temporal duration of human life. In religious ritual specifically, this departure locates the human both within the historical time of the ritual and beyond it, in what is conceived of as a perpetual present tense, a divine, eternal time. The photograph of Roy queers both the content of sacred time and its relation to human time. The image of the sleeping figure, appearing on the border between boyhood and manhood, is both sensual and aestheticized, a representation articulated by the narrator as well, who describes the photograph as "beautiful": "The blurriness of the photo gives it an ethereal, painterly quality. Roy is gilded with morning seaside light. His hair is an aureole" (Bechdel 2006, 100). Roy becomes a sacred icon, an object of veneration that, like traditional religious icons, is "gilded," wears a halo, and inspires "awe" in the narrator (and, presumably, Bruce) (101). Here, sacred time is accessed not by religious ritual but by desire and opens onto the queer body rather than the divine. The queer body here stands in the place of religious ritual, evoking both human and eternal time, as Roy's photograph rests simultaneously within and in excess of heterosexual family time, a both/and status embodied in Roy's position as both babysitter and object of Bruce's desire.[13]

The graphic narrative's staging of the photo, then, formally interrupts diegetic time and simultaneously embodies the queering of sacred time by a desire that both inhabits and exceeds heteronormative family time. This temporal opening of the comics form enables a reparative revisiting of the past, one that recasts the past via information brought from the present but that also generates a reciprocal opening of the present and future out of the past. All this emerges out of queer desire: the narrator wonders, in looking at Roy's photograph, why she is "not properly outraged" (100) and speculates that "perhaps I identify too well with my father's illicit awe" (101). The photograph thus aligns the narrator's identification with her father as a sexual subject with her own queer desires. Identification and queer awe constitute a reparative reach into the past from the present, a temporal extension that—in producing a compassionate vision of the then—generates a queer identification with her father in the present and opens a way toward a more expansive queer futurity.

This asynchronous conjoining of temporal moments works reparatively elsewhere in *Fun Home*, perhaps most emblematically in another photographic sequence, this one juxtaposing photographs of Bruce and Alison as college students. Here, as in the photo of Roy, the queer body becomes the vehicle of this conjoining, enacting Dana Luciano's (2007, 18) description, in another context, of the "body as a potential site of historiographic and temporal interventions." For it is in the juxtaposition of these photographs that Bechdel most clearly represents a version of queer kinship that entails the mingled care of the other and the self, a queer kinship that draws on what Sedgwick (1997, 14) describes as "a view of the other as at once good, damaged, integral, and requiring and eliciting love and care ... founded on and coextensive with ... the often very fragile concern to provide the self with pleasure and nourishment in an environment that is perceived not particularly to offer them."

The final panel in chapter 4, which contains these hand-drawn photographs, is linked to the preceding panel, and both are rendered, like the photograph of Roy, as images of hands holding photographs (see fig. 3). In the penultimate panel, occupying the top third of the page, a hand holds a photograph of Bruce, cross-dressed in a woman's bathing suit. In the final panel, two hands each hold a photograph, one of Bruce, one of Alison, with a third of Bruce (a reproduction of the photo of the cross-dressed Bruce) floating in the background (Bechdel 2006, 120). This final panel takes up two-thirds of the page, with both the photos and the hands roughly life-size, the hands cropped by the edge of the frame. The visual similarity between these panels and the Roy photograph is reinforced by the narrator's explanation of the photos' shared origin, as she notes of the top photo, "In the same box where I found the photo of Roy, there's one of Dad at about the same age," while a tag over the photo of Bruce in the bottom panel reads, "In another picture ... ," implying that this photo, too, came from that box. The final panel juxtaposes the two overlapped photos, one of Bruce "sunbathing on the tarpaper roof of his frat house just after he turned twenty-two" and one of Alison "on a fire escape on [her] twenty-first birthday" (120). The narrator delineates the similarities between the two photos—"The exterior setting, the pained grin, the flexible wrists, even the angle of shadow falling across our faces"—and pointedly links this to their shared queerness, asking of the two photographs, "Was the boy who took it his lover? As the girl who took this Polaroid ... was mine?" (120).

That these images constitute a reparative temporal intervention becomes apparent via Bechdel's introduction of them by way of Marcel Proust. On the page preceding these two panels of photographs, the narrator notes, "After Dad died, an updated translation of Proust came out. *Remembrance of Things Past* was re-titled *In Search of Lost Time*. The new title is a more literal translation of *À la recherche du temps perdu*, but it still doesn't quite capture the full resonance of *perdu*." Over an image of Bruce reading the second volume of Proust the narrator continues, "This means not just lost but ruined, undone, wasted, wrecked, and spoiled" (119). This meditation on Proust and

Figure 3 From Bechdel (2006), *Fun Home: A Family Tragicomic*, 120

translation is sutured to the photographs in the two final panels as the narrator observes over the panel containing the photo of the cross-dressed Bruce, "What's lost in translation is the complexity of loss itself" (120).

To fully understand this claim in the context of Alison's life, we must consider the final two panels' photographs in conversation with each other. At the bottom of the panel that contains the juxtaposed photos of Bruce and Alison, the narrator concludes of the similarities between the two photos, "It's about as close as a translation can get"; as a result, a reader might be tempted to read these two photographs in generational and teleological terms, as instances of pre- and post-Stonewall time in which Bruce settles for the cover of heterosexual marriage while Alison fulfills the queer future that Bruce was unable to claim. But the photo that hovers like a specter in the background of this panel complicates this reading of Bruce's moment as "ruined, undone, wasted, wrecked, and spoiled" (119): as the narrator observes, "He's wearing a women's bathing suit. A fraternity prank? But the pose he strikes is not mincing or silly at all. He's lissome, elegant" (120). Is this photo evidence of time ruined by remaining unclaimed, closeted in the past, or is the beauty of her father in that moment of grace an opening, a glimpse of futurity and a past that occurred differently—more queerly pleasurably—than it might have seemed to? Indeed, these images' occurrence as reproductions of photographs rather than as comic panels further disrupts a teleological pre- or post-Stonewall reading, for to the extent that photographs constitute frozen moments of time, these two are temporally equivalent; frozen in a queer instant of pained pleasure, in communication with a queer lover/photographer, they speak to each other across time, across generations, of queer desire embodied. What's lost here is precisely the complexity of Bruce's past, but insofar as Bechdel represents that complexity on the pages of *Fun Home*, the past also hovers as a future potential.

Conclusion

Reading Bruce's "lissome, elegant" bathing suit shot as a version of queer camp renders it emblematic of *Fun Home*'s reparative enterprise as a whole. That is, if we understand camp as a temporal sensibility enacting the survival of the then in the now, we can also see it as opening up the now to a new then, a then occurring in both the past and the future. Elizabeth Freeman (2007, 309) reads drag performance as a version of queer camp, as "ritualized modes of handing down possibilities for queer embodiment to audiences who may not know the exact referent, or even care about it, but for whom historical disjunction itself may well serve as an opening into a differential future." Bruce's queer embodiment here, with the rejection of heteronormative kinship that his refusal of conventional gender implies, models just such a possibility for Alison: recasting his "nelly" self enables her "butch" self (Bechdel 2006, 15). Representing her father—both verbally and visually—as "lissome, elegant" produces a possibility, that is, a reparative reinhabiting of a potential past that makes possible, via a reciprocal relationship among asynchronous temporalities, the envisioning of a different present and future.

Sedgwick (1997, 28), explicitly reading camp as "the communal, historically dense exploration of a variety of reparative practices," delineates what she calls "defining elements of classic camp performance" thus: "The startling juicy displays of excess erudition, for example; the passionate, often hilarious antiquarianism, the prodigal production of alternate historiographies; the 'over'-attachment to fragmentary, marginal, waste, or leftover products; the rich, highly interruptive affective variety; the irrepressible fascination with ventriloquistic experimentation; the disorienting juxtapositions of present with past, and popular with high culture." Her description resonates with *Fun Home* as a whole: its erudition; its antiquarianism; its multiple historiographies; its attention to details of popular culture, both verbal and visual; its multiple affective registers; its engagement with imaginatively inhabiting other subjectivities; and, not least, its comingling of high and popular culture. All these work temporally in *Fun Home* to connect the present to the past as a mode of queer survival into an as-yet-unimagined futurity.

This is the reparative effort that fuels Bechdel's memoir, a vision that moves beyond a queer temporal binary that opposes a shameful past to a proud future. Instead, *Fun Home* provides a more affectively complex vision of both past and future, a vision that calls to mind Sara Ahmed's (2011, 161) assertion that queer theorists "don't have to choose between pessimism and optimism. We can explore the strange and perverse mixtures of hope and despair, of optimism and pessimism, within forms of politics that take as a starting point a critique of the world as it is and a belief that the world can be different." Ahmed here proposes a reparative critical queer practice that starts from a recognition that any vision of futurity that is more than just the always already foreclosed property of heteronormativity must necessarily be undergirded by both hope and despair. This, I contend, is what a specifically queer feminist reparative reading would look like, a reading that does not foreclose futurity but understands its potential as complex, open, and grounded in the material reality of both the pain and pleasure of the queer body. It is this hermeneutic that *Fun Home* enacts. The memoir tracks shame in Bruce's past and present but also pleasure and awe; their comingling functions as a shared affect that queerly links Bruce and Alison, as in the youthful father's and daughter's shared "pained grin" toward their lovers/photographers (Bechdel 2006, 120). And Bechdel consistently links this affectively mixed queer affiliation to the collateral damage inherent in Helen's role as heterosexual wife, as well as the palliative recourse to artistic creation that Helen, Bruce, and Alison share. Moreover, Bechdel tracks a comingling of affective registers in various temporalities; the same figure who haunts Bruce—the butch dyke in the diner—produces the sustaining "surge of joy" that the narrator attributes to the young Alison (119). The memoir's insistence on the coterminous nature of multiple affects disrupts a queer past-shame/future-pride binary, producing temporal registers that, like Bechdel's narrative, move backward, forward, and around in time. In doing so, *Fun Home* opens space for a present moment that contains a reparatively compassionate view of both the young Alison and her parents.

The narrator ultimately links this reparative temporal process to Alison's claiming of her queer subjectivity in a series of panels that provide the most visually explicit representation of Alison's claiming of her "erotic truth" (214). The tag superimposed on the image of a naked Alison between the legs of her lover reads, "Like Odysseus on the island of the Cyclops, I found myself facing a 'being of colossal strength and ferocity, to whom the law of man and god meant nothing'" (214). Beneath this imposing two-thirds-page panel are two smaller panels, one of Alison's face hovering slightly above her lover's pubic hair and the other of Alison's face buried in that hair. Continuing the extended analogy to *The Odyssey*, the narrator notes of the first, "in true heroic fashion, I moved toward the thing I feared," and of the second, "yet while Odysseus schemed desperately to escape Polyphemus's cave, I found that I was quite content to stay *here* forever" (214; emphasis mine). The shift in narratorial voice—the use of "here" rather than "there"—erases the distinction between narrator and Alison, collapsing the past and present, as the queer then lingers in the queer now, and contentment, cohabitating with fear, illuminates both past and present. The addition of "forever" suggests a perpetual present that draws in a sense of both human futurity and a queer sacred eternity.

José Esteban Muñoz (2009, 35) understands "our remembrances and their ritualized tellings—through film, video, performance, writing, and visual culture—as having world-making potentialities," a contention we might expand to include the comics form. Opening up registers of queer time not available in purely prose or purely visual form, comics offer a unique opportunity for the enactment of a queer temporality. *Fun Home* seizes that opportunity, deploying it to produce an affectively complex instance of a queer world making that draws on an understanding of the past as saturated with both pleasure and pain. This nuanced vision relies on the formal possibilities inherent in the comic form, such that the reparative reading of the narrator's past enables a queer artistic futurity. As such, *Fun Home* offers a complex and compassionate meditation on the potentialities of queer time and a salutary reminder of the radical possibilities inherent in the graphic form.

Kate McCullough is an associate professor of English and Feminist, Gender, and Sexuality Studies at Cornell University. Her book, *Regions of Identity: The Construction of America in Women's Fiction, 1885–1914* (Stanford Univ. Press, 1999), considers the contribution of women writers to turn-of-the-century discourses of US nationalism. She is currently working on a project on queer time and narrative form.

Notes

Thanks to Naminata Diabate, Saida Hodžić, Frann Michel, Lucinda Ramberg, Theresa Tensuan, and especially Mary Pat Brady for help in thinking through the questions at stake here.

1 Gillian Whitlock (2006, 966) invented the neologism *autographics*, defining it as follows: "By coining the term 'autographics' for graphic memoir I mean to draw attention to the specific conjunctions of visual and verbal text in this genre of autobiography, and also to the subject positions that narrators negotiate in and through comics." Early feminist cartoonists include Mary Wings, whose work appeared in the 1970s, roughly a decade before the start of Bechdel's strip *Dykes to Watch Out For*; subsequent feminist cartoonists include Diane DiMassa, Erika Lopez, and Roberta Gregory in the 1990s, along with a more recent generation including Ariel Shrag, among many others, in the twenty-first century. Properly read, Bechdel's work must be situated in the context of both queer comics work and feminist, lesbian political and social circles.

2 On the temporality of the archives, see Cvetkovich 2008 and Rohy 2009. On the graphic form, see especially Chute 2006 and Warhol 2011.

3 Frames visually signal a unit of time while also setting the pace of time's flow as Eisner (2008, 26) notes: "The act of paneling . . . 'tells' time. . . . The act of framing separates the scenes and acts as a punctuator. Once established and set in sequence the box or panel becomes the criterion by which to judge the illusion of time . . . the device most fundamental to the transmission of timing. . . . These lines drawn around the depiction of a scene, which act as a containment of the action, or a segment of action, have as one of their functions the task of separating or

parsing the total statement." Frames, rather than simply organizing the space of the page, move time through that space, thus helping to both produce and direct the temporal flow of the story and the reading experience itself.

4   The line between memoir and autobiography is blurry; I follow Robyn Warhol's (2011, 1) delineation: "In its current critical usage, 'memoir' places the focus on the person or object being memorialized, but 'autography,' like the word from which it is derived, 'autobiography,' suggests that the subject of the narrative is the author/artist herself." By this definition, Warhol claims that *Fun Home* is both. For an extremely useful discussion of multiple narrative levels in graphic narratives, see Warhol 2011.

5   Chute (2006b) introduces the term *recursive* in a review of *Fun Home*. Examples of *Fun Home*'s use of temporal devices include the opening chapter's proleptic revelation that this allegedly "ideal husband and father" was having "sex with teenage boys" (Bechdel 2006, 17). Chapter 2, in contrast, scrambles a chronological narrative at the level of the images. The chapter opens with an image of the local newspaper of July 3, 1980, headlined, "Local Man Dies after Being Hit by Truck," an image that analeptically precedes a second image of the local paper, dated July 1, 1980, two days before the first newspaper image and the day before Bruce died.

6   Here and throughout I follow the general convention of referring to the child protagonist appearing in the visual representations as Alison and to the disembodied narrator, who speaks from the point of view of the adult self, as Bechdel.

7   The querying of generational locations echoes Bechdel's use of Daedalus-Icarus imagery throughout.

8   I draw here on the insights of Thomas A. Bredehoft's (2006) powerful reading of what he refers to as the architecture of the comics page.

9   Sedgwick (1997, 10) details the temporality of paranoia as follows: "The unidirectionally future-oriented vigilance of paranoia generates, paradoxically, a complex relation to temporality that burrows both backward and forward: because there must be no bad surprises, and because to learn of the possibility of a bad surprise would itself constitute a bad surprise, paranoia requires that bad news be always already known."

10 Many critics have focused on this photograph; see, for instance, Cvetkovich 2008; Nabizadeh 2014; and Watson 2008.

11 The two pages on which Roy's photo appears are not numbered but occupy pages 100 and 101.

12 While I agree with Dana Luciano's (2007, 272) characterization of Eliade's account as "ahistorical and overly simplified," like her I understand his schematic to be useful as a description of mainstream categorizations of religious temporalities.

13 This status of a queer desire that is simultaneously both in and beyond family time is pictured quite literally in an image of a strip of photographic negatives that appears on the page following the two-page spread of Roy's photo, in which the negative of Roy's photo appears amid three negatives of a normative family vacation: children frolicking on a beach (Bechdel 2006, 102). Here, the very source of the family album's evidence—the negatives of the photos themselves—is demonstrated to have always contained queer desire.

References

Ahmed, Sara. 2011. "Happy Futures, Perhaps." In *Queer Times, Queer Becomings*, edited by E. L. McCallum and Mikko Tuhkanen, 159–82. Albany: State Univ. of New York Press.

Bechdel, Alison. 2006. *Fun Home: A Family Tragicomic*. Boston: Houghton Mifflin.

Bredehoft, Thomas A. 2006. "Comics Architecture, Multidimensionality, and Time: Chris Ware's *Jimmy Corrigan: The Smartest Kid on Earth*." *Modern Fiction Studies* 52, no. 4: 869–90.

Champion, Edward. 2006. "Interview with Alison Bechdel." *The Bat Segundo Show*. www.edrants.com/segundo/bss-63-alison-bechdel/.

Chute, Hillary. 2006a. "An Interview with Alison Bechdel." *Modern Fiction Studies* 52, no. 4: 1004–13.

———. 2006b. "Gothic Revival." *Village Voice*, July 12–18.

Chute, Hillary, and Marianne DeKoven. 2006. "Introduction: Graphic Narrative." *Modern Fiction Studies* 52, no. 4: 767–82.

Cvetkovich, Ann. 2008. "Drawing the Archive in Alison Bechdel's *Fun Home*." *Women's Studies Quarterly* 36, nos. 1/2: 111–28.

Dinshaw, Carolyn, et al. 2007. "Theorizing Queer Temporalities: A Roundtable Discussion." *GLQ* 13, nos. 2/3: 177–95.

Eisner, Will. 2008. *Comics and Sequential Art: Principles and Practices from the Legendary Cartoonist*. New York: W. W. Norton. First published 1985.

Eliade, Mircea. 1959. *The Sacred and the Profane*. Translated by Willad R. Trask. New York: Harcourt, Brace and World.

Freeman, Elizabeth. 2007. "Queer Belongings: Kinship Theory and Queer Theory." In *A Companion to Lesbian, Gay, Bisexual, and Transgender Studies*, edited by George E. Haggerty and Molly McGarry, 295–314. Malden, MA: Blackwell.

———. 2010. *Time Binds: Queer Temporalities, Queer Histories*. Durham, NC: Duke Univ. Press.

Groensteen, Thierry. 2007. *The System of Comics*. Translated by Bart Beaty and Nick Nguyen. Jackson: Univ. Press of Mississippi.

Luciano, Dana. 2007. *Arranging Grief: Sacred Time and the Body in Nineteenth-Century America*. New York: New York Univ. Press.

Mautner, Chris. 2008. "Graphic Lit: An Interview with Alison Bechdel." *Panels and Pixels*, March 3. http://panelsandpixels.blogspot.com/2008/03/graphic-lit-interview-with-alison.html.

McCloud, Scott. 1993. *Understanding Comics: The Invisible Art*. New York: Harper Perennial.

Muñoz, José Esteban. 2009. *Cruising Utopia: The Then and There of Queer Futurity*. New York: New York Univ. Press.

Nabizadeh, Golnar. 2014. "The After-Life of Images: Archives and Intergenerational Trauma in Autographic Comics." In *Mapping Generations of Traumatic Memory in American Narratives*, edited by Dana Mihailescu, Roxana Oltean, and Mihaela Precup, 171–89. Newcastle upon Tyne: Cambridge Scholars.

Nealon, Christopher. 2001. *Foundlings: Lesbian and Gay Historical Emotion before Stonewall*. Durham, NC: Duke Univ. Press.

Rohy, Valerie. 2009. *Anachronism and Its Others: Sexuality, Race, Temporality*. Albany: State Univ. of New York Press.

Sedgwick, Eve Kosofsky. 1997. "Paranoid Reading and Reparative Reading; or, You're So Paranoid, You Probably Think This Introduction Is about You." In *Novel Gazing: Queer Readings in Fiction*, edited by Eve Kosofsky Sedgwick, 1–37. Durham, NC: Duke Univ. Press.

Stockton, Kathryn Bond. 2009. *The Queer Child, or Growing Sideways in the Twentieth Century*. Durham, NC: Duke Univ. Press.

Warhol, Robyn. 2011. "The Space Between: A Narrative Approach to Alison Bechdel's *Fun Home*." *College Literature* 38, no. 3: 1–20.

Watson, Julia. 2008. "Autographic Disclosures and Genealogies of Desire in Alison Bechdel's *Fun Home*." *Biography* 31, no. 1: 27–58.

Whitlock, Gillian. 2006. "Autographics: The Seeing 'I' of the Comics." *Modern Fiction Studies* 52, no. 4: 965–79.

Margaret Galvan

"The Lesbian Norman Rockwell": Alison Bechdel and Queer Grassroots Networks

Abstract Alison Bechdel's renown has been building since the success of *Fun Home* (2006). While scholars have focused on her contemporary production, her comics work within grassroots periodicals, including her long-running strip, *Dykes to Watch Out For* (1983–2008), has received comparatively little attention. By focusing on the grassroots context of *DTWOF*, this essay demonstrates how Bechdel's participation in grassroots periodicals shaped her work. Through the development of new reading practices and the notion of queer comics archives, I show how queer communities influenced Bechdel's visual rhetoric in the pages of *WomaNews*, the grassroots periodical where Bechdel first published her work and participated as a member of the collective. Informed by archival research, this analysis embraces grassroots contexts as an overlooked venue for exploring queer histories and tracing the development of queer comics.
Keywords comics, *WomaNews*, *Dykes to Watch Out For*, *Fun Home*, archives

> The project of feminist cinema, therefore, is not so much "to make visible the invisible," as the saying goes, or to destroy vision altogether, as to construct another (object of) vision and the conditions of visibility for a different social subject.
> —Teresa de Lauretis, "Imaging" (1984)

Origin stories are central within comics to understanding a character's trajectory through his or her roots and original context. And, yet, the beginnings of acclaimed artist Alison Bechdel's work are vague in her retrospective accounts. The lack of access to Bechdel's own origin story and those of her characters obscures how directly queer grassroots politics shaped the course of her work. She began drawing comics in the pages of New York City feminist newspaper *WomaNews* in the summer of 1983. Over the next three years, Bechdel developed her renowned strip, *Dykes to Watch Out For*, evolving it from *New Yorker*–esque single panels to multipanel thematic takes. The pages of *WomaNews* evidence Bechdel's growth as an artist not just in her comics but also in advertisements and other graphics for the collective that she created.

Despite how formative these early years and this grassroots publishing experience were for Bechdel's career, most readers and critics do not know about them. While some early iterations of her comic appear in her first two collections with Firebrand Books, many, including her single-panel works, do not. Further, none of these early comics is included in *The Essential Dykes to Watch Out For* (2008b), which is now the means through which most fans and scholars access and write about the series.[1] In an introduction to the volume, Bechdel (2008a, xiv) discusses her career and reduces *WomaNews* to an unnamed "local feminist newspaper," further obscuring her early work that is not included in the collection.

These hidden production histories are key to situating Bechdel within contemporaneous queer discourse and to recontextualizing the visual theorizing that her comics perform in dialogue with grassroots networks. In addition to her work on *WomaNews* (1983–85), she served as the production coordinator for the Minneapolis–Saint Paul gay and lesbian newspaper *Equal Time* for four years (1986–90) before she was able to make a living from her comics and associated work.[2] Bechdel also self-syndicated her strip in roughly two hundred periodicals over the course of two decades (1983–2008), which put her finger on the pulse of local social movement politics nationally and internationally over a decade before the Internet digitally networked people together. She chronicled this experience in a short-lived strip, *Servants to the Cause* (1989–90), which appeared in the pages of national gay magazine the *Advocate*. This strip follows a diverse cast of characters who work together on a fictitious queer periodical, and the plot intersects generational debates and identity politics. In this article, I unfurl how Bechdel's queer visual politics derived from her closeness to grassroots networks, drawing on archival research of her papers held in the Sophia Smith Collection at Smith College, Firebrand Book Records held in the Human Sexuality Collection at Cornell University, and the newsprint collection at the Lesbian Herstory Archives. Methodologically, I employ close analysis alongside historiography, using archival materials to inform both. I queer these methods through introducing new kinds of collective, visual analysis and centralizing archives as part of the analytical frame.

Archives are necessary to encounter these histories. I call for a greater engagement with archives in comics studies; the overreliance on published and available texts skews the visible reality of what we analyze (Galvan 2015). This alliance is not merely recuperative: we must be cognizant of how these archives operate to facilitate the discovery of these materials (Galvan 2017). In this article, through looking at these comics and their archives, I argue for an expansion of what we consider worthy of analysis under the banner of comics studies. Grassroots publications allow Bechdel and other cartoonists to express their politics in varied, image-text considerations that are not always explicitly comics but that benefit from analysis under this paradigm. As one can tell from a glance at the archives in play, these sorts of publications are not kept within archival comics collections but exist within queer-adjacent[3] and queer grassroots archives. Analyzing these comics through these spaces, I theorize queer comics archives and develop new methods of reading comics in queer communities that shift our focus from canons to the collective practices that shape the production and circulation of queer comics art.

In order to understand not only Bechdel's queer comics but also those of many of her contemporaries, it is necessary to review the publishing milieus that supported her work. Grassroots queer comics are overlooked by comics studies because they are often produced outside of comics communities. Throughout the years, anthologies like *Gay Comix* (1980–98),[4] *Strip AIDS USA* (Robbins, Sienkiewicz, and Triptow 1988), *Dyke Strippers* (Warren 1995), *Juicy Mother* (Camper 2005), *Juicy Mother 2* (Camper 2007), *No Straight Lines* (Hall 2013b), *QU33R* (Kirby 2014), and *Alphabet* (Avery and Macy 2016) have been an important means of gathering queer comics from across their disparate publication contexts. While these venues make the work more visible, we miss a sense of the local politics that intersect with the comics, as when they appear alongside articles in periodicals. Featured in a majority of these anthologies, Bechdel is central to this community of artists. Roz Warren dedicates *Dyke Strippers* to her, and *Gay Comix* devotes an entire issue to her work (Mangels 1993). In his introduction to *No Straight Lines*, editor Justin Hall (2013a) acknowledges both the power of queer periodical comics and the difficulties that have kept them from the recognition they richly deserve: "The weekly strips' publication in the gay newspapers gave them a timeliness and immediacy that was [sic] often used for direct political and social commentary. It also placed them even farther outside of the traditional comics industry than the queer comic books and tied them in even more strongly to the LGBTQ community and the queer media ghetto." These circumstances separated queer grassroots comics from the "traditional comics industry" of their time, and they continue to delay recognition for these comics.

This description neatly characterizes Bechdel's own career as she published *DTWOF* over the course of two decades (1983–2008). Interviews with Bechdel reflect the marginal position of queer comics publishing. Anne Rubenstein (1995, 114) opens an interview with Bechdel with this one-liner: "Alison Bechdel may be the most popular American cartoonist who you've never heard of." Six years later, Trina Robbins (2001, 82) echoes this sentiment in the introduction to her interview with Bechdel: "In a better world, she would already be a well-known mainstream creator." In the intervening years, Bechdel self-syndicated her own strip in around fifty periodicals nationally and internationally. Most of these venues were strictly grassroots, but she had more mainstream coverage in a few markets. Her publication list was always in flux, as grassroots periodicals went under with frequency. *WomaNews* stopped publishing in 1991, and *Equal Time* folded in 1994. With such losses, Bechdel would seek out new periodicals with similar geographic coverage so that her local readers would still be able to access her strip.

In March 2006, in advance of the release of *Fun Home* (2006a), which rocketed Bechdel to mainstream acclaim, Bechdel assessed her national coverage by labeling a map with the names of her publications and marking key cities she was not reaching (Bechdel 2006c) (fig. 1). Although she had thirty-five big cities and other environs under her belt, she identified fifteen cities that she wanted. Notably, she previously had coverage in these cities, including Phoenix (*Heatstroke*), Anchorage (*Identity Northview*), and Milwaukee (*Wisconsin Light*). More than just a snapshot of her coverage in the United States and Canada, the map presents a sense of her span across the decades. Granted, it does not show the whole picture—the roughly two hundred periodicals that published her comic over the course of two decades—

"The Lesbian Norman Rockwell" 411

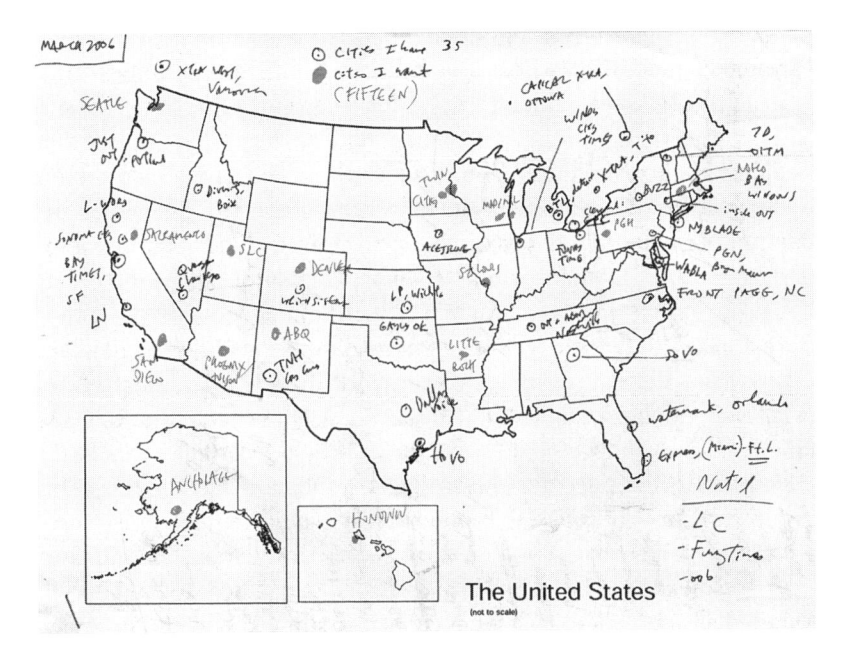

Figure 1 Bechdel's publication network in March 2006. Courtesy of Alison Bechdel Papers, Sophia Smith Collection

but it evokes what both Rubenstein and Robbins are getting at when they cite Bechdel's popularity in spite of her lack of mainstream renown. When Bechdel ceased publishing *DTWOF* in May 2008, many periodicals had been publishing her work for nearly two decades, including small outfits like *Bryn Mawr College News* (Bryn Mawr, PA) and *Sonoma County Women's Voices* (Sebastopol, CA) alongside more prominent and national publications like *Lesbian Connection* (East Lansing, MI), *Lesbian News* (West Hollywood, CA), *off our backs* (Washington, DC), and the *Washington Blade* (Washington, DC). Through her own efforts, Bechdel had a presence in grassroots publications across the nation, and her books and associated products were sold in an overlapping geography of bookstores.

And yet, this map and those interviews could have been framed very differently, for in 1993 Bechdel turned down an offer to produce a syndicated strip with the Universal Press Syndicate (UPS), which gets strips like Garry Trudeau's *Doonesbury* and Bill Watterson's *Calvin and Hobbes* into the funnies of thousands of major newspapers. In making her decision, Bechdel solicited the advice of fellow queer cartoonist Joan Hilty, who was familiar with different comics markets. Hilty (1993) responded by sharing materials critical of the UPS and hedging about her advice, explaining, "So, basically, I'm just flip-flopping about what to tell you. I guess that reflects my own mixed feelings about the profession: the exposure's great but the politics are daunting.... On the other hand, your work is so good—putting a lot of other comics to shame on both an artistic and narrative level—it deserves an even wider audience." Bechdel echoed this back-and-forth in notes to herself, where she drafted questions for the syndicate ("How does the editing process work?"; "How political/sexual/etc. can it be?") alongside questions for herself ("How much time will this take?"; "How bland would it have to be?"; "Could I work in 4 panels??") (Bechdel 1993). These personal questions indicate that she was leaning toward "no" because this opportunity would require her to create a strip format that would have taken time away from *DTWOF* and may have needed to be quite "bland." Based on politics and some well-founded assumptions about what constraints the strip would face, her refusal demonstrated why LGBTQ comics stayed out of the most visible comics communities until only very recently. Bechdel was able to turn down the offer in part because she was able to make a living through self-syndicated cartooning. In the early 1990s, she was also earning money through her stationery business, where she sold a catalog of *DTWOF* items, including mugs, mousepads, and calendars.

Self-syndication offered Bechdel financial solvency as well an important connection to the communities represented in her strip. If she had accepted UPS's offer and given up self-syndication, she would have lost her source material. While she was publishing *DTWOF* with smaller periodicals, not only did they send her a copy of every issue, but they also frequently corresponded with her. That is, the structures of self-syndication facilitated Bechdel's close communication with each periodical. This correspondence was often warm and friendly, as her activist interlocutors related as much to her as they did to her recurring cast of characters who became a feature of the comic in early 1987. Yet, shoestring finances made funding the comic a continual battle—one that various periodicals put extra effort into solving, thereby proving the import of Bechdel's strip to their readers. For example, in the July/August 1988 issue of *Valley Women's Voice* (Pioneer Valley, MA), the paper printed a notice above one of Bechdel's strips: "HELP!: Don't let Mo, Toni, Ginger, and friends leave the Valley. Only with your sponsorship ($) can we keep *Dykes to Watch Out For* in the *Valley Women's Voice*" (Bechdel 1988). In this notice, the characters are configured as "friends" who might have to move away if financial support doesn't come through. Ultimately, *DTWOF* stayed in the Pioneer Valley periodical through the funding of local cartoonist Rob Ranney and others, whose names were published alongside the comic in future issues. Across the country, members of the *Lavender Network* (Eugene, OR) raised $600 to fund Bechdel's comics through their July 1990 Save the Dykes event. Sally Sheklow (1990), Bechdel's contact at *Lavender Network*, communicated the success of the event through photographs and also included information about her creative project, *The Sound of Lesbians*, a musical comedy-parody. Through these items, Sheklow shared the vibrancy of the queer community in the Pacific Northwest and displayed a personal connection with Bechdel. These examples show how personal investment in Bechdel's comic formed the basis for her support among these varied collectives, linking her to diverse lesbian communities.

These grassroots networks infused Bechdel's comic with queer rhetoric from a range of local and nationally known grassroots periodicals. Bechdel demonstrated how much her characters' lives are in sync with political change in an eleven-year graphic time line that she included in her retrospective book, *The Indelible Alison Bechdel* (Bechdel 1998, 73–83). She created five parallel time lines—a general one for national happenings that year; one for Mo; another for Clarice and Toni; yet another for Sparrow, Ginger, and Lois; and a final one for Madwimmin Books. In this elaborate time line, Bechdel included panels and images from her strip and captioned these happenings, arguing for the importance of common lesbian lives in their parallel development alongside large-scale events. This time line also evoked her grassroots popularity, as these women could see themselves in her characters, living their lives amid global changes much larger than themselves. In doing so, it effectively illustrated the networked visual politics that Bechdel first developed in the pages of *WomaNews*.

Through engaging Bechdel and her work in *WomaNews*, I argue for new methods of reading comics that arise out of and integrate their grassroots contexts. Interacting with other content on the pages of the periodical, these comics establish particular techniques in expressing queer experience. Bechdel's comics do visual work akin to what contemporary lesbian theorist Teresa de Lauretis (1984, 67–68) argues that feminist cinema should do in "construct[ing] another (object of) vision and the conditions of visibility for a different social subject." As Bechdel glibly puts it in an interview, "I would love to be the lesbian Norman Rockwell" (quoted in Stephenson 1995). Further specifying this project in a retrospective comic, Bechdel asserts that her goal is to create "a catalog of lesbians! I would name the unnamed. Depict the undepicted!" (Bechdel 2008a, xiv). That is, to embody Rockwell in a lesbian way, Bechdel seeks to "catalog" a wide array of "undepicted" lesbian experiences, making visible a multiplicity of "different social subject[s]" and creating the possibilities to maintain these "conditions" through her business savvy and persistence. Well-known for the *Saturday Evening Post* covers where he illustrated everyday US culture for more than five decades, Rockwell further broadened the swath of the United States he covered in later work when he tackled topics like civil rights. In some of her work, Bechdel directly echoes Rockwell, as when she modeled the cover of her 1994 calendar on Rockwell's iconic Thanksgiving painting, *Freedom from Want* (1943), by positioning the recurring cast of *DTWOF* around a table to celebrate the protagonist's birthday (Bechdel 1994). By naming her comic *Dykes to Watch Out For*, she directed her readers to look at this project and be complicit in making visible these new subjects, an action that included not only reading her comics but financially supporting her through purchasing calendars and other items.

Not only do Bechdel and de Lauretis theorize each other, but we can build from them a theory of the archives that contain these works. Explicitly queer and queer-adjacent archives are the frame around Bechdel that further sustains these "conditions of visibility," making apparent "different social subject[s]" from those found in comics collections in other archives. Archives that collect not only personal papers but more extensively a world of queer experience—periodicals, books from grassroots publishers, movement T-shirts and buttons, and so on—allow us to see the process of "construct[ing]" queer subjectivity and make visible not only queer individuals but truly a "social subject" in her investment in collective politics and queer networks. To wit, we can see the quotidian queer community that Bechdel strived to "catalog," taking a page from Rockwell's depictions of everyday US communities. Heather Stephenson (1995, 6), the journalist who solicited the Rockwell soundbite from Bechdel, posits, "Bechdel sees herself as an archivist chronicling her generation through the details of lesbians' daily lives." This embodiment of Bechdel "as an archivist" speaks volumes, for as a lesbian, "her generation" is the queer one that has hitherto not been seen in such fullness or, in de Lauretis's language, as "construct[ed]." It is perhaps little surprise, then, that two decades later the critical reception of Bechdel's *Fun Home* (2006a) focused on the archival aspects of her work, including her precise reproduction of personal family objects. Though this personal archive reflects individual queer experience, established queer archives make visible political networks that sustain individuals and allow us to understand Bechdel as "the lesbian Norman Rockwell" in a manner that individual autobiography alone cannot grasp.

Queer Comics Archives

Archives are not simply an aesthetics of Bechdel's work: she engages existing archives and, like many lesbian feminists before her, actively creates her own archives to store material that otherwise might not be saved (Cvetkovich 2003 and 2008; Chute 2010; Eichhorn 2013; Kumbier 2014). These actions directly inform her artwork not only in subject matter but also, as scholars like Hillary Chute have discussed, in her rigorous process of drawing from physical examples (Chute 2010). Bechdel's dual engagement with existing archives and her own practice of saving materials came together in late 2008 when she donated a first accession of archival material to the Sophia Smith Collection at Smith College. She documented this process in a video posted to YouTube titled "The Memoirist's Lament," where she shows her many filing cabinets all over her house before she divulges that Smith College will be archiving these materials (Bechdel 2008e). With this reveal, the camera pans back from the material being shown and text appears across the screen: "god help them." She then transitions to looking inside the filing cabinets, culling folders that end up among those materials going to Smith College. She has since donated several more accessions and plans to send along additional materials, so her archival connection is active in the present day.

When she began to identify files to send to Smith, Bechdel was also in the midst of another creative project of organization as she suspended her twenty-year comic strip, *DTWOF*, in May of that year and curated a selection of strips to be published with Houghton Mifflin Harcourt, the same publishing house that released *Fun Home* (2006a). Both projects were completed in fall 2008, as Smith received twenty boxes of archival materials and *The Essential Dykes to Watch Out For* (2008b) was released. Due to the simultaneity of these endeavors, the archive weighs heavily on Bechdel's collection. And it is not only the space of the Sophia Smith Collection that inflects *The Essential Dykes*, but it is also the Tretter Collection of GLBT archives at the University of Minnesota, where she visited in March (Bechdel 2008c), and the Human Sexuality Collection at Cornell University, which houses the papers of her longtime publisher, Firebrand Books, where she visited in April (Bechdel 2008d), that shape this volume.

These three archival encounters erupt onto the pages of Bechdel's introduction to *The Essential Dykes*. As in *Fun Home* (2006a) and *Are You My Mother?* (2012), in the introduction she re-creates personal documents in the telling of her artistic genealogy but depicts herself entering a locked room called the archives and accessing the documents from there (Bechdel 2008a, vii). Once she has entered this space, she starts rummaging through the drawers, seemingly disrupting classification yet retrieving her files in precise chronological order (viii). In the comic, she builds a narrative of how she became an artist through her reading of these archivally housed documents. Key here is her sprawling rendition of the archive itself, pictured in a long vertical panel on the left-hand side of the page. She uses this verticality to great effect, depicting the space as filled with rows of infinitely tall filing cabinets. This image resembles, in part, the back room of the Tretter Collection, where she captured a photo of herself in awe during her visit (Bechdel 2008c), except the shelves of archival boxes are replaced by fantastically impossible filing cabinets, giant versions of those that populate her home. At the point of donating her own files to Smith, Bechdel acknowledges in her work the hybridity of the space where such files are organized and kept—a merging of domestic and institutional storage. In this piece, Bechdel creates a fantasy archive through which she relates her personal queer history, just as institutional repositories collect a larger scope of queer genealogy. She discussed these larger histories as she blogged about her visits to the archives at the University of Minnesota and Cornell University (Bechdel 2008c and 2008d). In nesting three archives into one representation in this comic, she underlines their interconnected nature and how archives not only contain grassroots networks but are themselves also part of a network.

This network of archives that collect intersectional queer and feminist histories comprises grassroots archives started by activists. Ann Cvetkovich's *An Archive of Feelings* (2003) jump-started critical conversations about radical archives and remains a vital cornerstone, much as Jacques Derrida's *Archive Fever* (1995) did for more general archival concerns. Cvetkovich's delineation of grassroots archival spaces not only illuminates Bechdel's own symbolic embrace of archives, but from Cvetkovich's description we can also fashion our own definition of queer comics archives, which preserve this doubly marginalized work—as comics are an art form often not taken seriously that marginalized folks then embrace to represent their experience. Following her analysis of different valences of queer archives, including an extended discussion of the Lesbian Herstory Archives, Cvetkovich (2003, 268) defines these entities:

> Ephemeral evidence, spaces that are maintained by volunteer labors of love rather than state funding, challenges to cataloging, archives that represent lost histories—gay and lesbian archives are often "magical" collections of documents that represent far more than the literal value of the objects themselves. . . . Queer archives can be viewed as the material instantiation of Derrida's deconstructed archive; they are composed of material practices that challenge traditional conceptions of history and understand the quest for history as a psychic need rather than a science.

Throughout this passage, Cvetkovich focuses on different registers of "history" and the "challenges" that grassroots archives present, nuancing these concepts through repetition. Through coalescing ideas of "history" and its "challenges" in the "challenge [to] traditional conceptions of history," Cvetkovich demonstrates how all the items in her opening catalog add up: as "material practices" that can perform these "challenges" through various methods. In Bechdel's representation of archives, we can see how she leverages her "'magical' collection of documents" to narrate the overarching trajectory of her career, selecting items that together culminate into "more than" the sum of their parts. In activating archival objects, Bechdel "challenge[s] traditional conceptions of history" and uncovers her lived lesbian history that shapes her long-running comic. Where Bechdel illustrates the multivalent possibility of queer archives, Cvetkovich communicates the ways that archives enact that multivalence.

"Material practices" differentiate comics collections in queer archives from comics held in other archives. To create a framework for understanding how comics operate in tandem with the queer archives that house them, I theorize the notion of queer comics archives. They "challenge traditional conceptions of history" not only through the comics' content but also in how they open up "material practices" that give us new ways to analyze the documents themselves and conceptualize the affiliated histories. In this analysis and conceptualization, we activate de Lauretis's "conditions of visibility" that permit us to recognize new individual and collective histories (de Lauretis 1984, 67–68). Archives in general allow us to read comics with a new fullness and to see the personal networks surrounding their creation. Queer archives empower us to see new comics not housed in other comics collections and to understand the importance of social activism to comics through studying them in their original queer publication contexts in addition to examining them as they touch the lives of gay and lesbian folks who donate their ephemera to the archives or who are preserved through their communication with the artists themselves. Collections-building "material practices" embody "queerness as collectivity"—an articulation of the relational queer theory that José Esteban Muñoz (2009, 11) theorizes in *Cruising Utopia*. Just as Muñoz maps queer collectivity through close reading, I develop new practices of close-reading comics that emphasize relationality and thereby unfurl how queer activisms shape such works. Departing from the traditional formalism of comics scholarship that "privileges art and artists with more cultural capital, not less" (Galvan 2015, par. 9), this approach decenters the individual, honoring the rich history of collaboration in comics by opening a conversation about the multiple ways that communities shape even single-authored works.

We must analyze queer comics as they originally appeared in the pages of grassroots periodicals. I read comics as but one panel on an entire spread of content and examine how other materials on the page intersect with the comic. I further understand the periodical as a space of exploration and trace how comics art and styles evolve in this context. Given the inherent stylistic freedom, I also look to other image-text creations and read them under the paradigm of comics studies. With these practices, we read beyond the static frame that closets comics. When we fixate on the frame and what's inside, as strict comics formalism would have us do, we fix straight edges to our interpretation rather than considering queerer readings that cross borders (Anzaldúa 1987). Many early exploratory works are never republished outside of queer publication networks, but such works—like comics-infused advertisements—are important to understanding a more nuanced queer theory inflected by the thought of local collectives. These modes of reading comics bring the surrounding community and production history to bear on what is created in the panel.

Such practices are not applicable only to comics that appear in grassroots spaces; rather, we must be generally attentive to original publication histories and to reading across publication contexts. Whenever a comic is republished in a new venue, its meaning—and sometimes also its content—shifts. With queer comics especially, moments of republication build community as the new setting makes the comic visible to a new audience. As we have already seen, queer periodicals enfolded Bechdel's comic into their own local communities and inscribed her comic with additional meaning when they raised money to support her work. In prioritizing periodicals as an overlooked place for the development of queer comics, I position this article in conversation with recent scholarship that brings attention to the importance of periodicals to queer thought through close-reading the content and production histories of specific collectives (Beins and Enszer 2013; Enszer 2015a and 2015b; McKinney 2015; Beins 2017).

Now, I turn briefly to one of these methods: reading the comic in the context of the page spread. The other techniques are in play here, too, as I examine an advertisement for the collective where Bechdel leveraged comics-like imagery, and this piece is an early creation, so we could ask how Bechdel revised her style going forward. In the March 1984 issue of *WomaNews*, Bechdel produced an advertisement for two upcoming *WomaNews* workshops, where participants would "learn practical skills" like "editing/proofreading" and "layout/pasteup" (Bechdel 1984b, 8–9) (see fig. 2). The women exhibit serious demeanors as they demonstrate the skills covered in each workshop. Their faces communicate dedication—an attribute that *WomaNews* would want to encourage in potential new collective members. The humor lies in the action of their hands. The writerly type, bent so earnestly over a sheet of paper for the "editing/proofreading workshop," concentrates

Newsbriefs

compiled by Hennie Spek and Kathy Stener

• Two white North American activists, Shelley Miller and Silvia Baraldini, were subpoenaed last February by a federal grand jury investigating the clandestine Puerto Rican independence organization, FALN. The two women refused to testify and denounced their subpoenas as an effort at political internment of public activists. Miller, a leader of the New Movement in Solidarity with Puerto Rican Independence and Socialism, stated that the use of the grand jury is "part of a strategy by the U.S. Government to destroy solidarity with Puerto Rican independence at its earliest stages."

The two were to be tried on Feb. 9 for criminal contempt. At a pre-trial hearing, the defendants presented the judge with an open letter from nearly 100 organizations and individuals denouncing the use of the grand jury as a repressive tool of political internment and supporting the stance of non-collaboration. This is the third trial in the past year in which supporters of Puerto Rican independence have been prosecuted for criminal contempt.

• Thousands of women rallied in Ouagadougou, the capitol of Upper Volta, on Oct. 4 to celebrate the changes brought to women by the socialist revolution of Aug. 4, 1983.

The president of Upper Volta, Thomas Sankara, has consistently emphasized the exploitation of women and has urged and aided Voltaic women to organize to accomplish their liberation. In a speech on Oct. 2, he declared that the revolution and women's liberation go together. Since the revolution, women have been increasingly more involved with the Defense Committees, and the Ministry of Social and Women's Affairs has been restructured to take account of the new involvement.

• Two hundred women from the U.S. and Canada were refused entry to Honduras, where they planned to hold prayer vigils for peace in the region near two U.S. military bases and in the capital, Tegucigalpa.

The visit was organized by the Women's Coalition to Stop U.S. Intervention in Central America and the Caribbean. The first group was prevented from boarding a Honduran airline flight in New Orleans, after the company received word of the government's decision. The second group arrived in Honduras on an Air Florida flight, but the aircraft was ordered to return to Miami with the women on board.

Outwrite

• In 1982, Jackie Fourthman, then 20 years old, pleaded guilty to third-degree murder and child abuse in the death of her 7-month-old son. She was sentenced to 9 months in prison to be followed by probation conditional on her not having another baby for 15 years. Fourthman was arrested late last year for leaving Indiana without permission of her probation officer and for giving birth to another son in Nevada.

The probation condition may be renounced as unenforceable because Florida's Second District Court of Appeals called it unconstitutional when James Burcell, Fourthman's estranged husband and father of the dead child appealed the court order that he not father another child for 15 years.

The Guardian

• Rosemary Hernandez, a battered woman and mother of two young daughters, was murdered in Park Slope on July 27, 1983. Her husband, the prime suspect, was arrested in November. A memorial fund has been set up for the children, whose guardians are family members in desperate need of financial help. Contributions from individuals, groups or agencies should be sent to: Children of Rosemary Hernandez, c/o New York Women Against Rape, 231 E. 14th Street, NY 10003.

ARTISTS CALL Against U.S. Intervention in Central America staged a silent march on January 28 in New York City, as part of a 3 month calendar of events. Hundreds of artists and their supporters converged at the Battleship Intrepid, and walked in a somber single file procession down the Avenue of the Americas to a rally in Washington Square Park. The demonstrators, each wearing a black vest and white name band carrying the name and country of a human rights victim in Central America, then stepped into the park stage and recited the name and country of the deceased.

• The Nestle boycott is over. After seven years the Infant Formula Action Coalition has suspended the boycott against Nestle and affiliated products, including Stouffer's and Taster's Choice.

Nestle was under boycott for contributing to world hunger by marketing its products in such a way that poor women in developing countries stopped breast feeding their children. Recently the company began to follow the marketing codes of the World Health Organization. Ten nations participated in the boycott.

Science Magazine

• A group of women met February 11 to start a Women's Tax Resistance group. They feel they can't continue to demonstrate for peace and a feminist future while paying for war and destruction.

The money they withhold will be turned over to women's organizations, battered womens' shelters, clinics, daycare, etc., all those human services, so vital to women's lives, that have been cut.

All women are invited to resist with them in one of the following ways: refusing to pay telephone tax or some part of the federal income tax, or choosing to live simply below a taxable income. They said they are not opposed to paying taxes but can no longer pay for patriarchal violence either at home or around the world—helicopters over Nicaragua, the shelling of Lebanese villages—while school lunches and food stamps are cut, and decent housing is denied to the women, men and children of our city.

For more information about support meetings for Women's Tax Resistance call Margaret Jolly at 989-6615. There will be a general Tax Resistance workshop on March 25. Women from the women's group will be there.

Harriet Hirshorn

• A New York State ERA was opposed by leaders of National Women's Organizations at a recent meeting with Governor Mario Cuomo. Cuomo launched his attempt to pass a state Equal Rights Law in his second State of the State message. Women at the meeting warned Cuomo that his state proposal could damage chances for a federal Equal Rights Amendment. They explained that should ERA-NY lose, it would be a defeat from which women's organizations could not dissociate themselves whether or not they supported the campaign. Despite this opposition, Cuomo plans to ask the state legislature to pass the amendment this year and next.

The Guardian

• Eight Haitian women at the detention center of the Immigration and Naturalization Service (INS) started a hunger strike to protest policies toward refugees. The strike, which started on Jan. 19, has spread to one-third of the Krome detention center's prisoners. Detainees from Bangladesh, Lebanon, El Salvador, Guatamala, India, and Iran have joined the protest, which began when prisoners learned that three other Haitians just arriving from New Orleans were about to be deported after the Supreme Court turned down their appeal for political asylum.

The original strikers were joined by 62 Haitian men on Jan. 24 after an INS guard struck a Haitian refugee. Seventy more detainees joined the strike the next day. INS officials have barred the media and Haitian support group representatives from the camp since the hunger strike began.

The Guardian

• In January, the National Organization for Women sponsored its first Lesbian Rights Conference in Milwaukee, WI. The decision to hold the conference followed fierce internal struggles to realign the traditionally mainstream position of NOW, which has usually side-stepped lesbian issues.

In 1984, NOW made lesbian rights one of its four national priorities and began to plan the conference then. The 3-day conference, titled "Power and Politics in 84," focused on improving state laws on lesbian rights. In addition, the 350 delegates from across the nation chose New Jersey as a target state in which to pass a gay and lesbian civil rights bill.

The Guardian

• Over 400 pro-abortion forces in Washington state rallied on Jan. 22 against a crusade to close the Everett Feminist Women's Health Center. Since its opening in August, the center, which offers low-cost abortions, has been under attack by right-wing and fundamentalist Christian groups. These attacks included threatening phone calls and verbal and physical abuse of Center clients, and culminated in the firebombing of the clinic on Dec. 3, 1983.

Speakers at the rally insisted that abortion is an economic and not a moral issue. This was corroborated by a representative of the Whatcom County Labor Council, which passed a resolution noting that since women comprise 52% of the work force, women's right to safe and legal abortion is a labor issue.

• Following testimony by Nat'l Gay Task Force Excutive Director Virginia M. Apuzzo on January 26, the Committee on Human Development of the U.S. Conference of Mayors endorsed legal protections for gay men and lesbians. The Committee unanimously approved a resolution stating that "recognizing the right of all citizens, regardless of sexual orientation, to full participation in American society, the Committee recommends that all levels of government adopt legal protections for the rights of gay and lesbian Americans. The Committee calls on its colleagues to consider executive and legislative remedies to guarantee equal opportunity and protection in the public and private sectors."

The full Conference of Mayors will consider the resolution at its June meeting in Philadelphia. Apuzzo outlined for the mayors a series of policy measures that localities should undertake to ban discrimination against lesbians and gay men. According to NGTF some forty cities already have at least some civil rights guarantees for lesbians and gay men, along with ten counties and seven states.

• 1,000 women marched to protest violence against women in San Juan, Puerto Rico on Nov. 29. Women shouted and carried banners, and a group of 30 women dressed up to present the different roles of women in society—all of whom are raped. Women dressed as nurses, secretaries, domestic workers, teachers, and one woman dressed as a bride. The marchers congregated around the Capitol Building where two women chanted a list of 118 women who have died at the hands of their husbands, boyfriends, and rapists.

Outwrite

• The case of a lesbian graduate teaching assistant who lost her position at Louisiana State University because of her involvement with an undergraduate is now pending in the Fifth Circuit Court of Appeals. Kristin Naragon challenged the termination of her teaching position, but the District Court upheld the University's position. In the appeal of the case, *Naragon vs. Wharton*, Lambda Legal Defense and Education Fund has filed a "friend of the court" brief. Lambda and the Louisiana Civil Liberties Union, which represents the plaintiff, argue that Naragon has been deprived not only of her right to professional training but of her constitutional rights to privacy, free association, and due process.

• Student doctors practicing vaginal examinations on unconscious women is a common and accepted practice in the teaching hospitals of England. In fact, according to a report on basic medical education "students on gynecology attachments find theatre sessions valuable for this reason."

The women—who have gone to the hospital as patients expecting health care—are not asked for their permission for these examinations.

Outwrite

Figure 2 "Advertisement: *WomaNews* Workshops and Page Spread." Originally in *WomaNews*, March 1984. Courtesy of Lesbian Herstory Archives

Community Announcements

"Black Women: Achievements Against the Odds," an exhibit which features 20 posters marking the contributions of Black women in American history, will run through March 31 at the Morris-Jumel Mansion, W. 160th Street and Edgecombe Ave. The exhibition is free with the museum admission of $1 and can be viewed from 10-4 p.m. (except Mondays)...**Lambda Legal Defense has an opening for a Public Information Director.** Strong writing & editing skills and working knowledge of the media helpful. Call 944-9488. Resume with references to Lambda Legal Defense, 132 West 43 St., NY, NY 10036. Minority and women candidates encouraged to apply...**Entries are now being accepted for the third annual San Francisco Gay Video Festival 1984**, which is part of San Francisco's Lesbian/Gay Freedom Celebration. The festival brings together the best in professional, avant-garde, and short features by independent lesbian and gay producers around the country. Deadline for entries is May 31. Accepted formats are 3/4" and 1/2" VHS. For information and entry forms, contact: John Canaly, FRAMELINE, 182-B Castro St., San Francisco, CA 94114 or call (415) 861-0843...**"Work and Families in the '80's,"** a conference on changing roles and expectations, will be sponsored by the Yale Undergraduate Women's Caucus. Topics will range from workplace innovations and childcare to men and families and decision making on parenting. The conference will take place on Friday, March 2 and Saturday, March 3 at Dwight Hall, Yale. For more info contact Debra Schwartz, (203) 776-7704 or the Yale Women's Center (203) 432-3813...**The Second Annual Black Women's History Conference** will take place on Saturday, March 24 and Sunday, March 25 on the Douglass College Campus of Rutgers University in New Brunswick. Cost for the conference is $41.50 and the deadline for registration is March 7th. Included in the weekend's events will be a concert on Saturday evening featuring Sweet Honey in the Rock. For more info, contact Viola Van Jones (201) 932-9603 or (201) 932-9729...**The Women's Coalition to stop U.S. Intervention in Central America and the Caribbean** encourages membership of national organizations with differences in racial/ethnic makeup, age, experience, and faith traditions to work towards peace in this hemisphere. Annual membership for organizations is $25, for individuals in local chapters, $5. Contact: Sr. Marjorie Tuite, 475 Riverside Dr., Room 812, NY 10115...A writer/editor seeks women who have given children up for adoption—either legal or covert—and are willing to write or talk about their experiences for an anthology bringing together women's voices and historical, cross-cultural, legal, and feminist perspectives on the institutions, customs and attitudes surrounding adoption. If you wish to participate, contact K. Kaufmann, c/o Plexus, 545 Athol Ave., Oakland, CA 94606...**Need a place to display your artwork? The Gay Women's Alternative's Lesbian Feminist Art Show** will include the works of painters, weavers, photographers, posters, etc. Call Linda Grishman at (212) 989-2958 for more information...**Tuesday, March 20, will be Gay/Lesbian Lobby Day in Albany.** The Lobby Day is being sponsored by the New York State Lesbian and Gay Lobby (NYSLGL). Topics range from funding for the AIDS Institute to the eventual passage of a gay and lesbian civil rights bill. All registered voters are eligible to participate. For further info, contact Richard Gottlieb—(212) 867-7500 (day) and (212) 757-7434 (night)...**The week of April 29-May 5 will be "Women's Week" at Virginia Polytechnic Institute and State University.** Lectures, workshops, entertainment and celebration with focus on women's lives, history, culture and accomplishments. Send your complimentary books, copies of periodicals & promotional materials for display to: Evelyn Newlyn, Chair Women's Studies Committee, Virginia Polytechnic Institute & State University, Blacksburg, VA 24061...**Yenga Productions is looking for original half hour and hour-long radio plays by women of color or adaptations of such works for summer production.** Deadline: March 30. Send a SASE for returns. Please include brief biographical sketch and send to: Yenga Productions, P.O. Box 25216-0, Durham, NC 27702...**International Women's Day on WBAI (99.5 FM) takes place on March 8 from 7:30am-11:30pm.** The program will include documentaries, panels, news, interviews & music on women's issues. Detailed description of program available March 1 from WBAI-FM, 505 8th Ave., New York, NY 10018. tel. (212) 279-0707...**Lesbian Health workers are available for services at Community Health Project on Thursday nights, beginning March 8, from 7-9 pm.** Call for appointment (212) 691-8282. Volunteers are welcomed and will be trained by the staff...**St. Mark's Women's Health Collective, New York's lesbian clinic will hold an orientation and training for new members on Friday, March 23 at 7:30pm.** The clinic is located at 9 Second Ave. between Houston and East First St., tele. 228-7482, Tuesday evenings 5-9pm. ■

THE NEW YORK CENTER FOR EATING DISORDERS

offers therapy for emotional eaters
• compulsive overeaters • anorexia
• bulimia

622-2575

A 6-week workshop for compulsive overeaters will begin shortly.

(212) 729-3400

FRANK C. DAVID, Inc.
FUNERAL HOME

Five minutes from Manhattan
JUST ACROSS THE 59th STREET BRIDGE
Convenient to all subways — Parking

MARIA CIMO   31st St. and 30th Ave.
Funeral Director   Long Island City, NY 11101

Serving the Women's Community since 1979

Massage • Shiatsu
Energy Balancing

MARJORIE CONN   582-3533

WANTED

Singles of all lifestyles

DON'T BE ALONE ANYMORE

DISCOVER THE NEW ALTERNATIVE

Free info write:

Superrific Connections Ltd.
51 East 42nd St.
Suite 517W
New York, N.Y. 10017

DEBBIE FIER
INNOVATIVE PIANIST/VOCALIST
Appearing with
Jean Fineberg on sax & flute
and
Nydia Mata on congas

Saturday
March 24
10 & 11:30 pm
at
Eric's
2nd Ave.
at 88th St.
New York City
$5.00

Womanews Workshops

Learn Practical Skills — FREE

EDITING/PROOFREADING WORKSHOP • SAT. MAR. 31
12-5 PM

Tired of long-winded prose?
Learn the fine arts of deletion,
insertion and transposition.

LAYOUT/PASTEUP WORKSHOP
SAT. APRIL 28
12-5 PM

Pasteup is not as hard as it seems.
Learn the fundamentals of wielding an
X-acto knife, sizing photographs and
using a T-square. No skills needed.

ALL WOMEN WELCOME
CALL TO REGISTER- 989-7963

325 SPRING ST. RM. 310

WHEELCHAIR ACCESSIBLE

FEMINIST PSYCHOTHERAPIST

THE CHOICE OF A THERAPIST IS A POLITICAL CHOICE

MELODY M. ANDERSON, C.S.W.

(212) 737-2032

The Woman's Newspaper
of Princeton

"A Woman's Place
is Where She Wants to Be"

PO Box 1303
Princeton, NJ 08542
(609) 924-1330

Complimentary copy with this coupon

GLOBAL LESBIANISM 2

Make connections with
lesbians around the world...

Connexions #10, the second Global Lesbianism issue brings you a view of the world through the voices of lesbians internationally.

A year's subscription to Connexions is only $10. Single issues—$3.50. Connexions, an international women's quarterly, 4228 Telegraph Ave., Oakland, CA 94609.

Connexions

W.B.A.I.

The Lesbian Show
Everywomans space
Woman Network News
The Velvet Sledgehammer
The Weekly Report from Intergay
Women and the World in the 1980's

"The Only Programming of its Kind in New York"

W.B.A.I. 99.5 FM
Listener-supported
Non-commercial radio

her energies on marking one big single *X* on the paper as if to cheekily pronounce, "No, no, and no; all of this has to go!" Below her, the woman engaged in the "layout/pasteup workshop" has been stymied by her overzealous approach to the tools of the trade—glue, paper, and scissors. The glue is all over the table, and cutout paper rectangles of various sizes are stuck all over her. Yet, she still determinedly holds the scissors in her right hand as she attempts to wrest control of her left hand from the glue's grasp. That levity and a bit of chaos enter the frame through the working hands implies that the activity of making *WomaNews* is not a mechanical endeavor but, rather, a creative, open, and human one. There is space for mess and occasionally flip decisions within a fervent framework.

Reading this piece as but one panel in a full-page spread, we can see how its meaning radiates as those looking at the advertisement could imagine the work of their hands in carefully editing the news briefs or in curating the advertisements to fill space on this and subsequent pages. We can also consider the page from Bechdel's perspective—these are the conversations and social organizations that influenced the evolution of her work and also those she edited and organized when she participated in page layout. The humor that Bechdel balances in the representations of the women gestures toward the flexibility that she enacts to match her style to fit not only the periodical's politics but also its limitations of page space. This matter of space became even more important when Bechdel moved from advertisements created to fit existing space to comics that she published across an array of periodicals. Her *DTWOF* comics blossomed alongside her participation in the *WomaNews* periodical. In the Firebrand reprints, we see these comics spanning two slim horizontal pages, while they take up a large full page in *The Essential Dykes* (2008b). When Bechdel sent her comics off to numerous periodicals, she included information about how to print and arrange this comic, giving the periodical a few horizontal and vertical possibilities so that the comic could fit various page layouts. When we expand our reading of a comic beyond the edges of the frame, as archives that house vast collections of queer periodicals allow us to do, we activate the notion of queer comics archives that free us to read comics in multiple contexts and fully engage "queerness as collectivity" (Muñoz 2009, 11).

In the following sections, I discuss Bechdel's development as a comics artist in conversation with the *WomaNews* collective through analyzing works she produced while a member of the collective. I assess these archivally held works through the close-reading methods of queer comics archives, first tracing the evolution of Bechdel's work through deliberate revision and then examining the importance of her comics-adjacent work for *WomaNews*. These accounts push back on the sense of Bechdel as a singular genius, since they show how Bechdel's participation in queer networks influenced her work. Queer comics archives make visible the networked world that queer comics thrived in and that has heretofore been little discussed in comics scholarship.

WomaNews and Revision

Bechdel started publishing in *WomaNews* in the July/August 1983 issue and spent the next two years evolving her comic in the pages of the periodical while also participating in its production. As she became a member of the collective in late 1983,[5] she produced one comic per issue along with other contributions. As she developed her hand, her earlier work explicitly served as the foundation for later work. Such was the case with a series of images of lesbians writing that Bechdel debuted in the October 1983 issue (figs. 3–8). These graphics accompany readers' letters. Bechdel consolidated these individual panels into a *DTWOF* strip in September 1984 (Bechdel 1984h, 16) (fig. 9) and substantially revised this strip for the first collection of her comics that Firebrand Books released in October 1986 (Bechdel 1986, 36–37) (fig. 10). This three-year period of intense refinement preceded her creation in early 1987 of the iteration of *DTWOF* that most readers are familiar with, which follows a dedicated cast of characters. To untangle Bechdel's process of making new lesbian subjectivities visible alongside her development as a politically informed comics artist, I track her revisions for these letter-writing lesbians.

These literary figures evoke the range of opinions that surround them on the letters page. The first image in the October 1983 issue of *WomaNews* shows an agitated woman, biting the tip of her pen while mulling over the next words to add to two pages of vigorously scrawled handwriting (Bechdel 1983b, 2) (fig. 3). This figure sits in a simple, square panel at the beginning of the letters page, in the top left of three columns, right next to the staff box.[6] The correspondence that surrounds this image has the same level of fierce passion

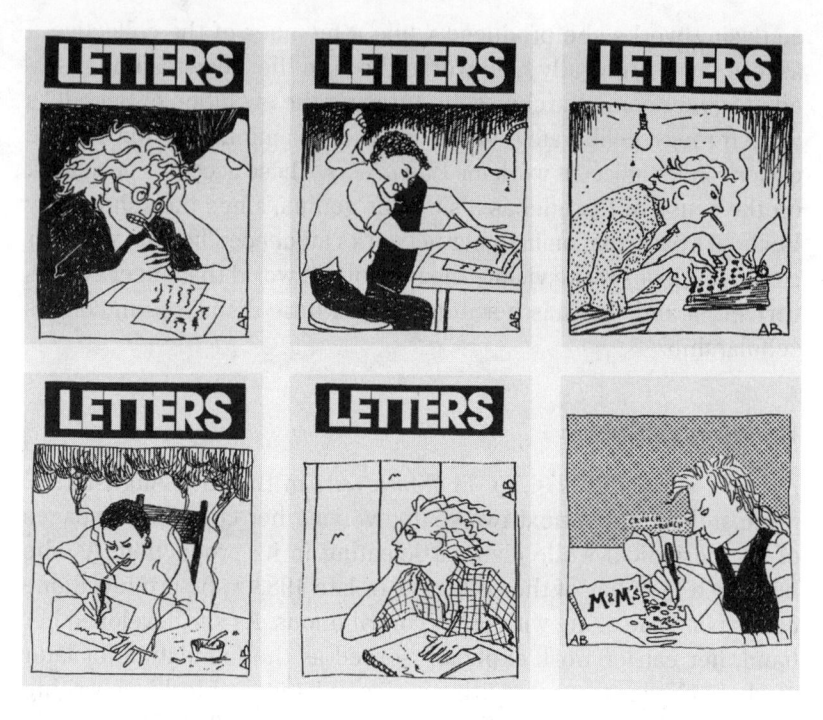

Figures 3–8 Letter-writing lesbians. Originally in *WomaNews*, October 1983–July/August 1984. Courtesy of Lesbian Herstory Archives

to it—if not more. In one of the dispatches on the page, for instance, Gloria Anzaldúa and Cherríe Moraga issue a public call, asking *WomaNews* readers to donate money to help get *This Bridge Called My Back* back into print with Kitchen Table: Women of Color Press (Anzaldúa and Moraga 1983, 2) after the dissolution of Persephone Press, reported in the pages of *WomaNews* two months previous (*WomaNews* Collective 1983, 13). Bechdel's figure—with her punchy persona and penmanship—taps into the unsettled energies on the letters page. The extreme color contrast deployed in representation—only scratchy, intense blacks or negative white space, no shades of crosshatched gray—visually underscores the raw nerves.

This intensity of feeling would continue in the women Bechdel drew for the letters page. All told, during her tenure at *WomaNews*, she created six letter-writing lesbians who were freely repurposed in the same section in subsequent issues. In all these images, the

"The Lesbian Norman Rockwell" 425

Figure 9 "Literary Dykes to Watch Out For: A Heloise C. Bland Lecture." Originally in *WomaNews*, September 1984. Courtesy of Lesbian Herstory Archives

Figure 10 "Literary Dykes to Watch Out For: A Heloise C. Bland Lecture." Originally in *Dykes to Watch Out For* (1986)

women are actively putting words on the page. The last of these figures first appeared in the July/August 1984 issue of *WomaNews*, a year after Bechdel's first contributions to the collective (Bechdel 1984f, 2) (fig. 8). This focused figure, in a jumper and with an apparent mullet, crunches on M&Ms, which are spilled across the selfsame page where she is composing. This woman and the five who precede her embody a wide variety of writerly affects—from those who smoke while writing (Bechdel 1984e, 2; Bechdel 1984d, 2) to those who contort their bodies to write (Bechdel 1983a, 2) to those who stare out into the distance for inspiration (Bechdel 1984g, 2) (figs. 4–7). In each iteration, the words of the letters surrounding these images supply the context, rather than Bechdel's words themselves providing contextualization.

This framing shifts when Bechdel further developed these writerly affects in the "Literary Dykes to Watch Out For" comic strip in the September 1984 issue of *WomaNews* (Bechdel 1984h, 16) (fig. 9). In this short strip, a narratorial voice, identified as "Heloise C. Bland" in the strip's subtitle, proposes, in the first, text-only panel, "to provide a brief psychological catalogue of the more common types of lesbians who write." In the following panels, we encounter six distinct women, represented not just as "types" but more specifically as species: Bland gives each of them a pseudo-scientific name in the accompanying boxes that describe each woman. These six species do not generally map one-to-one with their six *WomaNews* letters page predecessors; rather, their evolutions are more complex.

Although the letters-page lesbians show a range of affects, their association with the opinion page of a feminist periodical restricts their representation. In fact, their framing bespeaks these limitations—they are seen, more or less, in medium close-up, focusing their attention on the act of composition. We know relatively little about the worlds of these characters. These figures universally evoke collectivity by remaining open for identification with the varied letter writers of *WomaNews*. In her strip, Bechdel retains the universal quality of these women by transforming them into literary species.

To understand these species, we must grasp their natural habitat and behaviors, so we are treated to these figures in medium to medium-long shot, connected to their physical surroundings and the fullness of their bodies. In all the panels, we are told a story about the woman in association with her environment that shapes and is shaped by her writerly affect. The first four species are solitary, but the final two panels open up species of writers who are sexual (*Scriptus interruptus*) and social (*Procrastinatoria inertia*), and Bechdel increases the size of these panels in order to show these women engaged in composition through avenues of relation to other bodies. All these writerly species, however, have something, animate or otherwise, that inspires them to write.

The most newly evolved of the species in the strip is the one on the technological forefront, *Floppius discus*, who stares intently into a computer screen while jamming to tunes on her portable audio cassette player, the "Walkperson." Both of these technologies were newly available in the 1980s, with the personal computer highlighted in the American cultural zeitgeist in 1984 following an unprecedentedly popular Apple computer commercial during that year's Super Bowl.[7] This new, hip writerly persona exists alongside the orderly *Analus perfectus*, diligently at her typewriter with a cup of tea as day breaks. In the structure of the comic, this picture of perfection is formally contrasted with *Tequila nocturnalia*, the tortured writer—both smoker and alcoholic in this rendition—scribbling out words in the dead of night. But what about *Analus perfectus* vis-à-vis *Floppius discus*? We are in a moment of coexisting writerly technologies, but there is the future pull to the computer, borne out over time, further bolstering the forward motion of this figure. It is interesting, then, that in this strip, *Floppius discus* is the only overtly raced character. The future is more multicultural and complex than the white and tidy world of *Analus perfectus*, soon to be obsolete.

When Bechdel published this strip in her first *DTWOF* collection in 1986, she made further changes, forecasting the developing politics of her representations (Bechdel 1986, 36–37) (fig. 10). Indeed, looking from the version of "Literary Dykes to Watch Out For" in *WomaNews* to the one in her first published collection is akin to a lesbian spoof of the childhood "spot the differences" game in any *Highlights* magazine. If *Floppius discus* was the multicultural future foretold in the first iteration, then this future is building steam in the second version, where two more figures are visually reworked as women of color. These reworkings of *Ingestis poetica* and the woman listening to *Procrastinatoria inertia* do more than simply acknowledge the rising prominence of woman of color feminism. These personages also foretell the growth of the personal brand of lesbian feminist diversity that Bechdel more fully embraced when she relaunched *DTWOF* with a multiracial cast of recurring characters in 1987. It's hardly a coincidence that these two revised figures resemble two of her *DTWOF* characters, Sparrow and Ginger, respectively.

Overall, the collected version of this comic is more polished—from the neater styling of the typeface to the amount of detail lavished in representing each figure. In the revision process, some background elements were omitted to streamline the drawing—from the missing ashtray in *Tequila nocturnalia*'s frame to the reduction of the food items represented in *Ingestis poetica*'s workspace. In the revision of *Procrastinatoria inertia*, the "most prevalent type of lesbian writer," Bechdel changed the panel in numerous subtle ways that culminate in altering its meaning and its relationship to the reader. In both iterations, *Procrastinatoria inertia* has vaguely the same look—her T-shirt-and-jeans torso faces forward while she gazes semiwistfully off to the left in recounting her Connecticut childhood. In its first version, Bechdel directly aligned this figure with the readers of *WomaNews* by portraying her in a *WomaNews* T-shirt. This *WomaNews Procrastinatoria inertia* tells her tale at the bar to no one in particular—there is a couple getting handsy off frame to her right, and on her left, her one potential listener dozes while clenching a bottle of alcohol. With this T-shirt, Bechdel suggests that all readers are likely this woman at one point or another. In her revision and with her addition of an African American proto-Ginger in the frame, *Procrastinatoria inertia* takes on new meaning. By depicting the woman in a plain white T-shirt, Bechdel removed the associational ties to *WomaNews*, but we know, by the framing of the comic, that she is still not only a lesbian but ostensibly a dyke to watch out for, in the many valences of the phrase. Though the couple off frame to the right are still getting handsy in this version, this new *Procrastinatoria inertia*, in telling her tale, provokes a response—namely, one of proto-Ginger's apparent exasperation. Her annoyed expression isn't just about an irritating bar patron but gestures toward an exhaustion with this kind of white lesbian feminist, obliviously grandstanding about her privilege with no sense of the varied experiences of the feminists around her. Intersectional politics became an even more overt discourse in *DTWOF* in future years.

Queer Comics-Adjacent Material

In addition to her comics, Bechdel's image-text contributions to *WomaNews* included covers, advertisements, and graphics accompanying articles. Through these works, Bechdel implemented the visual language of comics and experimented with her form in ways that she later integrated into her comics. This technique was another form of revision, another instrument in her toolbox for creating more visible lesbian experiences. Across her advertisements promoting both social events and collective-building workshops, we can see her nascent visual politics, where she is thinking about how to portray a range of characters that represent collective experience.

Her advertisement for the *WomaNews* Fifth Anniversary Variety Show! embraced diversity by featuring five very different women locked arm-in-arm doing high kicks (Bechdel 1984c, 11; Bechdel 1985, 11) (fig. 11). Unlike the Rockettes, the famous New York City all-female precision dance troupe known both for high kicks and for a similitude of appearance among members of the group, the five women here differ from each other in every attribute: age, race, weight, cup size, height, shoe taste, hairstyle (Lambert 1987, par. 11). Bechdel's visual reference radiates particularly forcefully as the December date of this event—and, thus, the publication of the advertisement in the November and December/January issues of *WomaNews*—coincided with the Rockettes' performative mainstay, the annual holiday show (par. 18). For Bechdel to copy the Rockettes' signature high kick but radically depart from the accompanying display of only one sort of woman is especially progressive, given that the Rockettes were not yet a racially integrated troupe (Peterson 1984).

Bechdel's image suggests the unified movement of her dancers' high kick—other visual signifiers of similarity be damned. These women are linked together in political movement that builds strength from their diversity. Unlike the Rockettes, who pride themselves on similitude, success here is judged by difference—how many kinds of women can come together in coalition, high kicking (literally or metaphorically), arm-in-arm?

The wording of the ad suggests further coalitional broadening. The text framing the image is hand-drawn by Bechdel, as well, meaning that she was involved in the nitty-gritty details of the event. In the November version of the advertisement, the text beneath the image exclaims, "Singers! Dancers! Musicians! Surprises!" A number of possible expressions are enthusiastically encouraged; spectacles that fall out of the expected triptych are celebrated as "Surprises!" Further, prominently under the event information and taking up the same width as the image and its adjacent text, a line announces, "Performance space wheelchair accessible," welcoming sisters with disabilities. The text extends the range of expressions and bodies that can participate in both this variety show and collective. Moreover, this advertisement, in both the November and December/January issues, is embedded on the bottom right of the two-page calendar of events

430 American Literature

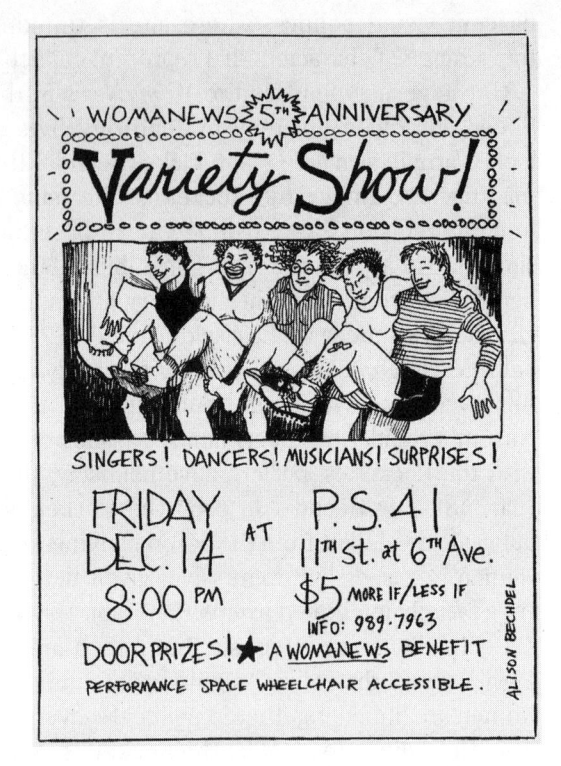

Figure 11 "Advertisement: *WomaNews* 5th Anniversary! Variety Show!" Originally in *WomaNews*, November 1984. Courtesy of Lesbian Herstory Archives

potentially of interest to those in the *WomaNews* community. Beyond the borders of this ad, we are immersed in a wide range of upcoming events for women of all sorts of dispositions.

In other advertisements, Bechdel showcased more ways that readers could support the collective. For the April 1984 issue, she devised a new advertisement for the sale of *WomaNews* T-shirts (Bechdel 1984a, 21) (fig. 12). In seeking to draw women into the collective by celebrating its politics as an active, fun, engaged endeavor, Bechdel employed multiple panels. In its arrangement of panels into a two-by-two grid, this advertisement reads as a comic. The narrative does not follow one woman in her *WomaNews* T-shirt but potentially four different women with diverse approaches. In each panel, cropping or perspective obscures the face of each woman, but contrasting visual cues—background texture, T-shirt, and hairstyle—suggest that we are looking at four different lived experiences. The illustrations encourage various

"The Lesbian Norman Rockwell" 431

Figure 12 "Advertisement: Get Yourself a *WomaNews* T-Shirt!" Originally in *WomaNews*, April 1984. Courtesy of Lesbian Herstory Archives

uses for the T-shirt, definitively echoed in exclamatory text in the space below each panel. In the top row of panels, Bechdel portrays two women altering the T-shirt to fit their daily lifestyles—the first woman rips off the collar, sleeves, and bottom hem of the shirt to create a punk look, while the second woman keeps a pack of cigarettes rolled in her right sleeve. By recommending alterations to the T-shirts in the very advertisement selling them, Bechdel and the *WomaNews* collective imagine a whole host of gender presentations in this garb. The *WomaNews* T-shirt and *WomaNews* itself are open for reinterpretation and negotiation on a regular basis.

The bottom row juxtaposes these diurnal activities by suggesting two nocturnal approaches to the garment. In these panels, both women are getting ready for bed while wearing their *WomaNews* T-shirts, but their shared experience diverges from there. Above a caption that intones, "Wear it to bed!" the first woman dons the T-shirt as her nightie, while diligently brushing her teeth, an action that suggests a quiet end to the evening. This speculation is supported by both the content of the second panel and its negating caption, "Don't wear it to bed!" Here, a woman removes her T-shirt in order to join an already naked partner awaiting her in bed; her evening is likely far from over. While this image is fairly innocuous in its portrayal of an imminent intimate encounter, the inclusion of lesbian sexuality as something that can be playfully tackled in a T-shirt advertisement gestures toward a feminist politics that embraces a wide range of sexual expression, just as the first row validates a gamut of gender presentation. Taken together, these panels celebrate a variety of sartorial choices, reflecting the array of political coverage but injecting it with humor through the comics medium. In this and other advertisements, *WomaNews* is explicitly evoked at the top, framing these representations. The collective nurtures Bechdel's visual politics and gives her the space to experiment with the comics form. Over the course of her career, grassroots spaces have continued to support Bechdel's growth.

Networking *Dykes* Online

Eight years after ceasing her creation of *DTWOF* in 2008, Bechdel released a Thanksgiving strip in November 2016 that responded to the presidential election of Donald Trump. She published the comic both in her local Vermont paper, *Seven Days* (Burlington), as well as on her personal blog, where she briefly prefaced it: "Since I stopped drawing *Dykes to Watch Out For* at the tail end of the Bush administration, people have asked me many times if I thought about my characters, and if so, what they were up to. And I would have to be honest. No, I didn't think about them, and I had no idea what they were doing. But last week they all started flooding back" (Bechdel 2016). She has since circulated two more strips in *Seven Days* and through her online outlets, the second coinciding with the Ides of Trump postcard-writing campaign in March 2017 and the third in July 2017 following the characters as they celebrate the Fourth of July. As she wrote on the release of this second strip, "I plan to continue doing these on an occasional basis as a way of staying sane" (Bechdel 2017). The commenters on her website and Facebook post thanked her for this strip and agreed with her sentiment about maintaining sanity. Despite the fact that Bechdel had not published a strip in nearly a decade, her community continues to affectively relate to *DTWOF*—evident in these responses and in Bechdel's statement that people asked after her characters.

These moments of interaction evidence how the transformation of grassroots infrastructure in the digital era facilitates community connection. Bechdel herself cites this direct interaction with her "strong community of readers" as a reason to start releasing her strips on her blog when she began the practice in early 2006 (Bechdel 2006b). Though common Internet wisdom advises against reading the comments, in queer communities this space facilitates an engagement that shapes future work. This dialogue echoes the correspondence with individual periodicals that I discussed at the outset of this article. In both instances, those who love her work communicate their support and discuss the future trajectory of her plot. In digital space, she often directly responds to these suggestions in the comment stream or by penning response posts on her blog (Bechdel 2006d). One of the hallmarks of comics is how they circulate among many publication venues, and I have argued throughout this piece that we must centralize queer periodical networks to understand the development of queer comics while simultaneously underlining how archives—grassroots archives in particular—preserve these networks.

By turning to the digital in closing, I urge us to pay attention to how the digital infrastructure of these spaces also facilitates "queerness as collectivity" (Muñoz 2009, 11). In digital spaces, we must regard both those new artists who have innovated the form of the web comic and those artists, like Bechdel, who take up the digital to supplement existing careers and how they re-create their physical communities in these new spaces. For Bechdel, this new infrastructure supports her identity as "the lesbian Norman Rockwell" as she connects more closely with readers while making lesbian experience visible in multiple forms (Stephenson 1995). On her blog, she not only distributes her comics, but she also shares sketches, textual reflections alongside accompanying photos, homemade videos, and various other new media image-text creations. This platform allows her to get back in touch with her beginnings at *WomaNews* and *Equal Time*, where she created comics-adjacent work in close proximity to her more formally legible comics. By embracing queer comics archives and affiliated spaces, we come to regard the role of queer community and transgress the borders of what constitutes comics in ways that better reflect and serve shifting queer activisms.

Margaret Galvan is assistant professor of visual rhetoric in the Department of English at the University of Florida. She is currently at work on a book, *In Visible Archives of the 1980s: Feminist Politics and Queer Platforms* (Univ. of Minnesota Press, under contract), which traces a genealogy of queer theory in 1980s feminism through representations of sexuality in visual culture. Her published work, which analyzes visual media culture through intersectional archival approaches, can be found in journals like *WSQ: Women's Studies Quarterly*, *Archive Journal*, and *Australian Feminist Studies* and in collections like *The Ages of the X-Men* (McFarland, 2014) and *Disability in Comic Books and Graphic Narratives* (Palgrave Macmillan, 2016).

Notes

I would like to express my gratitude to Alison Bechdel for her work, her precise record-keeping and archival donation, and her generosity in facilitating this research. Many thanks are due to the grant-funding institutions (the Graduate Center, CUNY; Smith College; NYC Digital Humanities) and the archives and archivists who have supported the development of this research over the past few years. Thanks also to key individuals who have been invaluable interlocutors: Nancy K. Miller, Meredith Benjamin, Melina Moore, Jack Gieseking, Jonathan W. Gray, Leah Misemer, and Hillary Chute. Thanks also to the editors of this special issue, Darieck Scott and Ramzi Fawaz, for their keen editorial insights.

1 Judith Kegan Gardiner (2011) explicitly analyzes *DTWOF* through this collection.
2 In an interview with Anne Rubenstein (1995, 116), Bechdel says, "And I started volunteering at a feminist newspaper called *WomaNews* where I did paste-up and production and wrote an occasional review."
3 In designating certain archives as queer-adjacent, I identify spaces that aren't explicitly queer but that contain a lot of materials relevant to queer experience, like the Sophia Smith Collection, for instance. This use of *adjacent* resonates with Eve Kosofsky Sedgwick's (2003, 8) discussion of the nondualistic nature of *beside* in *Touching Feeling* and how the spaciousness of that preposition allows "a wide range of desiring, identifying, representing, repelling, paralleling, differentiating, rivaling, leaning, twisting, mimicking, withdrawing, attracting, aggressing, warping, and other relations."
4 *Gay Comix* was a comics series that ran for twenty-five issues between 1980 and 1998 under three successive editors: Howard Cruse (#1–4), Robert Triptow (#5–13), and Andy Mangels (#14–25). In issue #15 (1992), Mangels renamed the series, *Gay Comics*, acknowledging the changing times and diminished presence of the underground comix scene that initially birthed the series. When discussing the series collectively, I refer to it by its initial title as that appears to be the general convention.

5   Two months after first publishing in *WomaNews*, Bechdel joined the staff box (masthead) as a named contributor, and two months later, in the December 1983/January 1984 issue, she appeared as a full member of the collective's staff, a position she continued to hold for a year and a half until the July/August 1985 issue.
6   Coincidentally, the October 1983 issue was the first in which Bechdel was listed in the staff box as a contributor to the collective.
7   Linda M. Scott (1991, 67–68) describes the huge public response following the advertisement in January 1984, which translated into big sales for Apple in the coming months.

References

Anzaldúa, Gloria. 1987. *Borderlands/La Frontera: The New Mestiza*. San Francisco: Aunt Lute Books.
Anzaldúa, Gloria, and Cherríe Moraga. 1983. "Bring *Bridge* Back!" *WomaNews*, October, letters sec. Lesbian Herstory Archives, Newsprint Collection, *WomaNews*.
Avery, Tara Madison, and Jon Macy. 2016. *Alphabet*. Walnut, CA: Stacked Deck Press.
Bechdel, Alison. 1983a. "Letters Page Caricature Graphic: Contortionist Letter-Writer." *WomaNews*, November, letters sec. Lesbian Herstory Archives, Newsprint Collection, *WomaNews*.
———. 1983b. "Letters Page Caricature Graphic: Pen-Biting Agitated Female." *WomaNews*, October, letters sec. Lesbian Herstory Archives, Newsprint Collection, *WomaNews*.
———. 1984a. "Advertisement: Get Yourself a *WomaNews* T-Shirt!" *WomaNews*, April. Lesbian Herstory Archives, Newsprint Collection, *WomaNews*.
———. 1984b. "Advertisement: *WomaNews* Workshops and Page Spread." *WomaNews*, March. Lesbian Herstory Archives, Newsprint Collection, *WomaNews*.
———. 1984c. "Advertisement: *WomaNews* 5th Anniversary! Variety Show!" *WomaNews*, November. Lesbian Herstory Archives, Newsprint Collection, *WomaNews*.
———. 1984d. "Letters Page Caricature Graphic: Chainsmoking Letter-Writer." *WomaNews*, February, letters sec. Lesbian Herstory Archives, Newsprint Collection, *WomaNews*.
———. 1984e. "Letters Page Caricature Graphic: Intent, Typewriting Female." *WomaNews*, December 1983/January 1984, letters sec. Lesbian Herstory Archives, Newsprint Collection, *WomaNews*.
———. 1984f. "Letters Page Caricature Graphic: M&M Letter-Writer." *WomaNews*, July/August, letters sec. Lesbian Herstory Archives, Newsprint Collection, *WomaNews*.

———. 1984g. "Letters Page Caricature Graphic: Pensive Letter-Writer." *WomaNews*, April, letters sec. Lesbian Herstory Archives, Newsprint Collection, *WomaNews*.

———. 1984h. "Literary Dykes to Watch Out For: A Heloise C. Bland Lecture." *WomaNews*, September. Lesbian Herstory Archives, Newsprint Collection, *WomaNews*.

———. 1985. "Advertisement: *WomaNews* 5th Anniversary! Variety Show!" *WomaNews*, December 1984/January 1985. Lesbian Herstory Archives, Newsprint Collection, *WomaNews*.

———. 1986. "Literary Dykes to Watch Out For: A Heloise C. Bland Lecture." In *Dykes to Watch Out For*, 36–37. Ithaca, NY: Firebrand Books.

———. 1988. "Dykes to Watch Out For: Groves of Academe." *Valley Women's Voice*, July/August. Lesbian Herstory Archives, Newsprint Collection, *Valley Women's Voice*.

———. 1993. "Questions for Syndicate." Alison Bechdel Papers, #08S-104. Sophia Smith Collection, Smith College, Northampton, MA.

———. 1994. "Dykes to Watch Out For 1994 Calendar." Box 66, folder 17: DTWOF 1994 Calendar: Review Copies (1993–1994). Firebrand Books Records, #7670. Division of Rare and Manuscript Collections, Cornell University Library, Ithaca, NY.

———. 1998. *The Indelible Alison Bechdel: Confessions, Comix, and Miscellaneous Dykes to Watch Out For*. Ithaca, NY: Firebrand Books.

———. 2006a. *Fun Home: A Family Tragicomic*. New York: Mariner Books.

———. 2006b. "Mo' Mo." *Dykes to Watch Out For*, March 1. http://dykestowatchoutfor.com/mo-mo.

———. 2006c. "The United States: March 2006." March. Alison Bechdel Papers, #08S-104. Sophia Smith Collection, Smith College, Northampton, MA.

———. 2006d. "What Is Real? A Short Disquisition." *Dykes to Watch Out For*, August 25. http://dykestowatchoutfor.com/what-is-real-a-short-disquisition.

———. 2008a. "Cartoonist's Introduction." In *The Essential Dykes to Watch Out For*, vii–xviii. New York: Houghton Mifflin Harcourt.

———. 2008b. *The Essential Dykes to Watch Out For*. New York: Houghton Mifflin Harcourt.

———. 2008c. "From the Archives." *Dykes to Watch Out For*, March 12. http://dykestowatchoutfor.com/from-the-archives.

———. 2008d. "Ithaca: Archival Kisses, Drunken Birds, Firebrand." *Dykes to Watch Out For*, April 13. http://dykestowatchoutfor.com/catching-up.

———. 2008e. "The Memoirist's Lament." YouTube, July 16. www.youtube.com/watch?v=cCuSglq5IAc.

———. 2012. *Are You My Mother? A Comic Drama*. New York: Houghton Mifflin Harcourt.

———. 2016. "Same as It Ever Was, Only Much Worse." *Dykes to Watch Out For*, November 23. http://dykestowatchoutfor.com/same-as-it-ever-was-only-much-worse.

———. 2017. "Postcards from the Edge." *Dykes to Watch Out For*, April 13. http://dykestowatchoutfor.com/postcards-from-the-edge.

Beins, Agatha. 2017. *Liberation in Print: Feminist Periodicals and Social Movement Identity*. Athens: Univ. of Georgia Press.

Beins, Agatha, and Julie R. Enszer. 2013. "'We Couldn't Get Them Printed,' So We Learned to Print: *Ain't I a Woman?* And the Iowa City Women's Press." *Frontiers: A Journal of Women Studies* 34, no. 2: 186–221.

Camper, Jennifer, ed. 2005. *Juicy Mother: Celebration*. New York: Soft Skull Press.

———, ed. 2007. *Juicy Mother 2: How They Met*. San Francisco: Manic D Press.

Chute, Hillary L. 2010. "Animating an Archive: Repetition and Regeneration in Alison Bechdel's *Fun Home*." In *Graphic Women: Life Narrative and Contemporary Comics*, 175–218. New York: Columbia Univ. Press.

Cvetkovich, Ann. 2003. *An Archive of Feelings: Trauma, Sexuality, and Lesbian Public Cultures*. Durham, NC: Duke Univ. Press.

———. 2008. "Drawing the Archive in Alison Bechdel's *Fun Home*." *Women's Studies Quarterly* 36, nos. 1/2: 111–28.

de Lauretis, Teresa. 1984. "Imaging." In *Alice Doesn't: Feminism, Semiotics, Cinema*, 37–69. Bloomington: Indiana Univ. Press.

Derrida, Jacques. 1995. *Archive Fever: A Freudian Impression*. Translated by Eric Prenowitz. Chicago: Univ. of Chicago Press.

Eichhorn, Kate. 2013. *The Archival Turn in Feminism: Outrage in Order*. Philadelphia: Temple Univ. Press.

Enszer, Julie R. 2015a. "'Fighting to Create and Maintain Our Own Black Women's Culture': *Conditions* Magazine, 1977–1990." *American Periodicals* 25, no. 2: 160–76.

———. 2015b. "Night Heron Press and Lesbian Print Culture in North Carolina, 1976–1983." *Southern Cultures* 21, no. 2: 43–56.

Galvan, Margaret. 2015. "Archiving Grassroots Comics: The Radicality of Networks and Lesbian Community." *Archive Journal*, no. 5. www.archivejournal.net/issue/5/archives-remixed/archiving-grassroots-comics-the-radicality-of-networks-and-lesbian-community/.

———. 2017. "Archiving *Wimmen*: Collectives, Networks, and Comix." *Australian Feminist Studies* 32, nos. 91/92: 22–40.

Gardiner, Judith Kegan. 2011. "Queering Genre: Alison Bechdel's *Fun Home: A Family Tragicomic* and *The Essential Dykes to Watch Out For*." *Contemporary Women's Writing* 5, no. 3: 188–207.

Hall, Justin. 2013a. "File Under Queer." In Hall 2013b, n.p.

———. 2013b. *No Straight Lines: Four Decades of Queer Comics*. Seattle: Fantagraphics.

Hilty, Joan. 1993. "Joan Hilty Letter to Alison Bechdel." September 14. Alison Bechdel Papers, #08S-104. Sophia Smith Collection, Smith College, Northampton, MA.

Kirby, Rob, ed. 2014. *QU33R*. Seattle: Northwest Press.

Kumbier, Alana. 2014. *Ephemeral Material: Queering the Archive*. Sacramento, CA: Litwin Books.

Lambert, Bruce. 1987. "Rockettes and Race: Barrier Slips." *New York Times*, December 26. www.nytimes.com/1987/12/26/nyregion/rockettes-and-race-barrier-slips.html.

Mangels, Andy, ed. 1993. *Gay Comics #19: Alison Bechdel Featuring Absolutely NO Dykes to Watch Out For!* San Francisco: Bob Ross.

McKinney, Cait. 2015. "Newsletter Networks in the Feminist History and Archives Movement." *Feminist Theory* 16, no. 3: 309–28.

Muñoz, José Esteban. 2009. *Cruising Utopia: The Then and There of Queer Futurity*. New York: New York Univ. Press.

Peterson, Gregory J. 1984. "The Rockettes: Out of Step with the Times? An Inquiry into the Legality of Racial Discrimination in the Performing Arts." *Columbia-VLA Art and the Law* 9, no. 3: 351–78.

Robbins, Trina. 2001. "Watch Out for Alison Bechdel (She Has the Secret to Superhuman Strength)." *Comics Journal*, no. 237: 80–86.

Robbins, Trina, Bill Sienkiewicz, and Robert Triptow, eds. 1988. *Strip AIDS USA: A Collection of Cartoon Art to Benefit People with AIDS*. San Francisco: Last Gasp.

Rubenstein, Anne. 1995. "Alison Bechdel Interview." *Comics Journal*, no. 179: 112–21.

Scott, Linda M. 1991. "'For the Rest of Us': A Reader-Oriented Interpretation of Apple's '1984' Commercial." *Journal of Popular Culture* 25, no. 1: 67–81.

Sedgwick, Eve Kosofsky. 2003. *Touching Feeling: Affect, Pedagogy, Performativity*. Durham, NC: Duke Univ. Press.

Sheklow, Sally. 1990. "Letter to Alison Bechdel," July 10. Alison Bechdel Papers, #08S-104. Sophia Smith Collection, Smith College, Northampton, MA.

Stephenson, Heather. 1995. "Alison Bechdel: 'I Would Love to Be the Lesbian Norman Rockwell.'" *Vermont Sunday Magazine*, June 4. Box 10, folder 30: n.d. Hot, Throbbing Dykes to Watch Out For: Promo Materials. Firebrand Books Records, #7670. Division of Rare and Manuscript Collections, Cornell University Library, Ithaca, NY.

Warren, Roz, ed. 1995. *Dyke Strippers: Lesbian Cartoonists A to Z*. Pittsburgh: Cleis Press.

WomaNews Collective. 1983. "Persephone Press Passes." *WomaNews*, July/August. Lesbian Herstory Archives, Newsprint Collection, *WomaNews*.

Joshua Abraham Kopin Identity and Representation in US Comics

Death, Disability, and the Superhero: The Silver Age and Beyond. By José Alaniz. Jackson: Univ. Press of Mississippi. 2014. xii, 363 pp. Cloth, $65.00; paper, $30.00; e-book available.

Graphic Borders: Latino Comic Books Past, Present, and Future. Ed. Frederick Luis Aldama and Christopher González. Austin: Univ. of Texas Press. 2016. x, 304 pp. Cloth, $90.00; paper, $29.95; e-book available.

The Blacker the Ink: Constructions of Black Identity in Comics and Sequential Art. Ed. Frances Gateward and John Jennings. New Brunswick, NJ: Rutgers Univ. Press. 2015. ix, 343 pp. Cloth, $90.00; paper, $29.95; e-book, $29.95.

Black Women in Sequence: Re-Inking Comics, Graphic Novels, and Anime. By Deborah Elizabeth Whaley. Seattle: Univ. of Washington Press. 2015. xiv, 242 pp. Cloth, $80.00; paper, $30.00; e-book available.

Speculative Blackness: The Future of Race in Science Fiction. By André M. Carrington. Minneapolis: Univ. of Minnesota Press. 282 pp. Cloth, $87.50; paper, $25.00; e-book available.

In April 2017, Marvel Comics vice president of sales David Gabriel told an interviewer that the company's recent slump was due to its move toward a more diverse roster of characters over the preceding year:

> What we heard was that people didn't want any more diversity. They didn't want female characters out there. That's what we heard, whether we believe that or not. I don't know that that's really true, but that's what we saw in sales. We saw the sales of any character

that was diverse, any character that was new, our female characters, anything that was not a core Marvel character, people were turning their nose up against. That was difficult for us because we had a lot of fresh, new, exciting ideas that we were trying to get out and nothing new really worked. (Griepp 2017)

After a quick backlash, Gabriel issued a correction. Even so, his framing and phrasing are enlightening; when he says "people didn't want any more diversity," he is staking a claim to having a monocultural audience. When he calls the situation "difficult for us because we had a lot of fresh, new, exciting ideas that we were trying to get out and nothing new really worked," he is suggesting that bringing diversity to comics is an innovation and one that has not worked out for his company financially.

The assumption embedded in Gabriel's statement, that the audience for comics is limited to straight white men who want the same kind of superhero story with characters from their childhood handed to them year after year, is common to both the popular discourse about comics and certain strains of academic discourse on the subject. With the growth in academic comics studies over the last decade, however, there has been a shift in the latter. Recent comics scholarship has emerged from many different kinds of academic departments—the traditional liberal arts disciplines, the fine arts, art history, communications studies, and information science—as well as from interdisciplinary scholars working primarily in ethnic studies, black studies, American studies, and women's and gender studies, among others. With important work coming out of a variety of discourses, one of the most exciting aspects of recent developments in the field is its necessary interdisciplinarity. While it has taken more than a century of academic scholarship to arrive at the idea that text, paratext, context, audience, and reception are all necessary components for understanding cultural production, comics studies is in a position to grow as a discipline in which scholars are and have always been able to close read a text itself and then discuss the way that text was produced, disseminated, and circulated. Scholarship within the field, like Ramzi Fawaz's *The New Mutants* (2016), Jeffrey Brown's *Black Superheroes, Milestone Comics, and Their Fans* (2001), and Tahneer Oksman's *How Come Boys Get to Keep Their Noses?* (2016), has taken extraordinary advantage of this possibility. One of the important consequences of this interdisciplinary method is that it becomes impossible to imagine an ideal audience for comics in the way that Gabriel does. Instead, this mode has enabled scholars to establish that comics, far from being only a popular cultural form that circulates among a particular audience and in particular ways, have been used and enjoyed by a variety of audiences through a variety of different but related forms (comic books, comic strips, graphic novels, webcomics, and so on).

Comics studies, therefore, is a discipline in which good work requires the acknowledgment of the multiplicity of audiences that comics reach. In particular, it demands acknowledgment that fans with many different kinds of intersectional identities exist and have always existed. In this context, it is easy to see that Marvel's strategy, which maintained a narrow view of the demographics of its audience, was always doomed to fail. Half-hearted, ahistorical gestures toward diversity are not enough to remediate the comics industry, the comics underground, or the academic comics discourse's mutual longstanding issues with the representation of women, people of color, and LGBTQ characters. Recent studies of comics and identity elucidate the obstacles that make it difficult for the voices of women, people of color, and LGBTQ cartoonists to make headway. What the following books show is that, against those obstacles, diverse voices have emerged anyway.

We can see this, for example, in José Alaniz's monograph *Death, Disability, and the Superhero: The Silver Age and Beyond*. Although the discourse on ability has clear and important political valences, the notion of disability as a kind of identity is often left out of conversations about diversity, both within the academy and outside of it, that focus on gender, race, and sexual orientation. One of the major tasks of *Death, Disability, and the Superhero* is to show that the scholarship on disability and disability activism is important to defining the intersectional frameworks that construe identity as a matrix rather than a data point.

In *Death, Disability, and the Superhero*, disability emerges as a particularly compelling lens through which to view superhero narratives because considering it means reconsidering the important but facile understanding of superhero narratives as adolescent male power fantasies. Instead, the book places the vulnerability of the body at the center of its understanding of the superhero. Focusing on the period of comics history beginning in the late 1950s, which comics fans know as the silver age, Alaniz demonstrates how the "anxieties and desires of the [post–World War II] age" (20) begin in this moment to assault the previously nigh-invulnerable superhero body. A comparison between the superhero and the "inspirational" figure of the supercrip, whose disability should elicit pity but instead provides an obstacle that, once overcome, renders the supercrip beyond pity, establishes the superability of the superbody as an important site for the examination of postwar anxieties and desires. What the superbody can and cannot do and how it arrives at a position outside of the bodily norm reveal for Alaniz exactly how postwar Americans, and in particular postwar American men, were afraid of what might become of their bodies in a changing world.

Death, Disability, and the Superhero includes an extraordinary wealth of images and takes a broad range of examples from the last half century of mainstream superhero comic books, but its most compelling cases are drawn from the Marvel comics of the 1960s and 1970s. Alaniz considers, among others, the Thing (whose exposure to galactic radiation turned him into living stone), Daredevil (an acrobatic hero who, as a boy, suffered an industrial accident that led to both blindness and supersenses that compensate for that blindness), and Dr. Doom (a supervillainous scientist who hides the disfiguring results of a lab accident behind a metal mask). Alaniz combines acute visual and textual observation with insights from the analysis of fan reactions that caused the early ending of storylines and the abandonment of characters like the She-Thing (a striking athlete and superhero who is cast as the Thing's love interest and is eventually turned into living rock herself) to understand the way that the "supercrip" archetype is reinscribed within the superheroic body. This archetype forces characters with disabilities to either paper over their experience of the world by attempting to pass as able-bodied or go into isolation on the fringes of culture and society, situations that mirror many of the challenges that disabled people face. In each chapter, Alaniz is particularly attentive to how disability reads in ways that are gendered and racialized, stressing that it appears above all as an assault on the typical white male body. Extending a perspective on how the undesirably racialized and feminized disabled come to be represented either as deserving of hatred and fear or as inspirational—rather than as individuals with important perspectives on the world, not all of which are informed by their bodies—*Death, Disability, and the Superhero* clarifies important issues in the study of the early twenty-first century's most important genre.

Situated in the context of a significant and growing scholarship, Frederick Luis Aldama and Christopher González's anthology *Graphic Borders: Latino Comics Past, Present, and Future* is an important intervention that recognizes that the category of Latina/o comics represents a range of output that is as broad as the medium itself. In their introduction, Aldama and González run through examples of common genres of Latina/o graphic narrative—science fiction, noir, erotica, superheroes, and autobiography, among others—to demonstrate that identifying a comic as Latina/o, either because the cartoonist is or the characters are, will explain little about the work in question. In this way, they resist the notion, common among both academic and popular discussions of ethnic literature, that in literary terms race and ethnicity represent a kind of genre with identifiable forms and tropes. Instead, they write that "Latino comic book creators" use the form to "open the reader's eyes to different ways of being in the world—ways typified by the respective Latino (Chicano, Dominican, Puerto Rican, Cuban) experience" (16). Common to the creators and characters discussed in the collection, then, is an alienation caused by their identity, which is perceived by the culture at large as being outside the national mainstream. The essays in *Graphic Borders* largely deal with the specifics of this alienation, which takes not only the national forms of Aldama and González's list but also those that intersect with culture, race, gender, sexuality, and class.

Graphic Borders is an entry in the University of Texas Press's World Comics and Graphic Novels and Nonfiction series, of which Aldama and González are also the editors. Given the laudatory transnational goals of that series, the essays' focus on comics artists from the United States and Mexico and on works produced for those markets presents an opportunity for further work on comics and creators with ties to other parts of Latin America. Similarly, although it is difficult to overstate the importance of Gilbert Hernandez, Jaime Hernandez, and Mario Hernandez (fondly known to comics fans as "Los Bros") and their 1980s comics anthology series *Love and Rockets* on both Latina/o comics and US alternative comics more generally, their presence here is overwhelming. Essays and an interview about their work make up the whole of the book's first section, and another deals in part with some of Gilbert's stories. Four out of the volume's fourteen pieces are explicitly about Los Bros. Essays on cartoonists like Roberta Gregory, Graciela Rodriguez, and Liz Mayorga, who are mentioned in the introduction, would have been a welcome addition.

Given the nearly impossible task of capturing the whole of the Latina/o experience in just one volume, however, *Graphic Borders* is admirably capacious. Importantly, it emphasizes intersections that make up Latina/o experience, with standout essays on blatinos in US popular culture, by Adilifu Nama and Maya Haddad, and gay Latina/o superheroes, by Richard T. Rodríguez. It also thinks across types of comics publishing, from mainstream superhero comics (Isabel Millán's essay on Marvel's Mexican–Puerto Rican Spider-Girl, Anya Sofía Corazón, and Brian Montes's essay on the blatino Miles Morales, otherwise known as the friendly neighborhood Spider-Man) to less covered but equally important forms like indie publishing (the essays on Los Bros), the comic strip (Héctor Fernández L'Hoeste's essay on *Baldo*), and the political cartoon (Juan Poblete's essay on the cartoons of Lalo Alcaraz). The picture of Latina/o comics that appears in *Graphic Borders* is a bright one, with recent growth in production and audience showing no signs of stopping. Even while celebrating these developments, however, Aldama and González are realistic about the importance of Latina/o creators to keeping the trend moving. "Simply put," they write, "mainstream DC and Marvel publishers are not interested in innovation—unless it sells.... For working Latino creators, maintaining control over their product is essential" (15).

Frances Gateward and John Jennings's edited collection *The Blacker the Ink: Constructions of Black Identity in Comics and Sequential Art*, while similar in construction to *Graphic Borders*, in some ways takes the opposite tack. While *Graphic Borders* is built around the idea that it is important to separate the identity of the creator from the genre of the work, Gateward and Jennings make "an attempt to start constructing ideas around 'Blackness' as a type of medium," later clarifying, "Blackness is a medium that Black people of the world have inherited and have added on to as the story has unfolded throughout history" (4). Interestingly, the volume puts forth a notion of the construction of blackness as an identity that resembles the collaboration common to the production of mainstream US comic books, which often feature contributions from separate writers, pencillers, inkers, colorists, and letterers, all of whom provide essential input. Gateward and Jennings make a compelling argument for the long-standing and continued relevance of sequential art as a method of understanding African and diasporic African identities, which sometimes speak with "one voice" and sometimes "ha[ve] a collection of many voices" (3). In this way, Gateward and Jennings suggest, there are both fundamental and contingent qualities of blackness that are essential to understanding black experience, and both of these can be seen by examining the history and form of black comics.

The essays in this volume generally deal with comic strips, comic books, and graphic novels and range across a wide swath of time periods and contexts. Although the collection is mostly focused on production in the United States, it notably features an essay by Sally McWilliams on *Aya*, a series of French graphic albums written by the Ivorian author Marguerite Abouet. More essays on international black creators and characters would have made a welcome addition. In other ways, though, the volume deals with many varieties of black identity, strains of black thought, and ways that black bodies have been represented in comics, including a piece by Patrick F. Walter on the intersection of postcoloniality and queer theory in the Vertigo series *Unknown Soldier* and another by Rebecca Wanzo on humor, citizenship, and the challenge to the cultural illegibility of black heroism in the comic strip *The Boondocks* and the superhero comic *Icon*. Importantly, although Gateward and Jennings begin and end their introduction by discussing Power Man, the urban superhero who has recently entered the broader cultural conversation as the subject of the Netflix / Marvel Studios television series *Luke Cage*, only a few of the essays deal with well-known mainstream superhero characters; for Gateward and Jennings, the crucial work on blackness being done in comics comes from other directions.

Although individual essays in both *Graphic Borders* and *The Blacker the Ink* deal with female characters or creators, they do so in the context of other categories. Deborah Elizabeth Whaley's strikingly designed *Black Women in Sequence: Re-Inking Comics, Graphic Novels, and Anime* is one of the first book-length works to deal specifically with the construction and experience of black women in sequential art rather than treating that experience as a subset of broader black or women's experiences. Although there is a distinct paucity of African American female characters and creators in mainstream and independent American comics,[1] it is simply untrue to say that they are not present. Indeed, *Black Women in Sequence* takes us beyond well-known characters like the X-Men's mutant weather goddess Storm to characters like Nubia (Wonder Woman's black sister) and the Butterfly (a character from a series of 1970s exploitation comics that Whaley identifies as the first black superheroine). Similarly, it is in the book's first and last chapters, in which Whaley considers the creation and consumption of sequential media by black women, often erased from conversations about fan culture, where *Black Women in Sequence* makes its most important contribution. There she acknowledges innovators in the field like Jackie Ormes, who drew comic strips for the *Pittsburgh Courier* in the context of early twentieth-century cultural-front leftism; Barbara Brandon-Croft, whose comic strip, *Where I'm Coming From*, was the first syndicated comic strip by a black female cartoonist; and the community of black creators and consumers of sequential media Whaley calls "Afrofans" (xi).

Black Women in Sequence is an extraordinarily ambitious work that draws on a range of discourses and methodologies to examine the way that black women are figured as what Whaley calls "sequential subjects" (8) across a broad range of time periods and media. In order to explore this topic, however, Whaley draws a rigid distinction between comics studies—which she says is narrowly focused on comic books, comic strips, and so on—and what she calls "sequential art studies" (13), which includes adjacent forms like animation and comics adapted into film. Approaching the topic in this way allows Whaley to include a significant number of examples from media outside of comics and graphic novels, but it also elides crucial differences among related forms and among disparate temporal and spatial contexts. Even so, *Black Women in Sequence* is an important addition to the literature on identity within comics, as it suggests possibilities for further research on a subject with very little coverage and in particular on figures like Ormes and Brandon-Croft. Whaley's work serves as an admonition to the field at large, a reminder of the vast variety of experiences contained within the matrices of intersectional identity and of the importance of specific attention to those experiences.

Although not primarily a book on comics, André M. Carrington's work in *Speculative Blackness: The Future of Race in Science Fiction* is focused on an adjacent paraliterary field. Speculative fiction, as a genre, encompasses many of the subgenres—superheroes, science fiction, utopia, fantasy, horror, paranormal romance—common in mainstream comics publishing, and the book's argumentative through-line is applicable to understandings of blackness within the medium of comics. As in *The Blacker the Ink*, which includes an essay by Carrington, *Speculative Blackness* is interested in teasing out blackness as a kind of mode. It is important, Carrington argues, that we consider a plurality of audiences when we talk about genre: "Whole segments of society experience genre traditions in different ways according to their sense of how these mediations pertain to their lives and the lives of others" (15). In order to make these arguments, Carrington draws on a long history of black speculative fiction fandom, providing a counterpoint to fan studies scholarship, which largely considers examples contemporaneous to its writing. His historical study of black fandom, which reaches the present in a consideration of the participatory practice of fan fiction, both honors the fact that black fans (who in debates about diversity within comics and genre fiction are often assumed to be newcomers) have been around for as long as there has been speculative fiction and clarifies the fact that fandom is historically contingent, responding to the differing needs of black audiences at different points in time. In order to work this point through, Carrington reads popular science fiction reparatively. Rather than focusing on the variety of ways that speculative genres are racist, already well-trod ground, he seeks out examples of the genre that have something to say about what a black future or a different version of a black past might mean for black identity in the present. In the encounter between blackness and speculative fiction, Carrington argues, we can see both the overwhelming whiteness of the genre, usually hidden from view, and the ways in which black people have found in speculative fiction a way to imagine otherwise.

In making his case, Carrington situates himself not only in the context of fan studies but also within the history of feminist science fiction critique, seeking to apply arguments made by writers and scholars on the role of women in speculative fiction to race. He honors this legacy by centering two chapters on black women—Nichelle Nichols's Lieutenant Uhura from the original *Star Trek* series and Storm. He has an additional chapter that focuses on the African American–driven publisher Milestone Comics's comic book *Icon*, which features the titular African American superhero. His focus on cultural production that is outside of much of the scholarship on speculative fiction, like television and comics, is also notable for what he chooses to leave out; even as he acknowledges the importance of black writers of science fiction like Samuel R. Delany and Octavia Butler, he seeks to move the study of black speculative fiction beyond the scholarship on those two authors.

Indeed, books like Carrington's mark an important point of maturation for the study of comics within academic literature, that is, their use as evidence in scholarship outside the specific field of comics studies. As the field grows and as the academic study of comics gains acceptance, critiques of this sort will become more common, and not all of them will be as receptive as Carrington's is. Even so, the five books in this review suggest a capacious future for the field, one that takes it away from narrow understandings of the medium like Gabriel's and toward broader and more inclusive histories and methodologies of comics.

Joshua Abraham Kopin is a PhD student in the Department of American Studies at the University of Texas at Austin. He serves on the executive committee of the International Comics Art Forum and is the president of the Graduate Student Caucus of the Comics Studies Society.

Note

1   Marvel did not employ a black woman as a comics writer until 2016, when it hired Roxane Gay and Yona Harvey to write *World of Wakanda*, a series focused on the fictional African nation home of the superhero Black Panther.

Reference

Griepp, Milton. 2017. "Marvel's David Gabriel on the 2016 Market Shift." *ICv2*, March 31. http://icv2.com/articles/news/view/37152/marvels-david-gabriel-2016-market-shift.

Shelley Streeby

Heroism and Comics Form: Feminist and Queer Speculations

Captain Marvel and the Art of Nostalgia. By Brian Cremins. Jackson: Univ. Press of Mississippi. 2016. xiv, 203 pp. Cloth, $65.00.

Frank Miller's Daredevil *and the Ends of Heroism.* By Paul Young. New Brunswick, NJ: Rutgers Univ. Press. 2016. xiii, 276 pp. Cloth, $90.00; paper, $27.95; e-book, $27.95.

Hellboy's World: Comics and Monsters on the Margins. By Scott Bukatman. Berkeley: Univ. of California Press. 2016. 263 pp. Paper, $24.95; e-book, $24.95.

Twelve-Cent Archie. By Bart Beaty. New Brunswick, NJ: Rutgers Univ. Press. 2015. ix, 221 pp. Cloth, $90.00; paper, $26.95; e-book, $26.95.

Instead of the disembodied abstraction that is typically the norm, I begin and end by remarking on my own embodiment as a white female scholar of popular culture reflecting on comics studies by reviewing four books written by white male scholars, all of whom make significant contributions in theorizing comics form. Queer theory teaches us to question the naturalization of norms, so while I observe that all four are male-authored texts that focus mostly on male characters, creators, and audiences, I do not assume bodies neatly match up with genders and sexualities. Instead, guided by queer of color critique, I emphasize each book's contributions in theorizing heroism and comics form while asking whether and how they engage, illuminate, limit, or even refuse analysis of intersections of gender, race, sexuality, and nation as intertwining social constructions. Three are studies of male superheroes. The fourth, Bart Beaty's *Twelve-Cent*

Archie, explores a world organized around a male character who is the antithesis of a hero: Archie is "a young man to whom things happen; he is not someone who makes things happen" (16). Overall, I am struck by the significance of gender (especially masculinities), sexuality (especially heterosexuality), race (especially whiteness), and nation (especially the United States) for the objects, creators, collaborations, audiences, and industries under discussion. On the other hand, imagining female, feminist, and queer readers and readings of comics is largely foreclosed, while maleness and masculinities are often reified and underexplored as historical constructs, even in work that makes significant contributions.

One of my guiding premises is that queer studies and especially queer of color critique have much to offer comics studies. As Siobhan Somerville (2014, 203) explains, *queer* since the 1980s functions both "as an umbrella term that refers to a range of sexual identities that are 'not straight'" and as an analytic that "calls into question the stability of any such categories of identity based on sexual orientation," thereby exposing the latter as constructions that "establish and police the line between the 'normal' and the 'abnormal.'" In addition to this guiding premise, I build on queer of color analysis modeled by scholars such as Roderick Ferguson, José Esteban Muñoz, and Fatima El-Tayeb, all of whom examine gender, race, sexuality, and nation as intertwining social constructions. Ferguson (2004, 149n1) defines queer of color critique as "a heterogeneous enterprise made up of women of color feminism, materialist analysis, poststructuralist theory, and queer critique" that interrogates such "social formations as the intersections of race, gender, sexuality, and class, with particular interest in how those formations correspond with and diverge from nationalist ideals and practices." Ramzi Fawaz (2016, 32) further theorizes the post–World War II "superhero as a distinctly queer figure of twentieth-century popular culture" by approaching "popular fantasy and its political effects" from the perspective of queer theory, which "is a body of knowledge that concerns itself with the ways queer or non-normative figures generate alternative desires, bring into view unexpected objects of passionate attachment, and facilitate the production of novel forms of kinship and affiliation." Although none of the books I discuss here draws much or at all on queer theory, all take up comics form in ways that both illuminate and swerve away from queer figures, alternative desires, unexpected objects of passionate attachment, and nonnormative social and sexual relations. The figure of the "little boy" as privileged subject and imagined reader and scenes of intergenerational transmission of comics among fathers, sons, and brothers also recur, suggesting that masculinities and relationships among men are central to almost all of these comics as well as the communities and networks that transmit their meanings.

The story of Captain Marvel and his alter ego Billy Batson, Brian Cremins tells us, "starts with a kid and his books" (3)—namely an editor and writer for Fawcett Publications, Bill Parker, who as a boy read about King Arthur and the Knights of the Round Table and later invented Captain Marvel. But Cremins focuses especially on cartoonist and critic C. C. Beck and writer Otto Binder as cocreators of "one of the best-selling characters of the 1940s" (8). By recovering Beck's theories of comics form in fanzines, letters, and other archival sources, Cremins does valuable work situating Beck as a figure "like [Will] Eisner" whose "body of work remains one of the great achievements in twentieth-century comics in the United States" (9). Cremins also explores Binder's career as a pulp science fiction writer and his invention of the animal character Mr. Tawny as his autobiographical surrogate. Here Cremins's remarks on the importance of fantasy and on animals as expressions of "a shadow self, one hidden from the world" (51–52) suggest that animals can function as queer figures, as in Jack Halberstam's (2011) work on animated animals. In a discussion of how Billy Batson's black valet, Steamboat, remains fixed in place while Billy's movement and mastery of spaces signal his heroism, Cremins also denaturalizes racial categories and explicitly names white supremacy as a problem. He foregrounds as exemplary the story of Steamboat's removal after objections from New York City junior high school students in the local Youthbuilders program. "If the form is as flexible and promising" as Eisner and Beck believed, Cremins argues, then it also "offers the means and opportunity" (103) to subvert racial stereotypes. Drawing on work in literature, psychology, and memory studies as well as fanzines, he examines relationships among the "medium of comics, the lure of nostalgia, and the art of memory" (4).

Cremins concentrates especially on Billy as "a fiction of lost innocence, a marker of the idealized notions of boyhood and masculinity in America in the 1940s" (56). He assumes the comic targeted boy readers (and, during World War II, soldiers) who found appealing the story's fantasy of "sheltered innocence" (75). Cremins also analyzes the comic as an extension of the boys' adventure genre, which goes back to the nineteenth-century dime novel, when white boy adventurers, often accompanied by a subordinate person of color, explored exotic, often racialized spaces far from home (see Saxton 1991 and Streeby 2002). While boys and masculinity are the main focus of this study, Cremins dedicates it to his grandmother and cites cartoonist Trina Robbins's memories of her "childhood discovery" of Captain Marvel, Billy, and most significantly Captain Marvel's sister Mary as a "pretty major inspiration" for her own career (quoted on 13). Cremins's brief mention of fanzines publishing photos of children in Mary Marvel costumes made me wonder about girl fans, as did Beck's remark in a footnote about how much his daughter and granddaughter enjoyed the series. At the end, Cremins analyzes a 1981 photograph of himself, surrounded by other "white middle-class boys" (148) and wearing a *Shazam!* T-shirt with an image from the Captain Marvel–inspired Saturday morning cartoon. With no memory of its origins, he speculates about the significance of wearing a T-shirt "with a character created for children in the 1940s" and concludes "the weight of nostalgia is literal," for the boys had "inherited a nostalgia for the popular heroes of the generations that preceded us" (149) even though the author did not read the original comics until much later.

In Paul Young's monograph on Miller's *Daredevil*, on the other hand, the author centers his own responses as a twelve-year-old boy and teenage fan, which he, unlike Cremins, remembers very vividly, even describing his study as a "masochistic project" and an "exorcism" (18, 20). Starting with the question, "Why did Miller's Daredevil blow my twelve-year-old mind?" (5), Young admits he still fears that writing a book will not "purge" either "the images or the rotating feelings of attraction and apprehension they inspire" (9). As "wretched" as he finds Miller's gender politics especially, he is "still haunted by what those images showed me and what they meant to me beyond what they depicted" (10). In a dialogue between Young as a boy and his older self, he explores the "hold" the comic exerted on his imagination in order to "shed some light" on Miller's success "and what that success meant for the discourse of superhero comics past, present, and future" (10). Throughout, Young frequently refers to his past as a minister's son growing up in small-town southern Iowa, foregrounding his and his brother's responses to comics, which continue today in their biweekly podcast, *To the Batpoles!* Along the way, Young also shows how Miller helped lead the creators' rights movement and contributed to the "mainstreaming of superhero comic books beyond their traditional market of children and lifelong fans" through "grim, violent, and/or erotic 'adult' content and successful Hollywood franchises" (5). Miller did so, Young suggests, through a range of formal strategies, including breaking with 1940s superhero conventions of reverence for life and modeling "looser, cartoonier drawing styles and non-Code-approved violence" (210). Young contends that Miller used subtlety, irony, and complexity to muddy the good/evil binary of previous superhero comics and raise thought-provoking questions about the relationship between justice and the law. In each chapter, Young credits Miller with achieving a self-consciousness and formal complexity that expose "the act of creating comics" (72) and the conventions of the genre.

Although Young incorporates insights from feminist film theory and at times addresses masculinity as a construct, I found myself a resisting reader when he moved from a particular, embodied, twelve-year-old, white-heterosexual-male "me" to a universalizing scholarly "we." Toward the end, Young alludes to Miller's saying, of *300*'s Spartans and vigilante superheroes such as Batman, that maybe "cultures need guys like that"; Young further clarifies, "I do mean guys—the reckless male narcissists who can't or won't make subtle distinctions between good and evil—to do the dirty work of 'preserving civilization as we know it'" (227). Clearly Young is criticizing the problem of reckless male narcissism and paternalistic investments in defending a racialized "civilization," but when he says Miller "lets us sit with that ugly possibility" and "squirm at our own enjoyment and/or disgust" (227), I feel the force of my own disidentification, as Muñoz (1999) put it. Although many female readers undoubtedly enjoy Miller's work, I am not part of the "us" who receives enjoyment, even if ambivalently mixed with disgust, from comics that explore whether white male narcissism is necessary or desirable to "civilization." I suspect that gender, sexuality, race, and nation shape such enjoyment in ways that also merit analysis and that considering their intersections in the field of superhero comics might teach us something about the construction of masculinities and imagined relationships among men.

Scott Bukatman also mentions his past as a young reader, but unlike Young he only started intensively reading Mike Mignola's *Hellboy* as a Stanford professor with research funds available to purchase new Dark Horse oversize library editions of the comics, which originally debuted in 1993. Bukatman insists he was not "returned to the world of my childhood," however, which he observes "isn't a place I especially want to revisit anyway" (6). Although he includes a chapter on convergences of technique and materiality in children's books and comics, he does not single out the figure of the boy reader, instead emphasizing how color can "provide a space apart that absorbs a reader" and "provides an antidote to pedantry" (99), enabling a "nonlinear mode of reading" (100). Bukatman suggests that *Hellboy* deviates from many other superhero comics in making its forensic detective protagonist "our surrogate" rather than "a figure of identification," such that "our interest is deflected or dispersed into the world itself" (198). Bukatman also emphasizes Mignola's "handmade ethos" (109) and "increasingly non-naturalistic" art, with its "refreshing attention to—and pushing of—the formal properties of the medium of comics" (9). Arguing that Mignola's art is not strongly shaped by a realism primarily indebted to cinema and television (9), Bukatman turns to a variety of media, "children's books especially, but also sculpture, pulp fiction, cinema, graphic design, painting, and medieval manuscripts" to "understand effects or possibilities in the medium of comics and to find vocabularies that will help articulate what it is that comics do" (10).

For readers seeking to explore queer possibilities in this beautifully illustrated volume, Bukatman's emphasis on *Hellboy* as "a comic steeped in the heretofore taboo genre of supernatural horror" (47) might be one place to start, since horror and the gothic are privileged genres in queer studies. The connections to Lovecraftian weird fiction and the occult detective could also open up questions about sexuality, gender, race, and nation, as could Bukatman's comparison of Hellboy to James Fenimore Cooper's Leatherstocking, who is "able to cross between civilization and destiny, retaining the morals of white culture while avoiding its decadence" (74). Hellboy's resistance to following his destiny might be understood as a queer deviation: "Resisting one's destiny is hard and lonely work—those horns can grow back" (77). Mignola's fondness for "nonchronological stories and his use of non-linear narrational devices" (181) might also be illuminated by recent work on queer time by Elizabeth Freeman, Halberstam, and others.

Gender and sexuality are rarely the explicit focus, though openings pop up here and there, such as a footnote where Mignola explains that he felt he needed more female characters but "couldn't draw" them since he was "terrible at drawing women" (227). Elsewhere, Mignola says he was surprised to discover that many of *Hellboy*'s fans are women and girls; it would be interesting to know more about audiences and to test the hypothesis that Mignola's focus on nonnaturalistic elements that work in ways other than through identification may enable female and queer affiliations and pleasures.

While the three books above focus on superheroes, Beaty's *Twelve-Cent Archie* explores "one of the most lowbrow examples of a particularly lowbrow art form" (3): "nostalgic" and "completely out of fashion" Archie, whose comics sold millions of copies a month in the 1960s and early 1970s (4). Although *Archie* superhero comics were briefly introduced, they lasted only sixteen issues collectively. Beaty calls this a failed "experiment" (195) since "an action hero" is something Archie is not, for *Archie* is "a comic about nothing" (192). But Beaty argues that, far from being a defect, this everydayness was one of the comic's great virtues: Archie was "the quintessential everyman—the typical American teen" (17) and *Archie* comics played with "the possibilities of everyday life in middle America, taken to certain logical or narrative extremes" (20). Beaty claims the greatness of *Archie* comics was inseparable from their nonliterary qualities as well as their attention to the quotidian. For instance, artist Harry Lucey was "one of the great masters of comic-book storytelling through body language" (21), known for "the amazing pliability of his characters and variety of their poses" (13), which supports Beaty's claim that body language is another way comics are closer to the visual arts than to literature. Contending that "scholars have focused nearly exclusively on those works that can be most easily reconciled within the traditions of literary greatness . . . or those of contemporary cultural politics," Beaty charges that such "cultural cherry-picking" leaves "enormous gaps in both the history and cultural analysis of comics" by excluding "the genuinely popular" (5) in the form of "children's comics and humor comics." These comics, he suggests, were "replete" with "self-referential formal play": they included "wordless comics, metareferential comics, and avant-garde and abstract visual tendencies" (6). Thus Beaty hopes to right "the scholarly wrongs done to Archie" by "addressing the works as both typical and exceptional" during Lucey's 1961–69 tenure as lead artist (6), works in which Beaty discovered "a level of complexity and interest that was totally unexpected." The comics' form—"their lack of continuity, their brevity, and their independent functioning within a larger narrative system"—contributed to that complexity, and Beaty especially praises "the efficacy and cogency of the interrelated short-story comics form as a significant alternative to graphic novels self-consciously modeled on literary parameters" (8). Indeed, one of the many pleasures of reading *Twelve-Cent Archie* is its exemplification of what we might call such a queer nonlinearity. Like the comics he studies, Beaty's book is nonlinear and can be read in any order, while each of his chapters is "like every Archie story," which can "exist independently of the rest" (7).

Beaty addresses these comics' queer potential most explicitly in his remarks on Jughead, who he suggests is asexual but whose "disdain for women" is often "read as a suggestion of queerness" (64). Beaty rejects such a reading since he finds no evidence that Jughead desires Archie and understands the couple instead as an "asexual male pairing" (65). If, however, we conceive of queerness not (only) as an identity but (also) as an analytic that denaturalizes socially and historically constructed identities, then a queer reading of Jughead's asexuality is certainly possible. Instead, Beaty emphasizes how the male creators of *Archie* comics centered an asymmetrical love triangle on Archie, Betty, and Veronica, thereby creating a "visual pleasure" that was "intended for a male heterosexual reader" (140), so much so that there is a "clear connection between the sales success of Archie comics and the degree of sexualization of Betty and Veronica" (141). He observes that Riverdale is "almost completely free of mothers and surrogate mothers," Betty and Veronica are physically identical except for hair color and Betty's ponytail, and a range of male body types exist while there is only one female body type. At the same time, he acknowledges *Archie* comics were "always popular with a young female audience" and speculates that the launch of *Archie's Girls: Betty and Veronica* in 1950 "heightened that appeal" (14). Concluding that *Archie* comics were antifeminist despite enjoying a "high proportion of female readers" (142), Beaty imagines girls could enjoy Betty and Veronica without emulating their behavior since theories of "resistant reading" teach us that people do not necessarily internalize what they read (141).

But while white girls were situated within antifeminist stories created by men, Beaty notes the absence of nonwhite characters in *Archie* comics, which resolutely ignored the social transformations of the civil rights era. Indeed, "Riverdale in the 1960s was a wish-dream of white privilege and normative sexualities, where all difference could be banished" (31). Reflecting on his own childhood in Canada, Beaty observes that "Riverdale was Edenic for a white kid growing up in a well-to-do suburb of Toronto in the 1970s," a version of his own "privileged world, only better." Although Beaty criticizes the normalization of whiteness in *Archie* comics, he embraces their pleasures. He ends the book by remarking on his enjoyment in watching his own son, who is now the same age Beaty was when he read his first *Archie*s, raptly immersing himself "in the world of Riverdale, just as I used to do" (212).

Beaty's speculation about Archie's female audience and the whiteness of *Archie* comics made me reflect on my own experiences reading them. I was born in 1963 in Ottumwa, Iowa, a deindustrializing small city that was then mostly white, though now home to a significant minority of Latina/os, and that is about forty-five minutes northeast of where Young grew up. I recall as a six-year-old buying *Little Archie* and *Hot Stuff* comics after lifting loose change from around the house, then biking around the neighborhood, stopping intermittently to read them covertly before my crime was discovered. *Little Archie* appeared from 1956 to 1983, thereby outlasting the 1972–74 collapse of *Archie* comics sales, and in 1969 I was reading them at the apex of their popularity. When I try to remember why they were so appealing, along with the color, the art, and the humor, I think of their cheapness (you could buy them with stolen change), portability (you could roll them up and carry them even when riding a bike), and most of all their ubiquity and easy availability (you could purchase them at the grocery store and many other places in my working-class town). Reading matter wasn't always easy to come by, and I remember urging my mother to buy them for me at the checkout stand partly because they were there and cheap enough that she might do it even though I had three little brothers also clamoring for things and my parents had a hard time getting by. Soon I moved on to *Mad* and *Cracked* and had mostly lost interest in *Archie* by my teens. As a twelve-year-old, I enjoyed the live-action *Shazam!* television show that preceded the

Saturday morning animated series depicted on Cremins's T-shirt, mostly because lead actor Michael Gray was a handsome teen idol often featured in *Flip* and *Tiger Beat* pinups. I was also drawn to *Isis*, a *Shazam!* spin-off featuring the ancient Egyptian superhero resurrected in the body of a female schoolteacher. I remember thinking *Archie* comics were corny and nostalgic for a fake America that never existed, but like Beaty I loved Lucey's art, and the love triangle meant two girls were crucial to the stories, which attracted me even though I didn't like either girl. As a working-class white girl, I disliked wealthy Veronica as everyone did but did not identify with Betty either, probably because she was blond and I was already baffled by how everyone thought blond girls were the prettiest for some weird reason, which I would later understand as white supremacy.

As a teen, I was drawn to the exciting visuals and alternative family teams that included women in *The Fantastic Four* and *X-Men* after spending hours combing through the cardboard boxes of a local store downtown that sold coins and comics to collectors. By the time I went off to college, I had fallen in love with the independent comics that suddenly appeared both in the local head shop across the bridge from the factory in Ottumwa and in my college town of Cambridge, Massachusetts, especially Los Bros Hernandez's classic *Love and Rockets*, which wrapped up science fiction, punk, and badass girls all in one gorgeous package. I especially adored Jaime Hernandez's Maggie the Mechanic stories, and since Lucey's *Archie* comics were a major influence on Jaime, my *Archie* fandom came full circle. In college and ever since, talking about comics with Chris Cunningham, a white gay man from Palestine, Texas, became one of my greatest pleasures. He shared with me how in a homophobic place he was sustained as a teen by the male bodies and queer families in the superhero comics I loved so much. I conclude with this autoethnographic fragment in order to suggest there are still many possibilities for enjoying and analyzing queer figures, alternative desires, unexpected objects of passionate attachment, and queer and nonnormative affiliations and kinship even in comics created by straight white men and aimed mostly at a transgenerational white male audience. And in thinking about form and heroism in comics studies today, there are still many questions left to ask about intersections of sexuality, gender, race, and nation.

Shelley Streeby is professor of ethnic studies and literature and director of the Clarion Workshop at the University of California, San Diego. Her books include *Radical Sensations: World Movements, Violence, and Visual Culture* (Duke Univ. Press, 2013), *American Sensations: Class, Empire, and the Production of Popular Culture* (Univ. of California Press, 2002), and *Imagining the Future of Climate Change: World-Making through Science Fiction and Activism* (Univ. of California Press, 2017). Streeby has an essay on reading Jaime Hernandez's comics as speculative fiction in *Altermundos: Latina/o Literature, Film, and Popular Culture*, and she is currently coediting *Keywords for Comics Studies* with Ramzi Fawaz and Deborah Whaley.

References

Fawaz, Ramzi. 2016. *The New Mutants: Superheroes and the Radical Imagination of American Comics*. New York: New York Univ. Press.

Ferguson, Roderick. 2004. *Aberrations in Black: Toward a Queer of Color Critique*. Minneapolis: Univ. of Minnesota Press.

Halberstam, Jack. 2011. *The Queer Art of Failure*. Durham, NC: Duke Univ. Press.

Muñoz, José Esteban. 1999. *Disidentifications: Queers of Color and the Performance of Politics*. Minneapolis: Univ. of Minnesota Press.

Saxton, Alexander. 1991. *The Rise and Fall of the White Republic: Class Politics and Mass Culture in Nineteenth-Century America*. London: Verso.

Somerville, Siobhan. 2014. "Queer." In *Keywords for American Cultural Studies*, 2nd ed., edited by Bruce Burgett and Glenn Hendler, 203–7. New York: New York Univ. Press.

Streeby, Shelley. 2002. *American Sensations: Class, Empire, and the Production of Popular Culture*. Berkeley: Univ. of California Press.

NEW FROM OXFORD

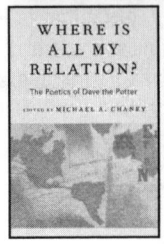

Oxford Studies in American Literary History

The Civil War Dead and American Modernity
IAN FINSETH

The Puritan Cosmopolis
The Law of Nations and the Early American Imagination
NAN GOODMAN

Empire of Ruin
Black Classicism and American Imperial Culture
JOHN LEVI BARNARD

Where Is All My Relation?
The Poetics of Dave the Potter
MICHAEL A. CHANEY

The Poetry of the Americas
From Good Neighbors to Countercultures
HARRIS FEINSOD

Emerson's Memory Loss
Originality, Communality, and the Late Style
CHRISTOPHER HANLON

Realist Poetics in American Culture, 1866-1900
ELIZABETH RENKER

American Enchantment
Rituals of the People in the Post-Revolutionary World
MICHELLE SIZEMORE

Forms of Dictatorship
Power, Narrative, and Authoritarianism in the Latina/o Novel
JENNIFER HARFORD VARGAS

Anxieties of Experience
The Literatures of the Ameericas from Whitman to Bolaño
JEFFREY LAWRENCE

Surveyors of Customs
American Literature as Cultural Analysis
JOEL PFISTER

Unscripted America
Indigenous Languages and the Origins of a Literary Nation
SARAH RIVETT

White Writers, Race Matters
Fictions of Racial Liberalism from Stoweto Stockett
GREGORY S. JAY

oup.com/us

OXFORD UNIVERSITY PRESS

Learn more. Teach better.

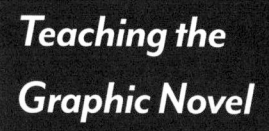

Teaching the Graphic Novel

Edited by
Stephen E. Tabachnick

353 pp. • 6 × 9

Paper $29.00

ISBN 978-1-60329-061-6

Available in the MLA series
Options for Teaching

> "This excellent collection lays out an impressive series of methods and techniques for teaching graphic novels. It comes at just the right moment, as the graphic novel has matured into an influential art form that has made a place for itself on the contemporary cultural scene."
>
> —M. Thomas Inge
> Randolph-Macon College

Modern Language Association | **MLA**

Join the MLA today and save 30% on all MLA titles.

bookorders@mla.org ■ www.mla.org ■ phone orders 646 576-5161

ⅢⅢ UNIVERSITY OF MISSOURI PRESS

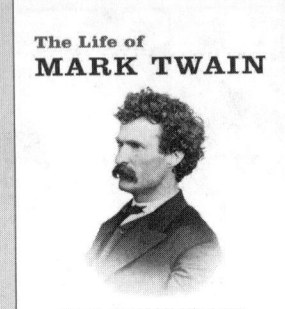

THE LIFE OF MARK TWAIN
The Early Years, 1835–1871
Gary Scharnhorst

"Gary Scharnhorst's monumental biography sets a new standard for comprehensiveness. This will prove to be the standard biography for our generation."—**Alan Gribben**, author of *Mark Twain's Literary Resources: A Reconstruction of His Library and Reading*

"Clear and engaging, Scharnhorst's prose keeps you rolling happily through this consummate American adventure."
—**Bruce Michelson**, author of *Printer's Devil: Mark Twain and the American Publishing Revolution*

$36.95 T · Cloth · 978-0-8262-2144-5 · 724 pp.

Orders: 800-621-2736 · upress.missouri.edu

Keep up to date on new scholarship

Issue alerts are a great way to stay current on all the cutting-edge scholarship from your favorite Duke University Press journals. This free service delivers tables of contents directly to your inbox, informing you of the latest groundbreaking work as soon as it is published.

To sign up for issue alerts:

1. Visit **dukeu.press/register** and register for an account. You do not need to provide a customer number.

2. After registering, visit **dukeu.press/alerts**.

3. Go to "Latest Issue Alerts" and click on "Add Alerts."

4. Select as many publications as you would like from the pop-up window and click "Add Alerts."

read.dukeupress.edu/journals

DUKE UNIVERSITY PRESS

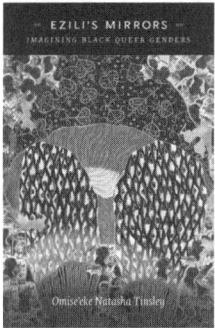

New books from
DUKE UNIVERSITY PRESS

Me and My House
James Baldwin's Last Decade in France
MAGDALENA J. ZABOROWSKA
104 illustrations, incl. 24 in color, paper, $28.95

M Archive
After the End of the World
ALEXIS PAULINE GUMBS
8 illustrations, paper, $24.95

Ezili's Mirrors
Imagining Black Queer Genders
OMISE'EKE NATASHA TINSLEY
8 photographs, paper, $25.95

Bodyminds Reimagined
(Dis)ability, Race, and Gender in Black Women's Speculative Fiction
SAMI SCHALK
paper, $23.95

dukeupress.edu | 888-651-0122
@DukePress | @dukeuniversitypress

ENGLISH LANGUAGE NOTES

Now published by Duke University Press

A respected forum of criticism and scholarship in literary and cultural studies since 1962, *English Language Notes* (*ELN*) is dedicated to pushing the edge of scholarship in literature and related fields in new directions. Broadening its reach geographically and transhistorically, *ELN* opens new lines of inquiry and widens emerging fields.

Sign up for new issue alerts at **http://dukeu.press/alerts**.

Laura Winkiel, editor

subscribe today.
Two issues annually

Individuals, $40
Students, $25

DUKE UNIVERSITY PRESS

dukepress.edu/eln
+1.919.688.5134 | 888.651.0122
subscriptions@dukeupress.edu

GLQ: A JOURNAL OF LESBIAN AND GAY STUDIES

Subscribe today.

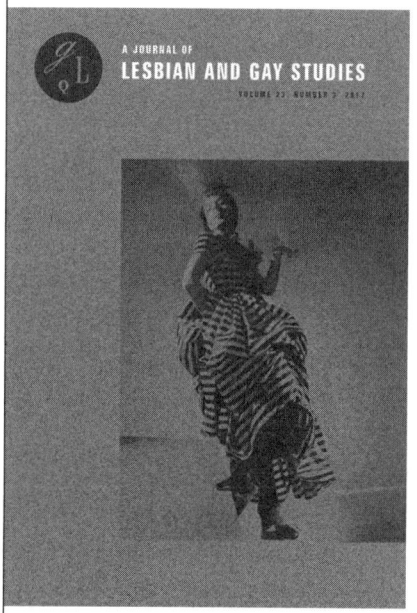

Providing a forum for interdisciplinary discussion, *GLQ* publishes scholarship, criticism, and commentary in areas as diverse as law, science studies, religion, political science, and literary studies. It aims to offer queer perspectives on all issues concerning sex and sexuality.

Sign up for new issue alerts at **http://dukeu.press/alerts**.

Jennifer DeVere Brody and Marcia Ochoa, editors

Subscription Information

Quarterly
Online access is included with a print subscription.

Individuals: $40 | Students: $25
Single issues: $12 | Double issues: $18

dukeupress.edu/glq
888.651.0122 | +1.919.688.5134
subscriptions@dukeupress.edu

DUKE UNIVERSITY PRESS

T*SQ Transgender Studies Quarterly

We're changing gender.

The Issue of Blackness

Paisley Currah and Susan Stryker, editors

TSQ offers a venue for interdisciplinary scholarship that contests the objectification, pathologization, and exoticization of transgender lives. Its mission is to examine how "transgender" comes into play as a category, a process, a social assemblage, an increasingly intelligible gender identity, and an identifiable threat to gender normativity.

Sign up for new issue alerts at **http://dukeu.press/alerts**.

Subscriptions

Quarterly. Online access is included with a print subscription.

Individuals: $45
Students: $28
Single issues: $12

dukeupress.edu/tsq
888.651.0122 | +1.919.688.5134
subscriptions@dukeupress.edu

DUKE UNIVERSITY PRESS